CREATIVE
HOMEOWNER®

W9-ATT-939

BARNS
SHEDS & OUTBUILDINGS

COMPLETE HOW-TO INFORMATION
DESIGN CONCEPTS FOR TEN BUILDINGS

CREATIVE HOMEOWNER® Upper Saddle River, New Jersey

Editorial Director: Timothy O. Bakke

Production Manager: Kimberly H. Vivas

Authors: John D. Wagner, Clayton DeKorne

Senior Editor: Mike McClintock

Associate Editor: Paul Rieder

Assistant Editor: Daniel Lane

Copy Editor: Ellie Sweeney

Editorial Assistants: Dan Houghtaling, Sharon Ranftle

Staff Photographers: John Parsekian, Brian C. Nieves

Photo Research: Stanley Sudol, Amla Sanghvi

Photo Assistants: Frank Krumrie, Dan Houghtaling, Daniel Lane, James Parlagi

Indexer: Sandi Schroeder

Technical Consultants: Jack P. Jones, Dave Crosby

Designers: Scott Molenaro, Robert Strauch

Design Assistants: Ed Jacobus, Charles Van Vooren

Illustrator: Ian Worpole

Cover Design: Clarke Barre, Robert Strauch

Front Cover Photography: H. Armstrong Roberts

Printed in the United States of America

Current Printing (last digit)
10 9 8 7

Barns, Sheds, and Outbuildings
Library of Congress Catalog Card Number: 00-107268
ISBN: 1-58011-075-4

CREATIVE HOMEOWNER®
A Division of Federal Marketing Corp.
24 Park Way, Upper Saddle River, NJ 07458
www.creativehomeowner.com

SAFETY FIRST

Though all the designs and methods in this book have been reviewed for safety, it is not possible to overstate the importance of using the safest possible construction methods. What follows are reminders—some do's and don'ts of work procedures and tool safety that apply to barn, shed, and outbuilding construction. They are not substitutes for your own common sense.

- Always use caution, care, and good judgment when following the instructions and procedures described in this book.

- Always be sure that the electrical setup is safe, that no circuit is overloaded, and that all power tools and outlets are properly grounded. Do not use power tools in wet locations.

- Always read container labels on paints, solvents, and other products; provide ventilation; and observe all other warnings.

- Always read the manufacturer's instructions for using a tool, especially the warnings.

- Use hold-downs and push sticks whenever possible when working on a table saw. Avoid working short pieces if you can.

- Always remove the key from any drill chuck (portable or press) before starting the drill.

- Always pay deliberate attention to how a tool works so that you can avoid being injured.

- Always know the limitations of your tools. Do not try to force them to do what they were not designed to do.

- Always make sure that any adjustment is locked before proceeding. For example, always check the rip fence on a table saw or the bevel adjustment on a portable saw before starting to work.

- Always clamp small pieces to a stable surface when working on them with a power tool.

- Always wear the appropriate rubber or work gloves when handling chemicals, moving or stacking lumber, or doing heavy construction.

- Always wear a disposable face mask when you create dust by sawing or sanding. Use a special filtering respirator when working with toxic substances and solvents.

- Always wear eye protection, especially when using power tools or striking metal on metal or concrete; a chip can fly off, for example, when chiseling concrete.

- Never work while wearing loose clothing, hanging hair, open cuffs, or jewelry.

- Always be aware that there is seldom enough time for your body's reflexes to save

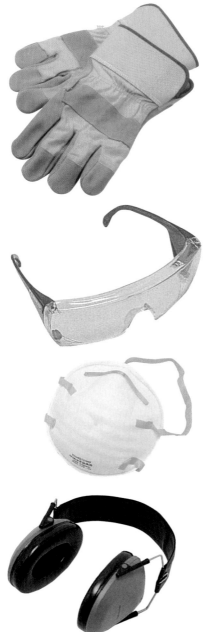

you from injury from a power tool in a dangerous situation; everything happens too fast. Be alert!

- Always keep your hands away from the business ends of blades, cutters, and bits.

- Always hold a circular saw firmly, usually with one hand on the trigger handle and the other on the secondary support handle.

- Always use a drill with an auxiliary handle to control the torque when large-size bits are used.

- Always check your local building codes when planning new construction. The codes are intended to protect public safety and should be observed to the letter.

- Never work with power tools when you are tired or under the influence of alcohol or drugs.

- Never cut tiny pieces of wood or pipe using a power saw. Always cut small pieces off larger pieces that are securely clamped or fastened to a stable work surface.

- Never change a saw blade, drill bit, or router bit unless the tool's power cord is unplugged. Do not depend on the switch being off; you might accidentally hit it.

- Never work in insufficient lighting.

- Never work with dull tools. Have them sharpened, or learn how to sharpen them yourself.

- Never use a power tool on a workpiece—large or small—that is not firmly supported.

- Never saw a workpiece that spans a large distance between horses without close support on each side of the cut; the piece can bend, close on and jam the blade, and cause saw kickback.

- Never support a workpiece from underneath with your leg or other part of your body when sawing or drilling.

- Never carry sharp or pointed tools, such as utility knives, awls, or chisels, in your pocket. If you want to carry such tools, use a special-purpose tool belt with leather pockets and holders.

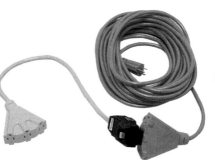

CONTENTS

How to Build Barns, Sheds & Outbuildings

Introduction

Written with the do-it-yourselfer in mind, Barns, Sheds, and Outbuildings gives you the information you need to plan, build, and finish a wide variety of utility buildings.

You'll find practical and detailed advice about building the simplest garden shed or backyard artist's studio, and the in-depth information you need to build a large gambrel dairy barn.

Part 1 begins with design and planning information to help you locate your building efficiently, decide on its design, and decipher architectural plans and building codes.

Individual chapters detail the basics of building foundations from simple shed foundations to poured concrete slabs; framing walls and roofs, including extensive sections on pole buildings and old-fashioned timber-framing techniques. There are also chapters on closing in the framing, including all types of roofing and siding, and installing doors and windows.

Other chapters cover the basic wiring and plumbing needs of your barn, and your options for interior and exterior finish and trimwork.

Part 2 presents ten designs—featuring several detail views—of various buildings, including sheds, barns for a variety of purposes, garages, and other utility buildings.

Skill Level: *Look for these estimates of job difficulty*

 Easy, *even for most beginners.*

 Challenging, *but can be handled by do-it-yourselfers with basic tools and carpentry skills.*

Difficult, *but still doable by experienced do-it-youselfers who have mastered basic construction skills, and have the tools and time for the job.*

CHAPTER 1

Planning

There's more to planning for a barn, shed, or other outbuilding than buying plans and a stack of lumber. First, you need to check with the local building department about codes governing the construction of the building as well as other restrictions on its size and location. You must then decide where to locate the building, taking into account the shape and physical characteris-tics of your property, the buildings on it, and the type of soil. When you've picked a site, you should analyze how you want to use the building: it's much easier to build for all options now than to add on later. Once you've settled on a basic plan, you can either buy a set of published plans, have them drawn, or draw them yourself in some cases, and then begin to erect the building.

Building Permits & Codes

Getting Permits

Most towns, cities, and counties require permits for buildings over a certain size or for any structure with a permanent foundation. Always check with the local building inspector early in the planning process. To find the phone number, look under your town's name in the phone book, and search for either "permits," "building inspector," or "inspector." Then call and describe the type of structure you plan to build and the size and basic characteristics of your lot. Ask whether you are required to submit a building plan, how long before beginning you must submit it, how long the review process takes, and whether you may reapply on appeal.

Also ask what a complete permit package contains. Some municipalities want just a site plan and two elevations (side views); others may want floor plans and detailed building specifications as well. If zoning is particularly restrictive in your town, they may even want to know the type of roof you plan to use and the color of the barn. Also, your permit application may require the opinions of a soil specialist or an engineer. You can get all this information by phone and then start to assemble your permit package using the pieces outlined in the sections below, including a site plan, floor plans, elevations, sections, and specifications, which combined are sometimes called, simply, drawings.

Restrictions

Many municipalities have restrictions that limit where you can build a new structure. A setback is the minimum distance between a building and the property line. An easement is the legal right for another property owner (or often a utility company) to cross or have limited use of another's property. Height and lot coverage restrictions limit how high you can build and what percentage of your lot can be covered by structures (including your house).

If local zoning permits you to maintain livestock, you will probably be restricted as to how close to your property lines you can locate a livestock structure. Always check with the local building department. You may find that your particular zoning does not allow livestock at all or restricts their numbers.

Codes

No matter how lenient the permit requirement may appear, it cannot exempt you from building your structure to conform with area building codes. These codes are the minimum building specifications required by law and are enforced by your local building inspector.

Codes ensure that standard building practices are used to make your building structurally sound and safe. To find out more about building codes, you can consult the many code handbooks available, even though every effort has been made in this book to represent common building practices that pass code inspections. That said, note that codes vary even regionally, especially where the weather or the risk of fire is severe, as in some Florida and California counties. The local building inspector is the expert in this regard, so ask about the code requirements and where you can find a reference for minimum specs.

Typical Code and Zoning Restrictions

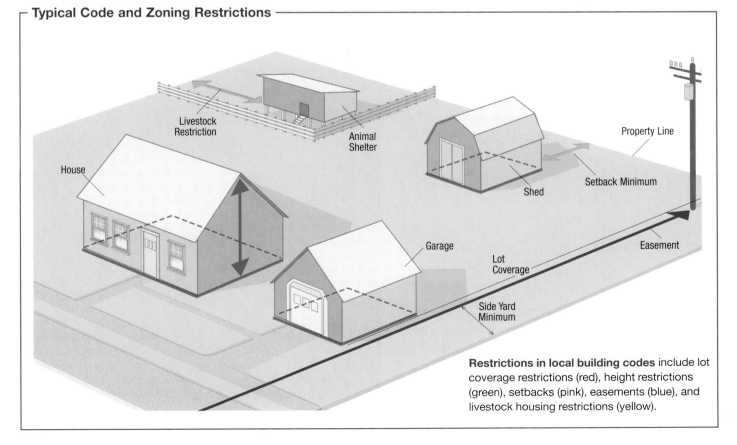

Restrictions in local building codes include lot coverage restrictions (red), height restrictions (green), setbacks (pink), easements (blue), and livestock housing restrictions (yellow).

Site Evaluation

There are four main things to consider about a potential site for your barn or outbuilding: access to both roads and utilities, soil type, drainage, and topography. If a number of places on your property satisfy these criteria, you might also consider other factors, such as solar orientation, weather protection, and the direction of prevailing winds.

Access to Roads

Good roads are expensive to engineer and build—even thousands of dollars per mile if you have to blast bedrock. They involve excavation, design for proper drainage, and careful selection of materials. You cannot just dump loads of gravel onto grass or bare earth and expect it to serve as a sound road surface for very long.

Also, once a road is in place, it has to be maintained. Gravel needs to be dressed every other year or so because the finer pieces sift down into the larger rocks. Blacktop cracks need to be sealed to prevent frost heaving that can tear apart all your costly work.

If you can position your barn so that it doesn't need a new road built to it, all the better. If you want to build your barn away from existing roads and your region endures winter weather (and a muddy spring), you will likely struggle with access over rutty roads and mud unless you construct a solid road bed. You will have to decide whether that's a price you're willing to pay to put off spending what it takes to build a good road.

Access to Utilities

You should always consult a licensed electrician in the planning stages. Depending on your circumstances, you may also need to contact the power company. Local utilities often regulate the maximum distance between a meter and a breaker panel and whether you can run an outdoor circuit to your barn directly from your house's main service panel or whether you need to have a separate subpanel installed in the barn.

Whether or not your local government requires it, all work should conform to the requirements of the National Electrical Code (available in local libraries). If you will be keeping livestock, bringing water to your barn is an absolute necessity. You're probably not going to want the expense of a new water main and septic system just for your barn; you'll want to hook it into your house's system, if possible. In regions with cold winters, water-supply pipes need to be buried 4 feet or more in the ground; the closer you are to your well and septic system or to the municipal water and sewage lines, the less time-consuming (and costly) this digging will be. Remember that some areas impose very strict standards for septic systems, and require perc tests, special permits, and inspections.

Soil

If you have a garden, you may already have an idea of what type of soil you have on your property—whether it's mostly sand, clay, silt, or loam. Before building a large structure, however, obtain a copy of a local soil survey map, which is available from the Cooperative Extension Service, to find out exactly what type of soil on which you'll be building. (A sample of what these maps look like is shown below.) The soil types are drawn onto aerial photographs with a key that explains the qualities of each

Load-Bearing Values of Soils

Class of Material	Load-bearing pressure (lbs. per sq. ft.)
Crystalline bedrock	12,000
Sedimentary rock	6,000
Sandy gravel or gravel	5,000
Sand, silt sand, clayey sand, silty gravel, and clayey gravel	3,000
Clay, sandy clay, silty clay, and clayey silt	2,000

Leveling a Slope

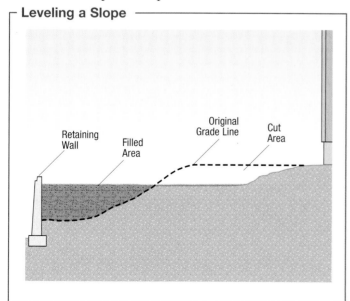

Retaining Wall

Filled Area

Original Grade Line

Cut Area

County soil maps are available from your Cooperation Extension Service office. They include aerial photos of the county with an overlay of coded soil types.

soil type, including engineering properties and how suitable it is for different types of construction methods.

Soils are rated for their load-bearing capacity—that is, how much weight per square foot they can support without having to be modified with soil stabilizers such as gravel, stepped landscaping, or retaining walls.

Bedrock, the most stable building surface, has the greatest load-bearing pressure rating. Sedimentary stone, such as sandstone, and gravel support slightly less weight; sand, silt, and clay soil support much less. Depending on your soil type, you can increase the width of the foundation footings to spread the load or even modify the soil itself by bringing in fill from elsewhere—an expensive option.

If you have any doubts about the bearing capacity of your soil, consult a soil engineer and the Cooperative Extension Service. Building on soil that can't support your structure will cause it to settle, crack the foundation, and rack the walls.

Drainage

Soil must drain thoroughly, especially in areas where the weather reaches freezing temperatures. Otherwise, moisture retained in the soil will freeze and cause frost heaving. Frozen soil can increase in volume as much as 25 percent, which presses the soil (and your barn's foundation) upward. In cold climates, prevent damage from heaving by

installing your footings below the average frost depth, which is available from your local building department.

It's also important to have good drainage around your structure for water that runs off the roof and groundwater that may run downhill and be blocked from its normal path by your structure. The soil around your structure should slope away from the foundation, generally at $1/4$ inch or more per foot for at least 6 feet. If needed, a swale, or shallow depression, can be used to direct surface water, and a perimeter drain made of perforated pipe can be used to direct groundwater away from your building into a drainage ditch or collection pond.

Topography

The topography of your site is the three-dimensional shape of your lot including major physical characteristics, such as standing water, large rocks, and trees. You can alter the topography of your lot, but it's expensive. Generally, it's better to adjust your barn to the topography.

A sloped site presents challenges when designing your foundation slabs. For example, you must excavate a flat pad, which could mean building a retaining wall. For walls, you can excavate the slope or use a stepped foundation. However, a sloped site isn't always a bad thing. If the lot slopes to the south, for instance, you will have a site that's warmer than surrounding flat areas because ground sloping 10 degrees to the south receives the same amount of solar radiation as level ground 700 miles to the south. Plus, mildly sloped sites are good for drainage, so if you prepare your barn's perimeter drains and swales properly, you will have a well-drained site and a dry barn.

Sun & Wind

In the Northern Hemisphere, the climate is slightly warmer on south-facing slopes and slightly colder on north-facing ones. To reap gains from passive solar heating, buildings should have the longest dimensions running approximately east and west with most windows on the south side and few on the north. In hot climates, you'll want to do just the

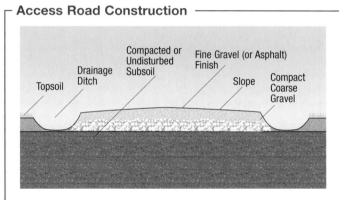

— **Access Road Construction** —

Topsoil — Drainage Ditch — Compacted or Undisturbed Subsoil — Fine Gravel (or Asphalt) Finish — Slope — Compact Coarse Gravel

A typical perimeter drain has several inches of gravel in the bottom, a perforated drain pipe to carry away water, and more gravel topped with filter fabric.

To keep perforated drain pipes from clogging, cover the gravel trench with filter fabric, or slip on a filter-fabric sleeve that lets water through but keeps out dirt.

opposite to prevent solar gain. Of course, other elements in your environment may not permit you to orient your barn this way.

When you position your barn, note that positive pressure from wind will drive cold air into the barn, and negative pressure on the far side will suck warm air out of it. As you orient your barn for sun and wind, keep in mind that, for the winter, you want to expose the wall with the most glazing to the south to collect solar heat while exposing the fewest openings to the ends of the barn that are perpendicular to the prevailing wind.

As for trees, there are different scenarios for dealing with either year-long prevailing winds that come from one direc-

tion or prevailing winter winds that shift from north to south between winter and summer.

The arrangement of trees is important, but so is the type of tree you plant. Deciduous trees bear leaves in the summer but lose them during the cold winter months. These trees are excellent for the south side of a barn because their leaves will shield the roof from the harsh summer sunlight and heat and—when the leaves drop—admit sunlight and heat in the winter. Carefully placed after close observation of prevailing winds, deciduous and coniferous trees can be used to direct cooling breezes toward your structure in the summer and block cold winds in the winter.

You can locate a small utility building, such as a utility shed that needs no permanent foundation, almost anywhere where it is convenient to your yard or garden.

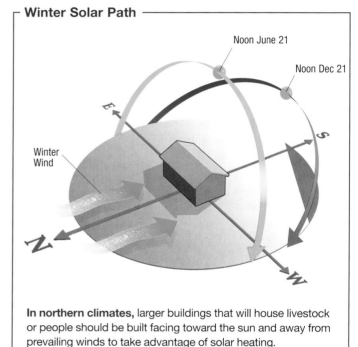

In northern climates, larger buildings that will house livestock or people should be built facing toward the sun and away from prevailing winds to take advantage of solar heating.

Wind Direction

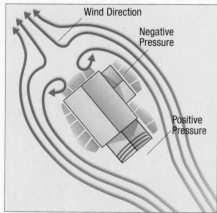

The direction of the wind and the pressures it creates affect how you should orient your building. The shortest side with the fewest windows should face into the prevailing wind.

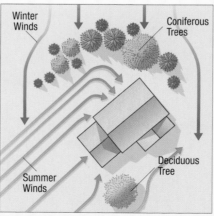

If seasonal winds blow from opposite directions, plant any type of tree where it will help channel summer breezes, but only put evergreens where they will deflect winter winds.

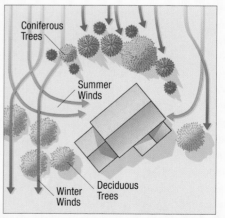

If winter and summer winds blow from the same direction, trees should be planted to direct summer breezes toward the building but direct winter winds away from the building.

Temporary Power

You can often bring power to saws and drills by running a power cord from a nearby house. Just be sure the cord is a heavy enough gauge to support the amp rating on your tool. An undersize cord can deprive a tool of the needed power and ruin the tool. This is because power encounters resistance in the cord and drops off over longer distances. You decrease this resistance by using heavier gauge wire. Generally use 10- or 12- gauge cords. They are not as flexible and light, but they will protect your tools in the long run.

If you can't get power nearby, you have two choices: make power with a generator, or install a temporary power pole. This setup includes a conduit mast, a meter base and meter, a turn-off switch, GFCI breakers, some outlets, and a rod hammered into the ground to act as a ground. Some utility companies will set up these poles for you for an installation fee and monthly power consumption charge. They will often have a minimum charge. An electrician can make one for you, but it will still have to be inspected by the utility company before the power is turned on. The building inspector may also want to take a look before it's approved for use.

If you do the work yourself, be sure to check specs with the local utility because there are often strict requirements about weatherproofing, pole height and depth in the ground, minimum distances from the service to the center of the street, and pole placement on the site. After you have the pole approved and power is flowing, you'll have to distribute it throughout the site through GFCI-protected cords and weatherproof outlet boxes.

A **portable generator** can supply power on a remote site. Fill it with oil and gasoline (top), start it and plug in your cords (bottom). Buy or rent a model with enough power to run your equipment.

Recommended Extension-Cord Wire Gauges

| For 115V: | | 25 ft. | 50 ft. | 100 ft. | 150 ft. | 200 ft. | 250 ft. | 300 ft. | 400 ft. | 500 ft. |
For 230V:		50 ft.	100 ft.	200 ft.	300 ft.	400 ft.	500 ft.	600 ft.	800 ft.	1000 ft.
Amp	0–2	18	18	18	16	16	14	14	12	12
Rating	2–3	18	18	16	14	14	12	12	10	10
of	3–4	18	18	16	14	12	12	10	10	8
Power	4–5	18	18	14	12	12	10	10	8	8
Tool	5–6	18	16	14	12	10	10	8	8	6
	6–8	18	16	12	10	10	8	6	6	6
	8–10	18	14	12	10	8	8	6	6	4
	10–12	16	14	10	8	8	6	6	4	4
	12–14	16	12	10	8	6	6	6	4	2
	14–16	16	12	10	8	6	6	4	4	2
	16–18	14	12	8	8	6	4	4	2	2
	18–20	14	12	8	6	6	4	4	2	2

Temporary Service Panel

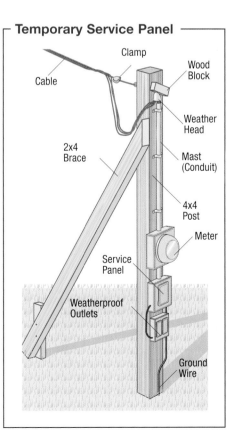

Clamp
Cable
Wood Block
Weather Head
2x4 Brace
Mast (Conduit)
4x4 Post
Meter
Service Panel
Weatherproof Outlets
Ground Wire

Design

Take your time when deciding on the layout, size, and overall design of your barn or shed. A great deal of effort goes into constructing a building—not just physical work but permits and financing as well. It is often worth the relatively minor effort and expense to expand a barn beyond what you expect to use today, just on the possibility that you'll need the space later. Ten years from now, for example, you may need an extra-large door for larger garden equipment.

If you already have a shed and need more space, it's not that expensive to build a second small shed or buy a prebuilt metal one. But if you're going to the trouble of building a large primary garden shed from scratch, you should think about the details you might want to add, such as wide, barn-style double doors and a sturdy ramp. If the shed will double as a workspace, you may want to add one or two windows, lights, and electrical outlets—or even a utility sink.

Designing for the Building's Purpose

The best thing to do when designing your structure is to list all possible uses you and your family can anticipate. Then sit down with this list and some graph paper, and figure out your space requirements.

For a storage shed, measure the equipment that you will need to store, and add at least a 12-inch buffer zone around the equipment so that you have room to walk around. If you want one room of an outbuilding to be a ceramics shop, for example, measure the potter's wheel, determine how much space you'll need to use it comfortably and safely, and be liberal when deciding on storage space.

Typical Garage Dimensions

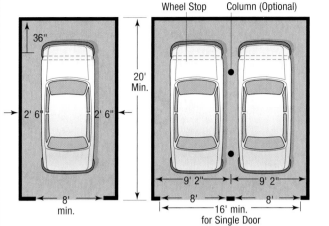

Typical Potting Shed

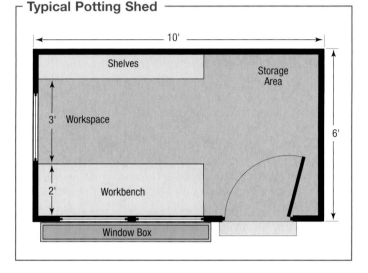

Typical Woodworking Shop

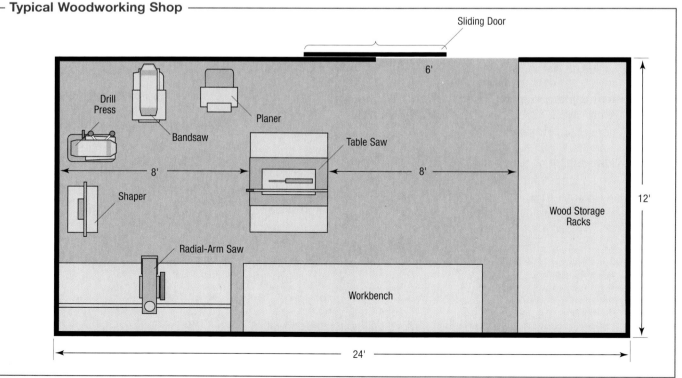

Typical Equipment Shed

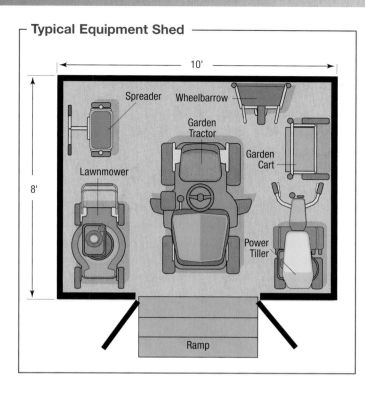

10'

8'

Spreader   Wheelbarrow

Garden
Tractor

Garden
Cart

Lawnmower

Power
Tiller

Ramp

For any kind of shop, whether you'll be working on cars or building furniture, you should mentally walk yourself through various projects to make sure you've allowed enough working space. For instance, in a woodworking shop where you'll need to rip a 4 × 8-foot sheet of plywood, you'll need at least 8 feet of clearance space in front of and behind the table saw.

Wiring & Plumbing

Also keep in mind your potential needs for electricity and water. If your eventual plan is to use part of a barn for living space or for keeping livestock, it makes sense to rough-in some of the plumbing—especially if it will be installed within a slab—so that the disruption is minor when you convert the barn to a heated structure. Adding wiring or heating after you've finished the building may not be as disruptive as adding plumbing, but it's still much less work to rough-in wiring and HVAC ducts in a building's unfinished frame than inside finished walls.

Leaving Your Options Open

Be sure to position entryways carefully, and keep in mind that although second-floor access may not be an issue today, it may be necessary in coming years. Think about how to design your structure to accommodate expansion. You may find it worth building an oversize header into one wall so that you can add a wing onto this side of the barn later and allow for a wide entryway.

The same is true for window and door headers. It is messy work to install window and door headers after a building is framed up, sided, roofed, and painted. But it is a cinch to install a header in the initial framing that could serve an additional window or door later. Just be sure to note these hidden elements in your plans for future reference.

Space Requirements
for Animals

Horses	Stall Size (feet)	
Mare/gelding	10×10	
Brood mare	12×12	
Stallion	14×14	
Pony	9×9	

Cattle	Pen Size	Stall Size (feet)
Cow	50 sq. ft/cow	9×9 minimum
Cow and calf	75 sq. ft.	10×10
Steer	75 sq. ft.	10×10

Swine	Pen Area	Outdoor Area
Sow	15 sq. ft.	35 sq. ft.
Sow and litter	30 sq. ft.	80 sq. ft.

Goats	Pen Size
Does	25 sq. ft./doe
Buck	8×8 stall plus 100-sq.-ft. pen
Kids	5 sq. ft./kid

Poultry	Floor Space
Chickens: Layer	2–3 sq. ft.
Broiler	1 sq. ft.
Roaster	2–3 sq. ft.
Chicks	1 sq. ft./chick before 10 weeks
Turkeys	3–4 sq. ft.
Ducks	3 sq. ft. (6 sq. ft. for confined breeders)
Geese	2 sq. ft. (5 sq. ft. for confined breeders)

Rabbits

1 sq. ft. × 18" high per rabbit

Requirements for
Feed/Bedding Storage

Item	Storage Space Needed
Hay	
Two-wire, 14 × 18 × 36-in. bales	5.25 cu. ft./bale (100 bales = 525 cu. ft.
Three-wire, 17 × 24 × 40-in. bales	9.44 cu. ft./bale (100 bales = 944 cu. ft.)
Grass hay (loose), 1 ton	450–600 cu. ft.
Alfalfa (loose), 1 ton	450–500 cu. ft.
Straw (loose), 1 ton	650–1000 cu. ft.
Feed	
Shelled corn, 100 lbs.	2.2 cu. ft.
Ear corn, 100 lbs.	3.6 cu. ft.
Oats, 100 lbs.	3.9 cu. ft.
Barley, 100 lbs.	2.6 cu. ft.
Soybeans, 100 lbs.	2.1 cu. ft.

This information is adapted from the MidWest Plan Service's Structures and Environment Handbook.

Animals require not only sufficient space inside a barn, but also enough area and properly fenced pasture outside to provide them with grass and room to exercise.

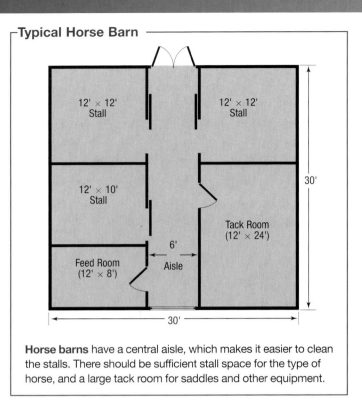

Typical Horse Barn

12' × 12' Stall

12' × 12' Stall

12' × 10' Stall

Tack Room (12' × 24')

Feed Room (12' × 8')

6'

Aisle

30'

30'

Horse barns have a central aisle, which makes it easier to clean the stalls. There should be sufficient stall space for the type of horse, and a large tack room for saddles and other equipment.

Guidelines for Animals

Animals have specific minimum space requirements, which are given in the table on the previous page. When building a barn for animals, you'll also need to consider storage space for feed, as well as providing sufficient water and perhaps electricity. Don't forget manure: if you have animals in stalls much of the time, you will want enough space near the stalls to drive in some type of tractor.

When you have animals in a barn, you also need to provide sufficient ventilation so that your barn is free of noticeable levels of ammonia and methane fumes. For a barn that doesn't vent well naturally, you may have to install a fan that provides for a minimum of four air changes per hour in winter and up to 40 air changes per hour in summer to keep the air clean, depending on how many animals you have.

Horses. In most climates, horses can be kept outside year-round, as long as they are provided with a three-sided shelter from storms. If you want to stall your horses, the barn should be designed to be warm in winter, cool in summer, and easy to muck out. A wide aisle between two rows of stalls works well. A dirt floor is the cheapest option, but it must be well-drained and kept covered in sawdust or straw. If your barn site is low or has drainage problems, make the floor out of 8 to 12 inches of crushed rock covered by a layer of tamped clay.

Cattle. For calves, milk cows, and beef cattle (cows, steers, or bulls), a three-sided open-front barn with access to the outside and individual feeding stalls is a minimum requirement. In most climates, cattle don't need to be kept warm in winter, but (like horses) they do require a wind-break and protection from rain and snow. An indoor pen for cows and their calves can have a dirt floor. Keep in mind when site planning that full-grown dairy cows or beef cattle may each need about 3 acres of forage pasture.

Pigs. For pigs, access to outside pastures is essential, along with an insulated, ventilated hutch for resting. In summer, pigs will need at least a roofed area to protect them from the sun. In cold winters, they'll need an enclosure to shield them from cold winds.

Sheep & Goats. Sheep and goats generally don't need any housing at all, unless they will be birthing during the winter. A 6 × 6-foot pen inside a larger barn generally is more than enough space for a doe or ewe and her offspring. A free space in the barn for shearing sheep will come in handy; if you plan on milking goats, allow an area for a milking station.

Poultry. Chickens, turkeys, and other domestic fowl require a closed-in building of their own, or a pen within a closed barn to protect them from wind, cold, and precipitation. The living area density for chickens should be no greater than 2 square feet per bird. Chicks need warmth and feeding space big enough so that half of them can eat at any one time. Turkeys require at least 3 square feet of housing per hen and 5 square feet per tom.

As requirements vary for animals region to region (and even among breeds) always consult the local Cooperative Extension Service and code authorities on your plans.

Feed Storage

Controlling rodents at the feed storage area is crucial. This can be as simple as storing food in a sealed garbage can. But if you use feed bins, it's going to take some planning to line them properly to keep out rodents. If your barn has a dirt floor, you should pour a small floor slab in a storage room to help control pests. Purchase bags of premixed concrete, and mix it on-site using a rented mixer or (for small rooms) hand tools and a wheelbarrow.

Drawings

Drawings are simply a set of plans or blueprints that you'll follow when building your project. Basic barn and shed plans are readily available in home centers, lumberyards, bookstores, and the like. If you don't find a barn plan that fits your needs, consider creating a customized version of one of the designs in the back of this book. If you try your hand at drawing plans yourself, be sure to hire an engineer or architect to review them for structural integrity and to bring the specifications up to current code standards.

Blueprints are drawn to scale; typically, a ¼-inch space on a blueprint represents a 1 foot space in the structure. Though the ¼-inch scale is common, some blueprints use a ³⁄₃₂-inch or ½-inch scale. Check the requirements of the local building department including the type and number of drawings you must submit.

Many Plans, One Building

If designers and architects were to put all the features of a building onto one sheet of the blueprint, it would be difficult to read and too complicated to follow. So at the design stage, an architect or engineer breaks the building down into different plans: a site plan, floor plan, elevation, wall sections, and the like.

Each plan shows how to build different features of the house. Depending on how complicated a building is, you sometimes need as many as ten pages, covering details such as plot plans, foundation plans, exterior elevations, section views, framing plans, rough opening dimensions, and finish schedules. A set of drawings also might include a complete materials list or a page of specifications for your project—information that is not on the drawings and blueprints themselves, such as the characteristics, qualities, and even model numbers of windows and doors.

Site Plan

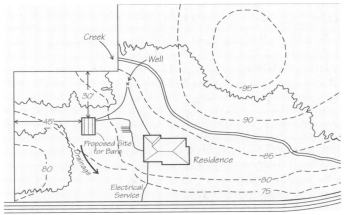

Site plans show from a bird's-eye view what your lot will look like with the new structure and any new roads or landscaping. Site plans need to show your property lines and how far the barn will be from each line. They will typically also show orientations to north, easements and right of ways, and existing structures.

Floor Plan

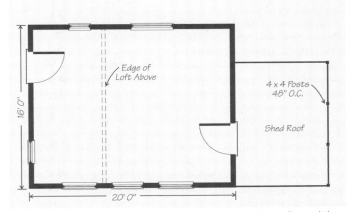

Floor plans give the location of exterior and interior walls and the location of windows and doors. If they're included in your project, the floor plans will also include location and types of major appliances, plumbing fixtures, and wiring, as well as exterior features such as stairs or a porch.

Elevation

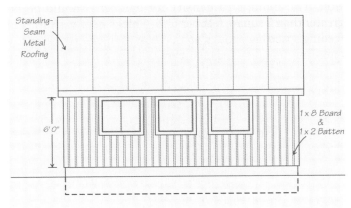

Elevation drawings are detailed one-dimensional renderings of the sides of a building. If two sides are identical (for example, the east and west walls), one drawing will suffice. Like floor plans, these can be a great aid when maintaining design and construction consistency during the building process.

Section

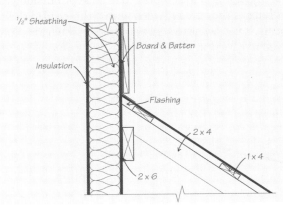

Sections are cutaway views of a wall, roof, or foundation that show what is contained within the structure. Sections can be helpful to show structures that are difficult to read on other building plans. Some inspectors may demand wall sections to see what will be within your finished walls.

Reading Blueprints

Blueprints may look confusing at first glance, but if you know the basics of how to read them, they eventually will become clear. First learn how to read the lines, because it is with various types of lines that a blueprint represents a structure's component parts. Then turn your attention to the symbols commonly used so you can have a complete understanding of what is shown. Bear in mind that some architects and engineers litter blueprints with construction notes.

Blueprint Lines

A solid line on a blueprint indicates an object's visible outline. You would see a solid line along both edges of a concrete wall where it meets the floor because those edges would be visible. A broken line indicates a hidden object. When a basement slab hides the footing below, a broken line can indicate the shape of that structure.

Aspects of a building, such as a window or door, often have to be located precisely in a wall or floor. This positioning is often handled with a centerline to establish the center point of an area. A centerline is indicated by a C and a broken line drawn perpendicular to the wall or window frame.

A section line indicates where an aspect of the building is shown in cross section. It indicates the point at which the structure is sliced and the section view is shown. A break line indicates a shortened view of an aspect of the building that has a uniform and predictable shape. A leader line simply points from a specific measurement or note on the side about a detail or other aspect of the building to that part of the building.

Blueprints also give dimensions, or distances between various points of a building. Lines play a role here, too. If the distance between two walls is 10 feet, the dimension 10'-0" interrupts a solid line with arrows pointing outward on both ends. Sometimes a dimension line has dots or slanted lines instead of arrows at its ends. An extension line establishes a reference away from the building lines where dimensions are noted.

Utility Symbols. To maintain consistency in the construction industry and avoid confusion, blueprint floor plans use standard symbols to show the positions of heating and plumbing components (such as radiators, thermostats, and water heaters) as well as parts of the electrical system (such as outlets, switches, utility panels, and smoke detectors).

Blueprints

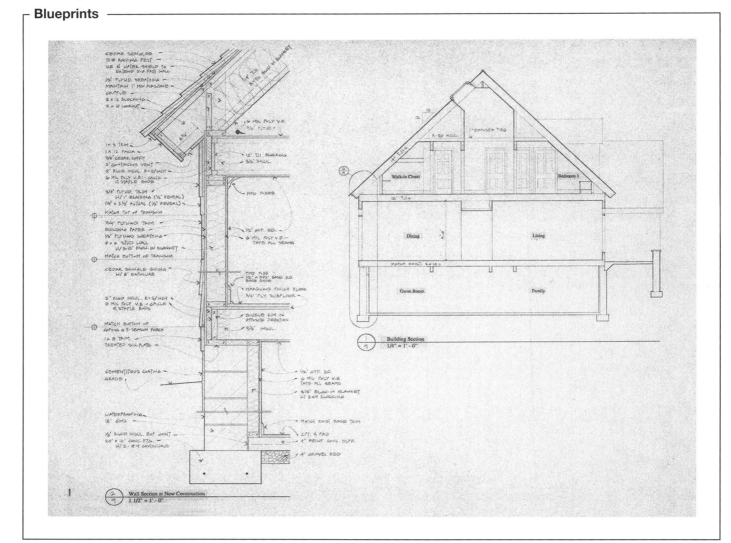

Utility Symbols

Blueprints include special symbols to represent features of utility and mechanical systems in the building.

Symbol	Name	Symbol	Name
———	Soil Line	⊳	Reducer
– – – –	Cold Water		Stop Cock
– · – ·	Hot Water		Return/Exhaust duct
—G—	Gas Line		Supply duct
– – –	Vent Line		Tank-type W.C.
—S—	Sprinkler Main		Water Closet
—D—	Drain Line		Lavatory
—FO—	Fuel Oil Line		Tub
	Check Valve		Corner Tub
CO.	Cleanout		Shower
HB	Hose Bibb		Urinal
	Floor Drain		Fuel Tank
	90° Elbow		Shower Head
	45° Elbow		Expansion Valve
	Tee Connection		Scale Trap
	Cross Connection		Compressor
	Wiring in Wall	B	Blanked Outlet
– – – –	Wiring in Floor	J	Junction Box
– – – –	Exposed Wiring	S	Single-Pole Switch
////	Conduit	S₃	Three-Pole Switch
	Weather Head	Sₗ	Lock Switch
GFI	GFCI Outlet	Sₚ	Pilot Light Switch
	Main Panel	Sₛ	Switch and Duplex Receptacle
	Duplex Receptacle		Ceiling Fan
	Triplex Receptacle		Clock Receptacle
	Duplex Split		Telephone
	Special Outlet		Signal Button
R	Range Outlet		Buzzer
	Ceiling Light		Bell
	Wall Bracket Light	TV	Smoke Detector
	Fluorescent		Intercom Station
P	Pull-Chain		Sound System

Wall Symbols

Blueprints also sometimes include graphic patterns to indicate materials. When a structure is drawn on a blueprint, the walls are represented as a line. But that line can be a brick wall, a wood wall, or even stucco over a wood frame.

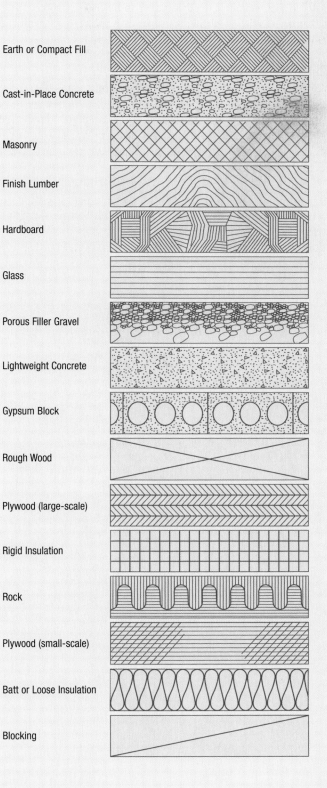

- Earth or Compact Fill
- Cast-in-Place Concrete
- Masonry
- Finish Lumber
- Hardboard
- Glass
- Porous Filler Gravel
- Lightweight Concrete
- Gypsum Block
- Rough Wood
- Plywood (large-scale)
- Rigid Insulation
- Rock
- Plywood (small-scale)
- Batt or Loose Insulation
- Blocking

CHAPTER 2

Tools & Materials

After you've chosen a site and a design, you're ready to begin building. But before you start, you need to make sure that you have the right tools, hardware, and materials for the job. A building project of any size requires accurate laying out, marking, and cutting. When even a ¼-inch error can lead to problems, it's a good idea to invest in some quality tools that, used properly, will improve both your accuracy and efficiency. And even the most meticulous planning isn't going to help if you don't build with the appropriate material. You need to be sure that you're using lumber that has been rated and graded for the situation. For example, you need to use plywood rated for exterior use in order to avoid delamination and possible rot.

Construction Levels

It is essential to build any structure plumb, level, and square. To do that, you will at least want to have a 4-foot spirit level for checking framing, and a line level and mason's string for checking long spans.

■ **Spirit Levels.** Spirit levels come in many lengths. A 4-foot model is best for working with framing. You can also extend its useful range by resting it on a long straight 2×4.

■ **Digital Levels.** Unlike spirit levels, digital levels beep when they are level or plumb. The tools never go out of whack because you can reset them electronically. Some electronic levels also work as inclinometers to give you the angle of rafters. That feature can be handy when you have to match roof pitches in separate, distant locations.

■ **Water Level.** A water level is basically colored water in a long clear tube with gradation marks on both ends. Because water seeks its own level no matter what the distance or terrain, you can use the tool for long-distance level checks. Once any air bubbles are removed, stretch the hose from one place to another (even up and down over rough terrain) and the water line at both ends will be level.

For grading sloped land and laying out level foundations, you'll need to use a transit, a builder's level, or a laser level. These tools allow you to sight a level line across large distances. These are expensive items, so you should rent them, if possible, when you're building from scratch.

Spirit levels are indispensable tools for carpentry. A 4-ft. level is needed for many aspects of framing and finishing; smaller levels are good for doors and windows.

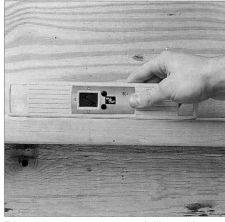

Digital levels are used much like spirit levels, but they have a digital readout. Most kinds will also emit a beep when they are held at level or plumb.

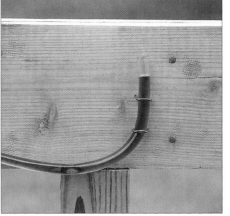

A water level is used for marking level points across long distances. They are especially useful for checking formwork before pouring a foundation.

Safety Tools

Common sense should tell you not to do construction work without first having some basic safety equipment, such as eye and ear protection. Wear goggles or safety glasses that have aerated side guards whenever you work with power tools. The U.S. Occupational Safety and Health Administration (OSHA) recommends that hearing protection be worn when the noise level exceeds 85 decibels (dB) for an eight-hour workday. When you consider that a circular saw emits 110 dB, however, it is clear that even much shorter exposure to loud noises can contribute to hearing impairment. Both insert and muff-type ear protectors are available; whichever you choose, be sure it has a noise reduction rating (NRR) of a least 20 dB.

If you're sensitive to dust, and whenever you cut pressure-treated wood, it's a good idea to wear a dust mask. Two basic kinds of respiratory protection are available: disposable dust masks and cartridge-type respirators. A dust mask will allow you to avoid inhaling dust and fine particles. Respirators have a replaceable filter. Both are available for protection against nontoxic and toxic dust and mist. Whichever you buy, look for a stamp indicating that the National Institute for Occupational Safety and Health/Mine Safety and Health Administration (NIOSH/MSHA) has approved it for your specific job. When you can taste or smell the contaminate or when the mask starts to interfere with normal breathing, it's time for a replacement.

Work gloves are also advisable at least when you're moving wood or doing other rough jobs. Similarly, heavy-duty work boots will protect your feet. Steel toes will prevent injuries to your toes from dropped boards or tools, and flexible steel soles will protect your feet from a puncture by a stray nail. Lastly, consider wearing a hard hat when you're working in the basement or work has started on the second floor and others may be working above you.

Squares

For accurate layout, you'll need a framing square. It's etched for layout of plumb and seat cuts for common rafters or hip rafters, plus degrees of angle for use as a protractor. A speed square—a heavy-duty aluminum right triangle—is great for guiding your saw and marking lumber, and also is etched with information. A combination square and a sliding T-bevel are helpful in marking cut lines on framing.

■ **Framing Square.** A framing square is an L-shaped tool made of steel or aluminum. It is indispensable when cutting rafters, marking cut lines on lumber, and making sure corners are square. Like the speed square, the framing square has figures etched into it. The figures sometimes include extensive rafter tables.

■ **Combination Square.** A combination square is a ruler with a sliding bracket mounted to it at 90 degrees. The bracket has a second surface, which you can use to make 45-degree cut lines on lumber. Some squares have a pointed metal scribe to mark work for cutting. This tool is handy, but the speed square will serve most of your needs.

■ **Sliding T-bevel.** Often called a bevel square or bevel gauge, this tool is useful for some complicated framing problems. You can set a sliding T-bevel at any angle and use it to transfer the same angle from one place to another.

Saws

Though framing doesn't demand the precise cuts that finish carpentry does, you still need high-quality saws with sharp blades. With power saws, a 7¼-inch circular saw is a practical choice. Look for one with good balance that is light enough for you to maneuver and easy to adjust for angle and depth. Make sure it has a comfortable handle. A table saw also adds tremendous capability to a project because you can rip sheets of plywood and boards quickly and accurately.

A **framing square** is a useful tool for checking stud layout, squaring up corners, and marking long cuts. For roof framing, a framing square with rafter tables is a useful addition to your toolkit.

A **combination square** has a sliding blade, ideal for making short measurements, checking right angles, and marking lumber cuts. Some combination squares have a spirit level embedded in the tool.

A **sliding T-bevel** has an adjustable pivot point between the blade and the handle. This enables you to mark angled cuts commonly needed on rafters, the framing for skylights, and miters on exterior trim.

Using Saws Safely

Set up a safe cutting station on heavy-duty boards or thick plywood fastened to sturdy sawhorses on level ground. When you cut large pieces, you must have something to support the wood that's hanging in midair; otherwise it will droop and bind your cut, increasing the risk of kickback.

Kickback happens when a blade binds in the cut or the teeth try to take too much of a bite, and the saw jumps back at you. It happens quickly and is quite dangerous. You can buy antikickback blades, which have modified tooth designs, but you can best reduce kickback by not rushing a cut and by stabilizing your work. Always stay away from directly behind the saw, and don't remove the saw from the workpiece until the blade has stopped.

When cutting wood where you'll install it, support the wood, preferably on sawhorses. Keep your hands as far as possible from the cut, and clearly sight your cut line to make sure it's free of obstructions such as nails or extension cords. Firmly place wood on a cutting surface; never cut wood held in your hand.

■ **Handsaws.** Crosscut saws are versatile handsaws about 24 inches long, with seven or eight teeth per inch. You can also buy specialized trim saws and rip saws. Backsaws—shorter, stiffer and broader than crosscut saws, with finer teeth—are good for detail and trimwork. Hacksaws are essential for cutting pipe, nails, and other materials too tough for a wood saw. Keyhole saws have a narrow-point blade handy for making small cutouts; stubbier versions with coarser teeth are called utility saws and are good for cutting outlet and other openings in drywall. Coping saws are used mainly to join curved-profile moldings.

■ **Circular Saw.** A circular saw is capable of quickly crosscutting, ripping, and beveling boards or sheets of plywood. The most popular saws are those that take a 7¼-inch blade. With this blade size you can cut to a maximum depth of about 2½ inches at 90 degrees. Some contractors use circular saws with larger blades for cutting posts in one pass, but a 7¼-inch circular saw is easier to control, and it allows you to cut anything as large as a 6×6 with a second pass. Smaller saws are also available, some of which are battery powered. These saws are often referred to as trim saws. Battery-driven models can be useful in situations when extension cords would get in the way.

Don't judge power saw performance by horsepower rating alone. Also look at the amperage that the motor draws. Low-cost saws may have 9- or 10-amp motors with drive shafts and arbors running on rollers or sleeve bearings. A contractor-grade saw generally is rated at 12 or 13 amps and is made with more-durable ball bearings. Plastic housings are no longer the mark of an inferior tool; however, a flimsy base plate made of stamped metal is. A thin base won't stay as flat as an extruded or cast base. To minimize any chance of electric shock, be sure that your saw is double insulated. Most saws have a safety switch that you must depress before the trigger will work.

■ **Reciprocating Saw.** This saw comes in handy for cutting rough openings in sheathing, fixing framing errors, cutting nail-embedded wood, or cutting the last ½ inch that your circular saw can't get to when you cut to a perpendicular line. Buy plenty of wood- and metal-cutting blades, but don't confuse the two. Wood blades have larger, more-offset teeth than the small-toothed metal-cutting blades.

■ **Power Miter Saw.** For angle cuts, you'll want to use a power miter saw, also called a chop saw. This tool is simply a circular saw mounted on a pivot assembly, which enables you to make precise straight and angled crosscuts in boards. You can buy chop saws that handle 10- to 15-inch blades. A 12-inch saw is often the best value for the money. Use a 60-tooth combination-cut carbide blade for all-around work.

You'll need a variety of handsaws for framing and finish work: crosscut saws are useful for making cuts where it's impractical to maneuver a circular saw.

A reciprocating saw, used for making rough cuts, is good for demolition work. It's also handy for cutting openings for a window, door, or roof vent.

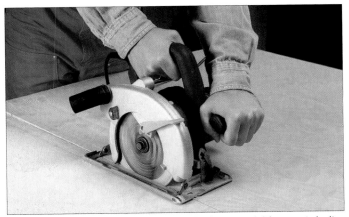

A 7¼-in. mid-priced circular saw is the best model for most do-it-yourselfers. Battery-powered models are available for sites located far from a source of electricity.

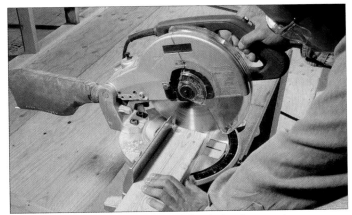

A power miter saw may be the right choice to speed up your production if you don't have enough room for a table or radial-arm saw in the work area.

Driving Nails & Screws

■ **Hammers.** Pros often use a 20- to 24-ounce waffle-head, or serrated, straight-claw framing hammer. Wooden (hickory) handles tend to absorb vibration better than fiberglass handles, so some people think wooden handles lessen your chances of developing repetitive motion ailments like carpal tunnel syndrome. If you're not used to manual labor, a 24-ounce hammer may be too heavy for you and you'll probably be better off with the 20- or 16-ounce size.

■ **Power Drill.** A corded or battery-powered drill is essential not only for driving wood screws but also for quickly and precisely drilling holes. If cost is an issue, buy a plug-in heavy-duty ⅜-inch drill with variable speeds. If you can afford the extra cost, you'll find a cordless drill even handier. Cordless drills come in an array of voltage ratings; the higher the voltage, the more powerful the drill. A 12-volt drill generally is powerful enough to fill all your needs.

■ **Nail Gun.** A pneumatic, or air-driven, nail gun, which uses a magazine that holds up to 100 or more nails, can take much of the tedium out of repetitive nailing. But you pay a price: nail guns are expensive and heavy, and you need compressors and hoses to run them. Nail guns really don't pay for themselves—purchased or rented—unless you have a great amount of nailing to do all at one time.

Most guns handle 6d through 16d nails. You'll need a compressor, gasoline or electric, and at least 100 feet of air hose. If you have a choice, go with the quieter electric compressor. Also, make sure you set the compressor's in-line regulator to the pressure required for the tool you'll be using.

Masonry Tools

Whether you're working with concrete, brick, or unit masonry (such as concrete block), you'll need many of the same basic masonry tools. You can easily rent many expensive items, so check before you buy a tool that you may not use often.

A framing hammer has a straight claw and a heavy head. It is used to drive nails. Lighter hammers are best for most DIYers, and for siding and finishing work.

A socket wrench kit or a set of combination wrenches is necessary for driving nuts onto bolts. If you're building a pole barn, buy extra-deep sockets and an extended handle.

An air-powered nail gun has a clip of banded nails that feed into the gun and are fired with a trigger squeeze. While handy, it is not cost-effective for the occasional builder of small projects.

A battery-powered electric drill offers convenience for barn projects, where there may not be enough power receptacles to go around. A ⅜-in. model will handle most DIY projects.

You'll need trowels and floats for the placing and finishing of concrete, and a bull float (made of magnesium or steel) or a darby (made of wood) to finish the upper layer of curing concrete. With a finishing trowel, you can create a smooth surface once the concrete is leveled; then you'll use edging and jointing trowels on the surface of the smooth concrete. An edging trowel makes a rounded edge on a concrete slab, which is safer and more durable than a sharp edge. A groover has a ridge down the center of its blade to form grooves or control joints. Jointers are metal rods (round or square) attached to a handle that you use to create various mortar joints when working with brick and concrete block.

Other Basic Tools

■ **Drill Bits.** The standard twist drill bit bores holes in wood, plastic, or metal. Spade bits quickly make large holes in wood, but not as cleanly as other bits. Masonry bits drill holes into brick and concrete. Hole saws make large, accu-

rate holes up to several inches in diameter. Single-twist auger bits have a small cone-shaped point at the tip to make them more accurate than traditional bits. Forstner bits cut holes with very little tear-out. An adjustable screw pilot bit will stop at a predetermined depth and cut a countersink.

■ **Wrenches.** Combination wrenches, adjustable wrenches, nut drivers, and socket wrenches have countless applications. You'll use pipe and spud wrenches when working with plumbing. For wiring, electrician's pliers, the multipurpose tool, and the cable ripper come in handy. Slip joint, diagonal-cutting, and needle-nose pliers have many practical uses.

■ **Woodworking Tools.** Use a tool belt when carrying nails and screws. Sanders, planes, and files help even out surfaces. Use measuring tapes to lay out the site and measure for cuts. Use knives and chisels to cut small amounts of material in places where a saw is not practical. You can use a pry bar as a lever in a variety of building situations. A screwdriver is often the only practical means of driving a screw.

Rubber float (A), striking tool (B), mason's trowel (C), wood float (D), 5-lb. hammer (E), magnesium float (F), jointer (G), brickset (H), notched trowel (I), and groover (J).

This basic collection includes a standard twist drill bit (A), spade bit (B), masonry bit (C), hole saw (D), single-twist auger bit (E), Forstner bit (F), and adjustable screw pilot bit (G).

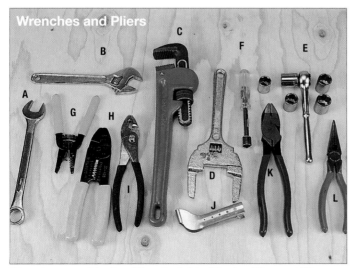

Wrenches: combination (A), adjustable (B), pipe (C), spud (D), socket (E), nut driver (F); pliers: electrician's (G), multipurpose tool (H), slip-joint (I), cable stripper (J), cutting (K), and needle-nose (L).

Tool belt (A), belt sander (B), smooth plane (C), scraper (D), long reel-type tape (E), screwdrivers (F), utility knife (G), measuring tape (H), sandpaper (I), wood chisels (J), wood files (K), and a pry bar (L).

Fasteners

Nails

The trick to choosing nails is to match the nail to the task. Codes often specify sizes of common nails for framing because they have an extra-thick shank and a broad head. You should use duplex, or double-headed, nails when you know you'll be removing the nail—in temporary sheathing, for example. Duplex nails allow you to snug the bottom nailhead up tight, but still give your hammer claw purchase to pull them out easily.

Besides common nails, you're likely to use ring-shank nails for subflooring; roofing nails and staples for applying felt paper, roofing shingles, and air-infiltration barriers (housewrap); and finishing nails for window- and door-jamb installations. Ring-shank nails have ridges on their shafts for extra holding power. Roofing nails have large heads to hold paper securely. Finishing nails are thin, with small heads that you can easily drive beneath the surface of the wood with a nail set.

Screws

There are many types of screws, but you'll probably use only a few in a barn project: wood screws or deck (buglehead) screws for joining lumber, and lag screws for making heavy-duty wood-to-wood attachments. Lag screws, sometimes called lag bolts because of their bolt-like heads, are heavy-duty screws that you drive with a socket wrench. They have wide threads for biting into wood like a screw but a hex-shaped head like a bolt. Lag screws are sized according to the diameter of their shanks: usually ⁵⁄₁₆, ⅜, or ½ inch.

Wood and deck screws are generally slotted or Phillips head, although there are other, less common head types. These screws are sized by their thickness, referred to by number. A screw's number indicates the diameter of its shank, the solid shaft of the screw measured at the base of the threads near the head. Common sizes are #6, #8, and #10. Of course, the length for any of these screws can vary. A #8 screw, for example, can be nearly any length up to about 3½ inches. The heavier the gauge, the more likely you are to find it in longer lengths.

Nail Sizes and Weights

Pennyweight	Length (in.)	Nails/lb. (Common)
2d	1	876
3d	1¼	568
4d	1½	316
5d	1¾	271
6d	2	181
7d	2¼	161
8d	2½	106
10d	3	69
12d	3¼	63
16d	3½	49
20d	4	31
30d	4½	24
40d	5	18
60d	6	14

Nail Types

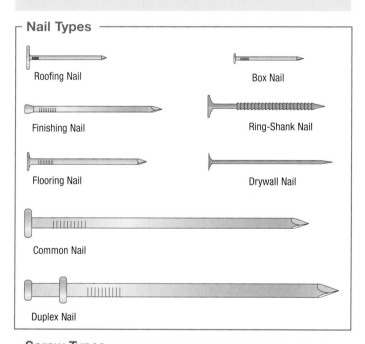

Screw Sizes

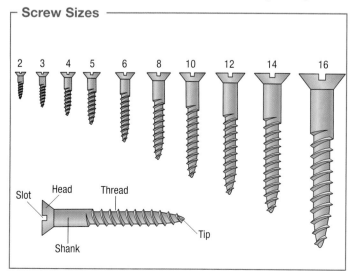

Screw Types

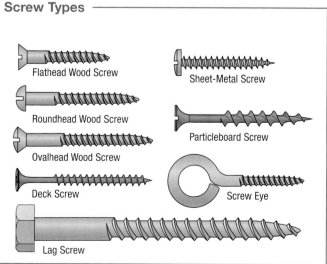

Bolts

Bolts fall into three main categories: carriage bolts, machine bolts, and stove bolts. Specialty bolts add many more categories. There are also about a dozen kinds of nuts and at least four kinds of washers. Each category of bolt, nut, and washer has a specific type of use and size requirement.

You probably won't find many framing applications for machine bolts, which have hex- or square-shaped heads, and stove bolts, which have rounded heads with a slot for a screwdriver. But carriage bolts, which have unslotted oval heads, can be effective when attaching structural lumber face-to-face or major timbers to posts. Carriage bolts have a square shoulder just beneath the head that digs into the wood as you tighten the bolt, which prevents it from slipping and spinning in the hole, and they are sized according to the diameter of their shanks as well as their length.

Another bolt you're likely to use, the anchor bolt, attaches the sill plate to the top of a foundation. Wedge-type bolts and J-bolts are the most common types.

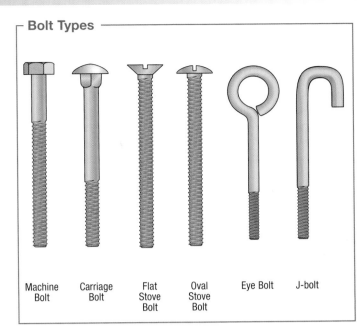

Bolt Types

Machine Bolt | Carriage Bolt | Flat Stove Bolt | Oval Stove Bolt | Eye Bolt | J-bolt

Framing Connectors

Major joints in framing, by code, need hangers, ties, anchors, or other metal supports for reinforcement. There often are special requirements in earthquake- or hurricane-prone areas. You can buy hangers and ties for a wide range of applications and for nearly every type of framing joint. For example, there are rafter ties for the joint between rafters and top plates, and joist hangers for joining ceiling or floor joists to header joists. Other commonly used fasteners include post anchors, which attach posts to concrete piers; truss plates, which hold together prebuilt roof trusses; panel clips, which join adjacent sheathing panels; and nail-stopping plates, which prevent drywall nails from being driven into pipes, wires, or ductwork.

Some connectors have nailing clips or teeth stamped into them, but these have little structural value and are used only to hold the hanger while you nail it in place. Some hangers require special nails; most use common nails.

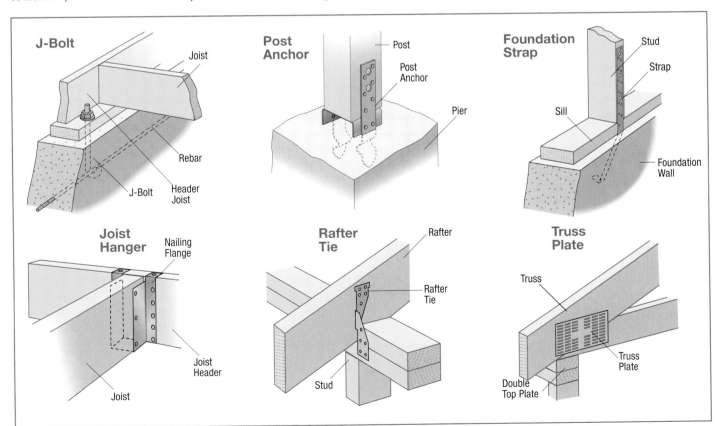

Lumber

Wood is one of the most important materials you'll buy for your project, so you should purchase the best quality you can afford.

Hardwood & Softwood

Wood is generally divided into two broad categories: hardwood and softwood. Common hardwoods include ash, birch, cherry, poplar, black walnut, maple, northern red oak, and white oak. Hardwoods come from slow-growing deciduous trees (trees that lose their leaves in winter); they are expensive and generally quite strong. Many hardwoods have beautiful grain patterns and are well suited to woodworking. But they are only used in the most expensive timber-frame construction.

Softwoods come from fast-growing, cone-bearing trees called conifers, or evergreens. Usually much less expensive than hardwoods and widely available at lumberyards, softwoods account for nearly all the lumber used in framing and construction. Though hardwoods are normally stronger because they're more dense, softwoods are certainly more than strong enough for utility framing.

Douglas fir, hemlock, eastern white pine, southern yellow pine, and spruce are all softwoods commonly used for framing. Douglas fir is used for most rough construction, especially along the Pacific Coast, where it is milled. In the South and East you're more likely to find southern pine. There are two other softwoods you might see, redwood and western red cedar, which aren't normally used for framing because of their expense. These species are excellent for exterior siding, trim, and decks because of their exceptional durability and natural resistance to decay.

Sawmills cut softwoods into standard dimensions and lengths. That's why the lumber is sometimes called dimension lumber. Unlike ordering hardwood, ordering softwood framing lumber generally doesn't require that you ask for a specific species of wood. You simply order by dimension and

grade. The lumberyard has already made a softwood choice for you by buying whatever wood is available for your region. The lumber is often simply stamped SPF for spruce, pine, fir; it can be any one of these softwood species. To understand lumber and how to use it properly, you need to know about the properties of a tree and the milling process.

Sapwood & Heartwood

There are two kinds of wood in all trees: sapwood and heartwood. Sapwood, as its name implies, carries sap to the leaves. The heartwood is the dense center of the tree. Trees that grow quickly (softwoods) tend to have disproportionately more sapwood. In fact, young trees consist of almost all sapwood. This is important to know when you buy lumber because sapwood and heartwood function differently in buildings. Heartwood, for instance, is used in exposed conditions or for special structural members because it is stronger and more durable. Sapwood is better suited for use as planks, siding, wall studs, and most other building components. And unless it's treated, sapwood lumber is more susceptible to decay than heartwood lumber.

Milled Dimensions

A piece of lumber has two sizes: nominal and actual. A 2×4 may start out at 2×4 inches (its nominal size) when it comes off a log, but it soon shrinks when it is dried. Then it shrinks again when it is planed. A 2×4 soon becomes 1½ × 3½ inches—the lumber's actual size. For wood lengths, the nominal and actual lengths are almost always the same. When you buy a 10-foot 2×4, it is usually 10 feet long (plus an inch or two).

Some lumberyards charge for lumber by the board foot, though increasingly yards are charging by the individual stick, or piece of lumber. If your lumberyard charges you by the board foot, here's how to figure it: take the nominal thickness, multiply it by the nominal width and the length, and divide by 12. A 10-foot 2×6 (usually written 2×6×10' in the industry) would be 10 board feet.

Lumber Grades and Cuts

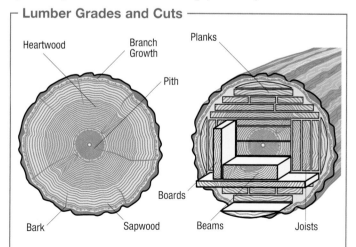

Two types of wood grow within all trees: sapwood and heartwood. Studs are typically sawed from the sapwood area, large-dimension and higher-grade boards and planks from the inner areas, and beams from the heartwood area.

Nominal & Actual Lumber Sizes

Nominal Size (in.)	Actual Size (in.)	Nominal Size (in.)	Actual Size (in.)
1×2	¾×1½	2×2	1½×1½
1×4	¾×3½	2×4	1½×3½
1×6	¾×5½	2×6	1½×5½
1×8	¾×7¼	2×8	1½×7¼
1×10	¾×9¼	2×10	1½×9¼
1×12	¾×11¼	2×12	1½×11¼
⁵⁄₄×2	1×1½	4×4	3½×3½
⁵⁄₄×4	1×3½	6×6	5½×5½

Grade Stamps

A typical grade stamp identifies the mill, the grading service's name, the moisture content, the grade, and the species.

The mill identification number isn't really important. The same with the grading service. The species mark is mostly a curiosity, too. But look closely at the biggest word in the grading stamp. You should see a word like STAND, which stands for Standard, the grade you'll use for standard residential-grade light framing. Next, look at the moisture designation. Here's where you'll see KD for kiln-dried, S-DRY, MC, or S-GRN. These are the moisture content ratings mentioned in the text below.

But no matter how much you know, the lumberyard will have already made most framing lumber choices for you, at least in terms of species. You'll simply specify the grade. Check the grading stamp at the yard to make sure you've picked up the right kind of wood.

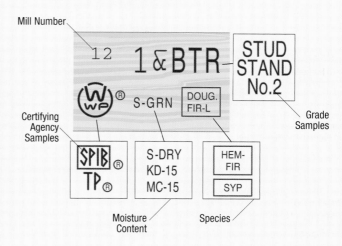

Grades

Besides sapwood and heartwood distinctions, many other wood features come into play, including moisture content, strength, number of knots, and appearance. A standardized system of grading rates wood for many of these qualities. The lower the grade, the poorer the quality.

Lumber grading for structural-grade lumber is complex, with categories, grades, and subgrades. For most framing, you'll find four lumber categories: select structural, No. 1, No. 2, and No. 3. The higher the number, the weaker the wood; the weaker the wood, the less distance you can span. A 2×8 hemlock-fir marked select-structural used as a joist and framed 16 inches on center might span 14 feet 2 inches, for instance, but a No. 3 grade only 11 feet. The wood gets weaker because there are more knots and less consistent grain as you move away from the select-structural grade. You also pay more for stronger wood. For structural framing—joists, rafters, ridgeboards—the typical lumber grade is No. 2.

When evaluating 2×4s, you'll find that there are three other names for the No. 1, No. 2, and No. 3 categories. Construction grade corresponds to No. 1; Standard-Better to No. 2; and Utility to No. 3. (A final category, Economy, is for nonstructural use.) For wall framing, use No. 2 (Standard or Better) for load-bearing and most other walls. Many yards don't stock weaker No. 3 (Utility). Because it's hard to sort this all out, and using utility lumber yields only marginal savings, you can safely buy No. 2 lumber and use it for your entire project.

All lumber has a high moisture content when it is milled. So it is either air-dried or kiln-dried for construction use. The acceptable maximum moisture content for framing wood at a lumberyard is 19 percent. Often the grade stamp for construction lumber will say "KD-19" (kiln-dried 19 percent).

Rough-Sawn Native Green Lumber

Available from some local sawmills, native green lumber's moisture content is usually high because it's sold unseasoned. Also, it's not cut as precisely as standard lumber. A

Rough-sawn green lumber can be ordered from some lumberyards and sawmills. It is beefier (a 2×4 being much closer to 2 in. thick), rougher, and more irregular than finished lumber.

2×8 can be 2¼ × 8½ inches, for instance, or 2 × 7¼ inches. It's unpredictable. Additionally, native green lumber is not as structurally stable as kiln-dried or air-dried dimension lumber. The wood is heavy and hard to work with, and it cracks and splits as it dries. Native green lumber is inexpensive, however, and it is often used to frame rough structures such as sheds or barns. Also, you can nail it in place soaking wet when you use it for board-and-batten siding.

Pressure-Treated Lumber

Pressure-treated (PT) wood is lumber that's been soaked under pressure with an insecticide and a fungicide, which ward off pests and decay, respectively. It's intended for use anywhere the wood contacts the ground (decks and piers), experiences sustained moisture levels (sills, outdoor stairs), or is subject to insect infestation (any exposed part of your structure in termite areas). PT lumber is mostly southern yellow pine, although some other pines, firs, and hemlocks are used occasionally.

Types. The most common kind of PT wood is treated with chromated copper arsenate (CCA), a compound that chemically bonds with the wood. CCA-treated lumber has a green tint from the oxidation of the copper. The retention level achieved during treatment determines its use. Lumber treated to 0.25 pounds of preservative per cubic foot is suitable for outdoor use above ground level. Lumber in contact with the ground should have a rating of 0.40. Even higher retention levels are available for special construction purposes such as wood foundations. For the most part, your lumberyard will carry one standard density.

CCA (and to some extent, all chemical treatments) is controversial. Some studies have shown that it dissolves back into the environment under certain circumstances. In response to these health concerns, some less-toxic alternatives are now available. ACQ Preserve with UltraWood water repellent and Kodiak are two types that manufacturers claim have less risk associated with them than those associated with CCA.

Cautions. Because CCA is potentially toxic, you should take precautions when working with it. Wear a long-sleeve shirt and long pants, work gloves, a dust mask, and eye protection. Do any cutting outside, and avoid sanding. Wash thoroughly before eating or drinking. Should you happen to get a splinter, remove it immediately—splinters from PT can be especially irritating. Clean up all scraps and sawdust, and either bury them or discard them in the trash. Never burn PT because the wood can release toxic gases.

Pressure-treated lumber (PT), easily recognized by its green tint, is commonly used on foundation sills.

Common Lumber Problems

As with any organic material that gains and loses water, wood swells when it is moist and shrinks as it dries. This can lead to warping (uneven shrinking during drying), checking (cracks along growth rings), bowing (end-to-end deviation from the plane of the board's wide face), twisting (spiral or torsional distortion), and cupping (deviation from a flat plane, edge to edge). Softwoods like pine, Douglas fir, and cedar are particularly vulnerable.

Given the demand on the nation's forests for wood, many lumber companies have shortened their harvesting cycles or have planted fast-growing trees. When these trees are harvested, they yield juvenile wood, which can give you problems. Juvenile wood encompasses the first 5 to 20 annual growth rings of any tree, and when it's used for lumber, it doesn't have the same strength as mature wood. You may get bouncy floors, buckled walls, weakened joints, and poorly fitting windows and doors. Even kiln-dried juvenile wood can warp because of non-uniform growth-ring distribution. Inspect the lumber you're buying, and look for telltale signs of juvenile wood, such as uneven grain distribution and warping, and refuse wood that is not up to par.

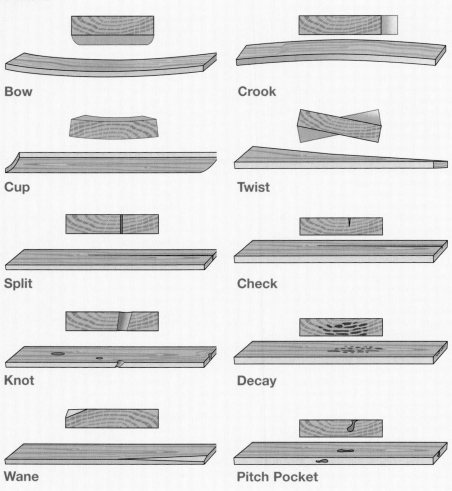

Bow

Crook

Cup

Twist

Split

Check

Knot

Decay

Wane

Pitch Pocket

Engineered Framing Products

Some engineered wood products were created in response to declining wood quality and rising costs. High-quality long beams of Douglas fir are expensive and few lumberyards will stock them. Engineered products using smaller pieces of lumber were created to fill the gap. You must use engineered products in strict accordance with manufacturers' span specifications. In addition, you must install them with specified techniques and, in some cases, special connectors.

■ **Glue-Laminated Lumber.** A glue-laminated beam is made up of smaller pieces of wood glued together lengthwise with waterproof glue. Glue-laminated lumber can be as long as you like—25 feet or longer. Each beam is specifically engineered to support an intended load. No matter what kind of glue-laminated lumber you install, you can't just nail it in place. You'll need framing connectors, shear plates, threaded rods, nail-on clips, or hangers at the connections.

■ **Laminated-Veneer Lumber (LVL).** LVL can replace steel or an oversize glue-laminated beam. It is made, as the name implies, by laminating ¼-thick plies together to a thickness of 4½ inches. You'll have to consult with the manufacturers' span charts to determine the size LVL to use on your job. Even when you get the span rating down, be careful, because you can't notch or drill LVLs for pipes, wires, and heating or air-conditioning ducts, and you have to use the proper connectors.

■ **Parallel-Strand Lumber.** Parallel-strand lumber is a kind of engineered beam, between 1¾ and 7 inches thick, made of thin strands of Douglas fir and/or southern yellow pine. The strands are glued together running parallel with one another. These beams are more dimensionally stable than LVLs or glue-laminated lumber beams, and they serve in the same applications. Parallel-strand lumber resists cupping and twisting when stored, which is a potential problem with some glue-laminated beams and LVLs.

■ **Wood I-Joists.** Wood I-joists are straight, dimensionally stable, and ideal for longer spans. I-joists are light and easy to install. The web, or center, of a wood I-joist is typically ½-inch plywood or oriented-strand board (OSB), and the 2-inch rails at the top and bottom are fir. Wood I-joists come in four sizes: 9½, 11⅞, 14, and 16 inches deep. Some connections may require special hardware.

Glue-laminated lumber is built up of finger-jointed dimensional lumber that must be sized for your application. The lumber is usually used as ridge beams, purlins, headers, and floor girders. Cambered beams are also available.

Parallel-strand lumber, similar to glue-laminated lumber, is made from individual strands of softwood lumber and an adhesive. These engineered beams may be up to 7 in. thick; you can order them in lengths up to 60 ft.

Laminated-veneer lumber (LVL) is a beam composed of wooden plies (like the layers of a plywood panel) glued together. The beams can be ordered in depth from 9¼ to 18 in. and anything up to 60 ft. long.

Wood I-joists can take the place of lumber joists in floors and ceilings. They are made with solid- or engineered-wood rails (the upper and lower part of the I) and ½-in. plywood or OSB webs. Web stiffeners and framing connectors may be required.

Plywood & Panel Products

Depending on your design, you might need plywood for floor decking and wall and roof sheathing. Plywood comprises an odd number of thin veneer layers of wood, called plies. The veneers are cross-laminated so the grain of one ply runs perpendicular to another. The veneers are glued and sandwiched together and then heated to over 300°F under 200 pounds per square inch (psi) of pressure. Standard plywood thicknesses are ⁵⁄₁₆, ⅜, ⁷⁄₁₆, ¹⁵⁄₃₂, ½, ⅝, ²³⁄₃₂, ¾, and 1⅛ inches. If you order ½- and ¾-inch plywood for your job, you'll most likely get ¹⁵⁄₃₂- and ²³⁄₃₂-inch plywood, respectively. Panels are almost always 4 × 8 feet after factory trimming. Corner to corner, panels sometimes can be slightly out of square, but not enough to cause problems.

Every piece of plywood has a face veneer and a back veneer. These are the outside plies. The plies under the face and back veneers are called crossbands, and the center ply is called the core. The core can be either veneer or solid lumber. Some plywoods even have fiberglass or particleboard at their cores. Veneer-core plywood is stronger than lumber-core plywood, but lumber-core plywood can hold screws better at its edges.

Used in the right applications, plywood is strong and adds stiffness to walls and strength to floors. Besides conventional sheathing plywood, you can buy treated, fire-retardant, and waterproof plywood for special applications.

Other Panel Products

Panel products other than plywood, called nonveneer or reconstituted wood-product panels, are sometimes used for sheathing. (Check this with your local building department.) Some of these panels are just as strong—and cheaper—than plywood. The products are called reconstituted because they're made from wood particles or wood strands that are bonded together with adhesive into 4 × 8-foot sheets.

- **Structural Particleboard.** Also called flakeboard or chipboard, particleboard is simply a panel of wood particles held together by hot-pressed resin. Some exterior-rated products have a layer of resin or wax on the outside to repel water. The glue used in these products is urea formaldehyde or phenol-formaldehyde adhesive. Some building-code organizations allow you to use structural particleboard as an underlayment or a subfloor.
- **Oriented-Strand Board.** Usually called OSB, this product also uses strands of wood, but the layers are crossed so that the direction of the grain of each layer is at 90 degrees to the previous layer, just as plywood is cross-laminated to give it strength. The three to five layers of strands in OSB are bonded together with phenolic resin. These panels have a smooth face and are often rated for structural applications. Waferboard, sometimes called strand board, is a similar product, but without the alternating layers of OSB.
- **Composite Board.** Basically a hybrid of plywood and particleboard, composite board has a reconstituted-wood-particle center but a face and back of plywood veneer. Where codes allow, you can use composite board as wall sheathing and floor underlayments.

Rating Panel Products

When you purchase structural panels, a grading label tells you what you're buying. The leading grading association is the American Plywood Association (APA), and you're most likely to see its stamp. (See next page, bottom right.)
- **Panel Grade.** Panel products are rated in a number of categories. If you look at a typical APA grade stamp, you'll see the panel grade on the top line. This entry designates the proper application for the panel—rated sheathing, rated flooring, rated underlayment, and the like.
- **Span Rating.** Next you'll see a large number or numbers, indicating the span rating. This rating is the recommended center-to-center spacing in inches of studs/joists/rafters

Common Wood Panel Products

Plywood consists of several thin layers glued together with their grains running in alternating directions. Plywood comes in several thicknesses, grades and ratings that indicate their use.

Structural particleboard is made from wood chips and sawdust glued together typically with urea formaldehyde resin into 4 × 8-ft. sheets. Its uses are often restricted by local building codes.

Oriented-strand board (OSB) is made from opposingly placed strips of scrap wood, held together with waterproof adhesives. OSB is allowed by many codes as subflooring and sheathing.

Tips on Materials, Deliveries & Storage

Stage deliveries so that your materials aren't backlogged, and you'll never run short of what you need. A good approach is to produce all your cut lists at the beginning of the job, break them down into work stages (foundation, rough framing, rafters, sheathing, roofing, windows and doors, siding and interior finish), and assign delivery dates for the materials needed for each work stage.

Using your site plan, with a clear outline of the footprint of your barn, designate some material drops. Lumber is heavy, so have it dropped close by. If you use trusses, which are fragile until set in place, don't schedule delivery until your truss crew is on hand. Windows and doors can go into a nearby garage. Trim lumber or siding, should be set in a clean, dry area, up on blocks.

Though it may be sunny and dry when materials are delivered, you should protect your deliveries against the elements. Many lumberyards have pallets that they will offer for free to keep the wood off the ground. Covering it with plastic is a good idea, but leave the ends of the wood open to breathe.

Finally, plan your deliveries to take advantage of any labor-saving tools the lumberyards offer. If the delivery truck has a lift, have them place rafter lumber on the second-floor deck.

Have drywall delivered after the exterior has been sheathed and windows have been installed, and store it indoors.

over which you can place the panel. If you see numbers like 32/16, the left number shows the maximum spacing in inches of the panel when used in roofing—32 inches of allowable span with three or more supports—and the right number gives the maximum spacing when the panel is used as subflooring—16 inches of allowable span with three or more supports.

- **Thickness.** The grade stamp also identifies the thickness of the panel—⅜ inch, ⁷⁄₁₆ inch, ¹⁵⁄₃₂ inch, ²³⁄₃₂ inch, and so on.
- **Exposure.** The stamp also lists the exposure and durability classification for plywood. Exterior indicates exposure to weather is possible; Exposure 1 designates suitability for wall and roof sheathing; Exposure 2, for applications that will have low moisture exposure, such as subfloors.
- **Mill & Standards Numbers.** The mill number simply identifies the manufacturer. The remaining numbers on the label—the national evaluation report (NER) and performance-rated panel standard (PRP)—indicate that the panel meets all construction requirements and requisite codes.
- **Veneer Grades.** Plywood is also rated for veneer grades, and that rating appears on the edge of the plywood in combinations of letters. There are six categories in veneer ratings: N, A, B, C Plugged, C, and D, indicating descending order of quality. N is a smooth surface of select woods with no defects, but you won't be using N in framing. It's for use in cabinetry. For construction-grade plywood, the face-and-back-veneer grades are combinations of letters. B-C, for example, is suitable for sheathing, while you'd use A-B when both the face and back veneers will show. A-C or A-D is suitable when only the A side will show, and C-D is used for concrete forms.

Common Plywood Types

For most outbuilding projects you'll be using ½-inch or ⅝-inch BC or CDX plywood—Exposure 1 for wall and roof sheathing and Exposure 2 for subfloors. If you're finishing a barn or shed with plywood alone, you may want to consider AC, which has one "good" side without any repair plugs or major defects.

Another alterative is Texture 1-11, which has grooves cut into it to resemble board siding. T1-11 comes in 4 × 8-foot and larger panels. For high walls, you need to cover the seam between the first and second courses with trim in order to maintain the illusion of board siding.

Typical Plywood Grade

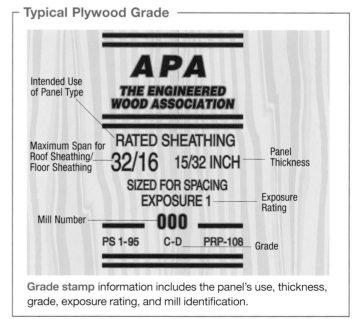

Grade stamp information includes the panel's use, thickness, grade, exposure rating, and mill identification.

Ladders, Scaffolds & Fall Protection

Most accidents in the construction industry are a result of falling. The risks increase as you move higher on a building. However, you can work safely by using the ladders, scaffolds, and fall-arrest devices on the market today. When you use these systems properly, you can protect yourself and anyone else working on your project, and increase overall job productivity.

Ladders

There are three basic kinds of ladders: stepladders, fold-up (articulated) ladders, and extension ladders. Stepladders are stable on a level surface, but you should never use one on a slope. The hazard with a stepladder is that the higher you go, the more unstable the ladder is. If you find you're working with your feet on or near the top three steps, you should move to a scaffold work platform or extension ladder.

Fold-up ladders are great for working mid-distances between 4 and 12 feet off the ground. These ladders are handy because you can extend the ladder and lock it straight to act as a standard, one-section ladder, lock it in an A position to act as a stepladder, or fold it into an M shape or into an upside-down U shape as a mini-scaffold on which you can place certified scaffold planks.

Extension ladders are used mostly for high outdoor work. Depending on the performance rating you use, these ladders will support the weight of a worker plus material (shingles, lumber, one end of a beam). Extension ladders are available in a wide range of sizes, typically from 20 to 50 feet.

You'll find each kind of ladder in metal (usually aluminum) or fiberglass, and many stepladders and extension ladders made of wood. The type you'll choose depends on the work at hand and how much you want to spend.

■ **Ratings.** Ladders are rated for the weight they can hold. You'll see a sticker on most ladders identifying their type. Type III ladders are light-duty and can carry 200 pounds per rung or step. Type II are medium-duty and can carry 225 pounds per rung or step. Type I ladders are heavy-duty industrial ladders and can hold 250 pounds per rung. Type IA ladders are extra heavy-duty and can hold 300 pounds per rung. Type I ladders are well worth the extra money for their greater safety margin.

■ **Safe Use.** When you use a straight ladder, set it against a vertical surface at the proper angle. As a rule of thumb, the distance between the base of the ladder and the structure should be one-quarter the ladder's extension. If your ladder extends 16 feet, for example, it should be about 4 feet from the wall. Anything steeper increases the risk that the ladder will topple backward when someone is on it, especially near the top. Anything shallower risks that the ladder may kick out or slide. Bear in mind these two rules for safety: allow the top of the ladder to extend about 3 feet past your work area; and if you're working near electrical lines use a fiberglass ladder.

Platform Jacks

It's often more practical to work from a platform rather than a ladder when you're framing. You can create a sturdy work platform using various kinds of brackets, called jacks, attached to a ladder, the roof, or vertical 4×4 posts.

■ **Roof Jacks.** Roof jacks are nailed directly through sheathing into rafters, allowing them to sit on the roof surface. The arms of the roof jacks that support a plank are adjustable, so you can level scaffold planks for roofs of various pitches. The plank provides a work surface for applying both shingles and tar paper.

■ **Ladder Jacks.** These metal brackets that hook onto extension ladders provide stable, level support for 2×10 scaf-

┌ **Ladders** ─────────────────

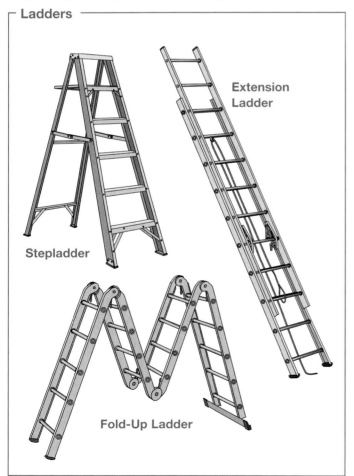

Extension Ladder

Stepladder

Fold-Up Ladder

┌ **Roof Jack** ─────────────────

fold planks or an aluminum platform. To use the jacks, you need two ladders, one for each end of the plank or work surface. There are two configurations for scaffold ladder jacks: inside-bracket and outside-bracket types. Inside ladder jacks suspend a plank or work platform beneath the ladders as they rest against a structure. Outside ladder jacks support a plank on the front face of the ladders as they rest against a structure. Either way, the jacks hook onto the rungs of the ladder at the junction of rungs and rails.

■ **Pump Jacks.** Pump jacks are metal brackets that travel up and down on 4×4 posts. The vertical part of the L hugs the post and the horizontal part supports a plank or work surface. Other brackets, which you attach to structural members of the wall, hold the 4×4 uprights to the structure. To raise the work platform, you pump the L-shaped jacks with your foot. To lower the platform, you turn a crank.

OSHA rules require rails on the back side of a pump-jack platform (the side against which a worker leans back when working on a structure). You need a 42-inch-high top rail, a 21-inch midrail, and a 4-inch toe board.

The planks that make up the work platform can span a maximum of 10 feet. The uprights can extend a maximum of 30 feet into the air. At their bases, the upright supports must bear on feet that keep them from sinking into the ground. If people are expected to be working below the pump-jack platform at any time, you must string plastic netting on the guard rails to keep things like dropped tools and materials from falling.

Scaffolds

Prefabricated scaffolds are aluminum- or steel-tube-framed structures that you assemble on site. You can make your own wooden scaffold, but prefabricated units are generally safer. Scaffolds provide an ideal working surface for such tasks as installing exterior sheathing or siding. Scaffolding is certainly good to have on site, but it's expensive to rent and prohibitive to buy. You may find other ways to work at heights—such as pump jacks in particular—that are more cost-effective for your project.

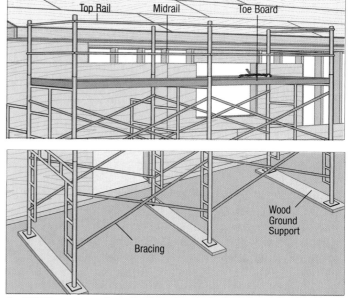

An **OSHA-approved scaffold system** includes a top rail, midrail, toe board (top), and wood supports beneath the baseplates (bottom).

Fall-Arrest Systems

One efficient way to protect against falls from a roof is a personal fall-arrest system. A full-body harness with a ring at the center of its back clips into one end of a lanyard, or tether. The other end of the lanyard clips into a rope-grab ascender, a one-way clamp that catches the rope if there is any downward pull, so you can go up but not down. You can release the ascender to descend. To use an ascender, clamp it onto a rope, and clip the rope into an anchor that's securely fastened into the ridgeboard or framing member. If you fall when wearing a personal fall-arrest system, you'll fall only as far as the slack of the lanyard and rope. A fall-arrest system costs around $350 for a starter kit, which includes all you'll need for most jobs.

As a practical matter, most novice do-it-yourselfers should work only on walkable roofs. These are roofs with a relatively low slope that you can negotiate safely without special fall-arrest systems.

┌─ **Ladder Jack** ─────────

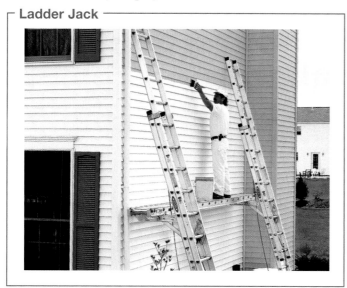

┌─ **Pump Jack** ─────────

CHAPTER 3

Foundations

All permanent structures need to be firmly attached to the ground—that is, built on a foundation. In fact, a well-designed and properly built foundation is the key to the safety and durability of a building. The type of foundation you will need to build depends on the design, size, and intended use of your building, the soil type on your site, and the depth of frost penetration in the area. Small, light buildings, such as storage sheds and chicken coops, often can be built on wooden skids set on the ground. Larger buildings will need concrete footings, and concrete or block foundations. Barns built on masonry piers or interlocked poles have their own foundation requirements.

Types of Foundations

Barns and sheds often require different foundations than houses. Many houses, at least in the northern half of the United States and Canada, have perimeter wall foundations made from concrete block or poured concrete, providing a basement or crawl space underneath the house. While you could build a barn with a full basement if you wanted to— big nineteenth century dairy barns often have a floor at least partially below grade—it is an extra expense almost never undertaken in outbuildings. Depending on the size and type of outbuilding, you're likely to use one of these foundations.

- **Concrete Slabs & Footings.** A slab is a thick layer (often 4 to 6 inches) of poured concrete reinforced with welded wire. You can combine slabs with foundations to hold up buildings by pouring a thickened edge (basically a footing and foundation in one) that is reinforced with steel bars. A slab is laid directly over a layer of compacted gravel in many barns to provide the finished floor. If you don't need a finished floor, you can pour a concrete perimeter foundation and leave a dirt floor.
- **Skids.** Pressure-treated timbers, such as 6x6s, often can handle sheds under 100 square feet that won't have to bear heavy loads. The skids should rest on trenches filled with compacted gravel to prevent excessive movement.
- **Wall Foundations.** You can use poured concrete or stacked concrete block reinforced with rebar. Less common wood-wall foundations, generally called permanent wood foundations, are used in regions with cold winters, particularly in Canada, because they can be built in weather too cold to pour concrete. Pressure-treated wood rated for ground contact is used for this foundation.
- **Pier & Beam.** This system is simply a combination of a footing with some type of foundation wall bridged by beams to support a floor.
- **Poles.** This unique system is one of the most efficient ways to build large barns. It consists of large-diameter poles commonly set below frost depth on concrete footings.

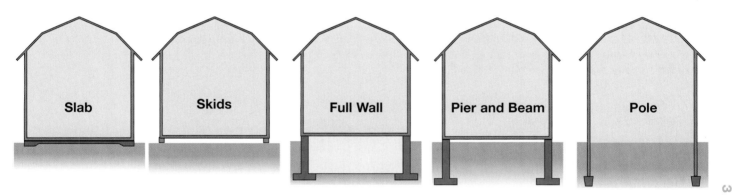

| Slab | Skids | Full Wall | Pier and Beam | Pole |

Plumbing & Electrical

If your outbuilding will have plumbing or electrical wiring, you need to make preparations for these systems before you begin to build the foundation. You'll need to dig trenches and install your below-grade pipes for your water-supply lines and drainpipes, as well as underground conduit for wires, before you place any rebar or wire-mesh reinforcement. If you want footing drains to deal with runoff, this is the time to install them. Local building codes will dictate the types of pipe and conduit permitted and how deep these pipes need to be. Wires can usually be 12 to 18 inches below grade; in areas with cold winters, plumbing pipes generally will have to be at least 48 inches below grade.

If you're pouring a slab foundation, you can use plastic pipe to create spaces in the concrete slab. The idea is to leave holes in the finished floor for a toilet flange, floor drain, and other mechanical fittings. In some localities, floor drains are required by code. Even if you won't be pouring a slab, you'll still want to install the main supply and drainpipes and any underground electrical conduit before you begin construction. If you're pouring a foundation, you can insert plastic pipes through the forms to provide mechanical access.

Provide mechanical access by cutting through plywood foundation forms and inserting plastic pipe before pouring concrete.

Site Preparation

The amount of site preparation required varies with the project. A dirt-floor pole barn located in a flat, well-drained area on stable soil might only need weeds cleared before you excavate. A slab-on-grade foundation on a sloped spot in a heavily wooded part of your property that also has poorly draining soil will require a great deal of work involving chain saws and heavy equipment. In areas with poor drainage, you will need to excavate enough soil to accommodate a layer of tamped gravel. If there's any doubt in your mind about your site, have an engineer test the soil. Improper site preparation will inevitably lead to uneven settling or heaving.

Marking a Layout

To lay out the rough corners of a basic building you'll need four 2×4 stakes and a 50- or 100-foot measuring tape. To find the location of your building's corners, measure from your property line, or from an existing structure on your property. To make sure your layout is square, measure the diagonals (they will be the same length in a square or rectangle), or use the 3-4-5 triangulation method. To lay out large foundations, especially those being built on a slope, it's wise to use a transit level or builder's level.

If you're not going to need excavation with heavy machinery, you can tie mason's string to nails on the corner boards and keep these lines as your layout marks. Once the layout is square, if the strings will get in your way, use spray paint to mark the ground underneath the lines. If you need to excavate the site, however, you'll need to build batter boards, which move the stakes outside of the building layout. Otherwise, a bulldozer or backhoe will excavate your corner boards along with the dirt.

Excavation

You can excavate for a foundation or a small slab with just a shovel or posthole digger and a lot of backbreaking work. Extensive excavation is best left to a contractor with the necessary heavy equipment. Although a professional operator can dig a hole with accuracy, machinery also can damage your yard. It pays to mark a particular route you want the operator to take to the site, and trees or bushes that you don't want knocked down or damaged.

Always have the local utility company inspect the site and locate and mark all the utility lines you'll need to avoid. Also, be sure your contract is explicit about soil and trees that are removed. Never bury stumps and wood scraps near the foundation because that may cause termite problems.

Preparing and Leveling a Site

For most slab construction or to cut into a slope, you'll need to hire a contractor to operate a bulldozer or backhoe.

A 4 x 4 post, powered by elbow grease, makes an effective hand tamper to compact soil and gravel in a foundation.

Rent a gasoline-powered vibration compactor for large jobs. These machines solidify ground and gravel under concrete.

Begin excavating the soil within your string lines by undercutting and rolling up sod, which you can use elsewhere.

Transits & Laser Levels

Even though you might not be familiar with them, it may be worth your while to rent a transit or a laser level and gain some experience with one of these tools. Their accuracy is the best way to be sure that your foundation is level and square.

Transits

A transit looks like a short telescope attached to a scale that is mounted on a plate on top of a tripod. The scope pivots both vertically and horizontally—unlike a builder's level (sometimes called a dumpy level), which only pivots horizontally and therefore can't be used to calculate a slope.

With a perfectly leveled transit you can sight a level line in a full circle, sight perfectly right-angled (90-degree) corners from a fixed spot, or exactly lay out a 1 percent slope for a trench that will hold a drainpipe.

To use a transit, you'll need to level the scope because even a minuscule error in leveling can be amplified to a significant amount over the length of your layout line. When you set the tripod into the ground, adjust the plate on which the transit sits (called the leveling plate) as close to level as you can, either by eye or with a spirit level built into the transit. Lock the plate so that the Vernier scale (which measures vertical tilt) reads in a level position. Aim the transit at 0 on the horizontal scale, and then use the leveling screws to further adjust the transit until it reads level. Repeat this process at 90, 180, and 270 degrees, releveling the plate each time. Once you've leveled it in the fourth direction, the transit should be perfectly straight.

To mark level points with a transit, you'll need to have all four batter boards set up. The simplest way to do it is to sight all four batter boards in the scope, and then have a helper make a mark where the crosshairs intersect. Measuring down uniformly from these marks will always give you points at the same level. You can use this method to check whether form boards are level and deep enough to contain your pour.

Laser Levels

Laser levels are similar to transits: they also pivot horizontally and vertically, enabling you to mark a level plane or sight perfect corners. However, a laser level doesn't require a second person to make marks. It sends a beam of light where you've sighted it, allowing the user to mark a line while working alone.

Laying Out Corners

To lay out the four corners of a building, attach a plumb bob under the tripod head, and set the transit directly over where you have set your first corner. Sight the transit along a string (after unlocking the vertical pivot screw) until the string is lined up in the scope's crosshairs. Set the horizontal scale to 0, and then rotate the scope to exactly 90 degrees. Have a helper place a batter board along where you've sighted, and mark exactly on the board where the crosshairs line up. This creates a line at an exact right angle to the string line you first sighted. From this perfect corner, you can lay out the remaining two sides of the building by measuring them. In the end, all four angles will be exactly 90 degrees.

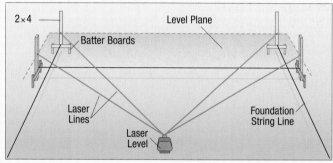

To level a site, rotate the scope of a transit or laser level and mark level points on poles at the corners. Batter boards set at a fixed distance below these marks indicate the new grade.

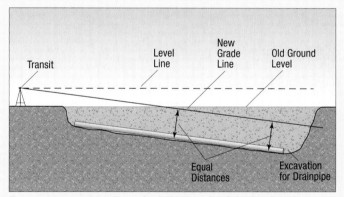

To mark a precise slope, lock the scope of the level at the incline desired, for example, on a drainage pipe. Use a pole to make marks on stakes a fixed distance below the sloped line.

To use a transit, one person sights through the scope, while another makes reference marks where the first person indicates. A laser level, which casts a beam of light, can be used by one person. Both are accurate to distances up to 200 ft.

Squaring Corners

A simple system for creating a perfectly square building layout is the 3-4-5 method of triangulation. Starting at corner A, measure 3 feet along one guideline and mark point B. Starting again from corner A, measure 4 feet along the guideline perpendicular to the first one, and mark point C. Adjust the AC line until the distance BC is exactly 5 feet. Angle BAC is now a true 90-degree angle. You can double-check the squareness of corners and the overall layout by measuring the diagonals between opposite corners. The two distances should be equal if the layout is square.

3-4-5 Triangulation

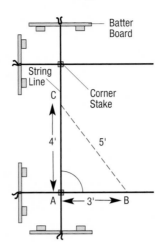

Diagonal check

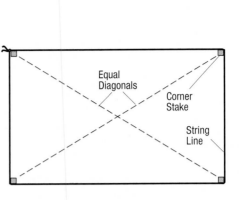

Making Batter Boards

TOOLS & MATERIALS

- Circular saw
- Clamps
- Power drill-driver
- Short sledgehammer
- Spirit level
- Line level
- Measuring tape
- Work gloves
- Safety glasses

- 2×4 stakes
- 1×4 boards
- 1" drywall screws
- Mason's string

1 Cut 16 stakes (4 for each corner) from 2×4s, about 3 ft. long, with pointed ends. These stakes support the horizontal batter boards.

2 Set pairs of 2×4 stakes at roughly right angles to each other, 2 or more feet outside the corners and parallel with the lines of the foundation.

3 Make batter boards by cutting 2-ft. 1×4s. After drilling pilot holes, screw the batter boards to the stakes, using clamps to hold the boards in position.

4 Use a level to check the batter boards. This allows you to stretch level string lines along the perimeter of the building foundation.

5 Tack nails into the batter boards. Then fasten guidelines to the nails in the boards to establish the exact building corners and overall outline.

Frost Depth & Frost Heaving

Water expands in volume by about 10 percent when it freezes, which can exert enough pressure to break apart concrete from below. To avoid this problem, called frost heave, piers and footings need to reach below the frost line, which is the average maximum depth of frost penetration. This map shows the average depth of frost throughout the U.S. In the western and northern parts of the country, as well as in Canada, freezing patterns vary so much that zoning is all but impossible. Even within zones, frost depths can vary depending on local weather patterns, altitude, and soil. Local building codes strictly regulate foundation depth and construction. To be safe, you should always consult the building inspector before starting a foundation project.

Vapor Barriers

To avoid problems with condensation and moisture buildup on your foundation, you should lay a vapor-retarding ground cover over the grade before you fill in your excavation with gravel. This is recommended particularly for the areas in dark green on the map at right. The barrier should be 6-mil-thick polyethylene sheeting, which is available at most home centers. Lay the barrier in the bottom of the excavation, and cover it with a few inches of sand to prevent the gravel from tearing holes in it. Individual sheets should overlap one another by at least 6 inches to prevent leaks. In areas with severe termite problems, you might want to replace the sand with special termite sand or add some kind of chemical-based termite protection.

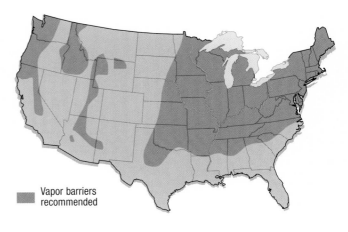

■ Vapor barriers
recommended

Termite Protection

In regions where termite infestation is a problem, steps must be taken to block the termites between the ground and the wood (typically the sill) at the foundation. Never bury any wood debris near a building, and make sure that you've cleared away grade stakes and footing forms. Place metal termite shields between the foundation and the sill for wall foundations. For slabs, a few inches of termite sand or diatomaceous earth on top of your vapor barrier should deter any termites from living underneath your floor. In some regions, the sand must be treated with an insecticide; consult with the building inspector. Bear in mind that in the most southern regions there are flying termites that can bridge typical ground approach defenses.

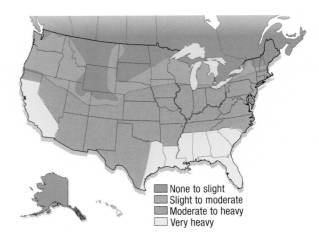

■ None to slight
■ Slight to moderate
■ Moderate to heavy
□ Very heavy

Concrete Basics

Concrete is a mixture of portland cement, sand, gravel, and water. You can purchase the dry ingredients separately or buy them premixed, generally in 80-pound bags.

Mixing Options

For large-scale projects, however, you should order ready-mix concrete. It is sold by the cubic yard and delivered in a truck ready to pour. For smaller jobs— say, form-tube piers for a small storage shed—you can mix your own concrete by adding water according to the instructions of the bag or by following the table, "Concrete Ingredients by Proportion," at right.

But don't get too ambitious. One cubic yard, only enough for an 8×10-foot 4-inch slab, would require about 40 of those 80-pound bags. For mid-size jobs or those that a concrete truck can't drive to, it makes sense to rent a portable power mixer. For estimating purposes, you can make about 1 cubic yard of concrete with five 94-pound bags of portland cement, 14 cubic feet of sand, and 21 cubic feet of gravel.

Ordering Concrete

Before you call, have an estimate for your order. Most ready-mix contractors will require only a day's notice. It's important to double-check your measurements of length times width times depth (and your calculations) to specify the order in cubic yards. Always round up your numbers so that you don't run short of material.

Mix Variations

When hand-mixing, you may be tempted to adjust the mix proportions—say, by adding more water to make the concrete easier to mix and pour. However, as water content can drastically affect strength, the best policy is to order ready-mixed concrete or precisely follow directions on the bags.

The standard proportion of water to cement produces concrete with a compressive strength of 3,000 to 4,000 pounds per square inch (psi). Adding less water makes mixing more difficult and could weaken the mix.

Ready-mix concrete is also available with additives unavailable to the DIYer. One type produces microscopic air bubbles. This air-entrained concrete is more resistant to cracking than concrete you mix on site. There are also additives that accelerate the curing time for concrete poured in cold weather. You can order ready-mix concrete to a greater compressive strength than hand-mixed concrete, to support a greater building load.

Curing

The process of hardening concrete and bringing it to its full strength is called curing. Concrete begins to harden as soon as it is mixed, and can support your weight within a few hours. Most of the curing takes place in the first two weeks, but it takes a month to reach near its peak hardness. Most concrete needs to be kept moist over seven consecutive days above 50° F to cure properly. If the temperature is above 70° F, the concrete may cure in five days; high-early-strength concrete needs only three. Curing concrete can be sprinkled periodically with water and covered with plastic sheeting, burlap, canvas, or straw to limit dehydration. There are also liquid curing compounds that you can roll onto concrete.

Curing in Extreme Heat. Concrete will dehydrate too quickly in hot weather, robbing it of the water it needs to cure. In extreme cases, a steady hot, dry breeze can accelerate evaporation so that the surface begins to set before it can be smoothed. There are some solutions, such as adding flaked ice or cooling down the aggregates with a sprinkler before adding them to the mix. To eliminate the risk of wasting your efforts on a job that doesn't last, don't pour in temperatures over 90°F. It's also important to remember that if the mix makes contact with a hot surface, moisture may burn off. It's wise to spray some cool water on forms that are sitting in the sun as well as on the reinforcing bar, which can get quite hot to the touch.

Mixing Concrete

TOOLS
- Mason's hoe
- Wheelbarrow
- Shovel
- Work gloves

MATERIALS
- Concrete mix
- Water

1 If concrete is too wet, ridges made in the mix with a trowel won't hold their shape. The concrete will be easy to mix and pour, but will not settle evenly nor provide its rated strength.

2 If concrete is too dry, you won't be able to make any ridges in the mix. It will be difficult to work. Mainly, the concrete will not cure properly and will not develop required strength.

3 When the concrete is mixed correctly, the ridges will hold most of their shape; only a little water will be visible on the surface. Place the concrete quickly, before it becomes too stiff to work.

Curing Concrete

TOOLS
- Garden hose
- Paint roller

MATERIALS
- Curing compound
- Straw
- Tarpaulin/plastic sheeting

1 To keep concrete sufficiently moist during the curing process, you can periodically spray the finished surface lightly but thoroughly with water from a garden hose.

2 A chemical curing compound, applied to concrete with a paint roller or air-powered paint sprayer, is one way to prevent water loss during curing. Apply it after the surface has set up.

3 Another way to prevent concrete from drying prematurely is to cover the slab with plastic sheeting held down with lumber or bricks. Burlap or straw can also be used but must be kept moist.

Concrete Finishes

Floating concrete after jointing and edging will drive the large aggregate below the surface and further smooth the concrete. Different tools—a wooden float, metal float, or even a stiff-bristled broom—will leave behind very different finishes. Steps and walkways can be given additional color and texture with extra aggregate added to the surface. Don't overwork the surface of air-entrained concrete, however: it can impair the concrete's frost resistance by removing air near the surface.

A wooden-float finish is slightly rough, just enough to be slip-resistant for safety, and also glare-free.

A steel-trowel finish is smooth, and is best suited for interior applications such as finished floor slabs.

A broomed surface is rough and very slip-resistant; this finish is ideal for outdoor steps and walkways.

Concrete Ingredients by Proportion

	Air-Entrained Concrete				Concrete without Air			
Maximum Size Course Aggregate Inches	Number of Parts per Ingredient				Number of Parts per Ingredient			
	Cement	Sand*	Coarse Aggregate	Water	Cement	Sand*	Coarse Aggregate	Water
⅜	1	2¼	1½	½	1	2½	1½	½
½	1	2¼	2	½	1	2½	2	½
¾	1	2¼	2½	½	1	2½	2½	½
1	1	2¼	2¾	½	1	2½	2¾	½
1½	1	2¼	3	½	1	2½	3	½

Note: 7.48 gallons of water equals 1 cubic foot. One 94-pound bag of portland cement equals about 1 cubic foot.
* "Wet" sand sold for most construction use.
The combined finished volume is approximately two-thirds the sum of the bulk volumes.

Perimeter Footings

For larger structures and in areas subject to frost heave, footings are the first step to a complete perimeter wall foundation or floor slab. (Some slabs are monolithic, which means that both footing and slab are poured at once.)

Assembling the Forms

Using your batter boards and strings as guides, dig the footing to the required width and depth. In some cases, part of the footing may extend above grade. If the soil is loose at the bottom of the trench, compact it with a tamper to prevent the concrete from settling. If you remove large rocks, fill the depressions and tamp them down firmly.

Drive stakes for the forms 18 to 24 inches apart. Clamp on the form boards before fastening them. Attach 1×2 braces across the top of the forms every 2 feet or so to keep them from spreading when you pour the concrete.

To keep cracks from forming, place steel reinforcing bars (#4 rebar) horizontally. You may need several rows for deep footings. Before you pour the concrete, make sure the form boards are level and plumb. Brush the insides of the forms with a light coat of motor oil or form oil; this will make them easier to remove after the concrete cures.

Pouring the Concrete

Pour or shovel wet concrete into the forms, flush to the top. As you pour, use a shovel or mason's hoe to work out any air pockets. Use a wood float, flat trowel, or short length of 2×4 to smooth the top surface of the footing. After pouring the concrete into the forms and smoothing and leveling it, set anchor bolts into the concrete 1 foot from the ends of each wall and 6 feet on center. The bolts are used to secure the sill plate that anchors the structural frame to the foundation. If the footing will support a block wall, you'll need to add rebar to tie the wall to the footing.

Building Footing Forms

TOOLS & MATERIALS

- Power drill with screwdriver bit
- Mason's twine
- Shovel
- 4' spirit level
- Measuring tape
- Hammer
- Clamps
- Short sledgehammer

- Concrete • Gravel
- Two-by formwork boards
- 2×4 stakes • 1×4 batter boards
- Duplex nails • Galvanized screws
- Plywood gussets • Form oil or motor oil

1 After setting up batter boards and marking the perimeter, begin excavating the soil within your string lines. Remember, the footings must rest below the local frost-depth line.

2 Drive in the stakes to support the form boards. You can build them from 1×4s or 2×4s, with an angle cut into the tip. Most footings are twice the width of the wall.

3 Use a clamp to fasten the form boards to the stakes temporarily. Check the boards for level, adjust them as needed, and then nail or screw the boards to the stakes.

4 Secure any butt joints in the formwork with ½-in.-thick plywood gussets. Use a power drill and 1½-in. screws to fasten these in place across the exterior face of each joint.

5 Use 1×2 spreaders to bridge the forms every few feet. These braces ensure that the weight of the concrete as it is poured will not cause the forms to bulge.

Pouring Concrete Footings

TOOLS & MATERIALS

- Pliers
- Hacksaw
- Wire cutters
- Mason's hoe
- Wheelbarrow
- Shovel
- Mason's trowel
- 2×4 screed

- Rebar • Wire
- Bricks, blocks, or wire chairs
- Plywood gussets
- Screws
- Concrete
- Anchor bolts

1 Support rebar at the proper height— generally at least an inch or two off the ground—with pieces of brick. Wire supports called chairs work better than bricks if you can find them.

2 Secure the rebar to the chairs or supports with wire ties, twisted tightly with pliers. This keeps the supports from being forced out of position by the concrete during the pour.

3 Around corners, you'll need to bend the rebar. Adjoining pieces of rebar should be lapped by several inches to provide unbroken support. Secure the laps together with wire ties.

4 Transport the concrete to the formwork using a wheelbarrow, bucket, or other container, and pour it into place. Use a shovel to distribute the concrete evenly throughout the form.

5 Fill the forms completely, using a hoe or shovel to spread it around evenly. Tamp the concrete as you work in order to eliminate any voids or air bubbles, particularly in corners.

6 To ensure a smooth and durable edge to the footing once it has cured, use a mason's trowel to fill corners, and work along the inside edges of the form boards.

7 Using a 2×4 screed board, cut a few inches longer than the total width of the footing, to fill the forms evenly and strike off any excess concrete above the level of the formwork.

8 Embed steel anchor bolts—usually 6-in. J-bolts—into the screeded concrete at 6 ft. on center and within 1 ft. of each corner or door opening. These bolts will hold the sill.

Slabs

The concrete slab, often called a slab-on-grade (the grade being the surface of the ground) is a monolithic piece of concrete, usually 4 to 6 inches thick, poured onto the ground over a bed of gravel within forms. Local codes specify the thickness of slabs for different purposes.

Soil preparation beneath a slab is crucial. Before you form a slab, prepare the soil to ensure proper drainage around and beneath it. In cold climates, this might mean replacing the soil to 50 percent of the frost depth with gravel. In some parts of the country, a polyethylene vapor barrier should be placed between the soil and the gravel base.

Formwork

Around the edges, a slab is formed by boards: 2×6s, 2×8s, 2×10s, 2×12s, or a combination of these, depending on the slab thickness and desired height above grade. Use 2×4 scab boards to hold the form boards together as you place them around the perimeter. Be careful to keep them plumb: check periodically with a spirit level. Brace and stake the boards in place using 2×2s or 2×4s, either driven into the ground or run diagonally as kickers. Also use a water level or transit to check that the forms are level across their tops.

When positioning the slab form boards, use mason's string as a guide. A batter-board system for defining form placement works well and provides a precise string outline to follow when forming the slab perimeter.

Reinforcement

You must reinforce concrete slabs with steel rods called rebar and welded-wire mesh. Within footings, you lay #4 rebar, and in the main area of the slab itself, use #10 reinforcing mesh. The rebar will also serve as an anchor for the J-bolts, which hold the sill plates in place once the concrete dries, and you start framing. (You can also place the J-bolts in the wet concrete.) Most codes call for J-bolts no more than 6 feet apart. Be careful not to put J-bolts where doorways will be.

Slab Footings

Most slabs are thicker around their outside perimeters where the slab will carry the load of the structure. This thicker section is called the footing. The footing and slab are integrally one piece of concrete, poured at the same time. To create the footing for slabs, simply dig farther down into the ground where you want the footing so that more concrete can be poured in there for a deeper section of slab. If you have sandy soil that won't allow you to do this, you can use 2×8s or 2×10s to form the sides of the footing.

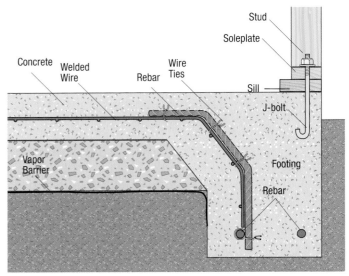

Concrete slabs need to be built on a bed of compacted soil and 4 to 6 in. of gravel. Rebar and welded-wire mesh add strength and tie the thinner slab to the thicker footings.

Welded wire comes in rolls that you can spread out over the excavation between forms. Overlap and wire-tie together sections of welded wire required to cover a large slab.

Anchor bolts are set into the top course of block or into concrete. With a framing square, measure from the outside edge of the block or slab to the bolt; then mark that distance in from the sill's edge.

Pouring a Slab

TOOLS & MATERIALS

- Compactor • Mason's twine
- Measuring tape • Line level
- Rebar chairs • Shovel
- Sledgehammer • Wheelbarrow
- Broom • Screed
- Float • Edging trowel
- Jointing trowel

- Rebar • Wire
- Duplex nails
- Two-by form boards
- 2×4 or 1×4 stakes
- Welded or woven-wire mesh
- Bricks, blocks, or wire chairs
- Wire ties
- Gravel

1 To strengthen the concrete, lay welded wire within the slab, generally on short supports called chairs. You can also use bricks or rocks to keep the wire above the soil.

2 If the slab will also be the finished floor, control joints will hide any cracks in the bottom of the joint. They can be formed into the pour or cut with a concrete saw after the slab hardens.

3 After you have evenly distributed the concrete throughout the form, you'll use a screed board to strike off the excess and fill in the hollows. Use a 2x4 slightly longer than the width of the slab.

4 As concrete pours from the ready-mix truck, use hoes and shovels to spread it evenly throughout the slab forms. You'll need several helpers to do this while the mix is still plastic.

5 Depending on the slab's use, you can smooth (with a float) the rough surface left by screeding (such as for a floor slab) or texture it with a broom for better traction (for a patio).

Estimating Concrete for Slabs

To figure out how much concrete to mix or order, you can use the chart at right. If you prefer, total up the volume inside the forms in cubic feet (length × height × width); then divide this figure by 27 to convert it into the ordering standard of cubic yards. To avoid a shortfall, it's smart to build in a reasonable excess factor of about 8 percent by changing the conversion factor to 25. Remember that an 80-pound bag of concrete mix will make only two-thirds of a cubic foot. Large orders measured in cubic yards will require a rented power mixer (and many bags of premixed concrete) or delivery from a concrete truck.

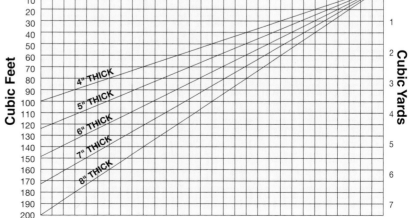

Square Feet

Cubic Feet

Cubic Yards

4" THICK
5" THICK
6" THICK
7" THICK
8" THICK

Piers & Posts

Pier or tube-form foundations are concrete pillars that support wood posts, joists, or plates. You will often find these foundations supporting decks on houses, but they work as well on outbuildings. Piers are susceptible to shifting out of plumb in areas that experience freeze-thaw cycles or shifting soil. So whether you use formless piers or tube forms, prepare the soil where they sit with the proper gravel and drainage to reduce the danger of frost heaving, and be sure to use the correct anchor, bracket, or strap to keep your framing in place on the pier.

To avoid frost heave, which can crack concrete and disrupt the structure above, piers must extend below where groundwater usually freezes in the winter—the average frost depth. This depth is available from the local building department.

Holes for piers need to be deep and narrow. They are best dug with a power auger, either one that runs off a tractor's power takeoff or a rented portable unit. Otherwise, use a posthole digger—a shovel will dig a hole with too wide a mouth. Minimize settling by digging down to the required depth and pounding the dirt at the bottom of the hole with the end of a 2×4. The concrete pier must rest on a solid base.

Pouring Piers

If the sides of the holes aren't crumbling, you could use them as rough forms. In that case, build a box staked at ground level to contain the concrete above grade. To avoid mixing in dirt and weakening the concrete, however, you can use lightweight form tubes, available at lumberyards and masonry-supply yards. You cut them to the height you need, and backfill them securely in the ground.

Setting Piers with Form Tubes

TOOLS & MATERIALS

- Posthole digger or power auger
- Mason's hoe • Mason's trowel
- Wheelbarrow or plywood
- Spirit level • Hammer
- Wrench • Work gloves • Handsaw

- Fiber tube
- Cement mix
- J-bolt with washer and nut
- Post base anchors
- Pressure-treated posts
- Galvanized nails
- Wire ties

1 Dig holes for your piers with a post-hole digger or power auger to below the frost depth. Rocky or wooded soil will be difficult to work. Fill the bottom with 2 in. of gravel for support and drainage.

2 Insert a fiber form tube into the hole. It should protrude from the soil level about 6 in. Cut off any excess with a handsaw. Plumb the inside of the form with a spirit level to ensure straightness.

3 Check the form tube for plumb and level with a spirit level. Then backfill around the form with soil. Remove large rocks from the fill; small rocks can be added near the bottom of the hole.

4 Pour concrete from a wheelbarrow directly into the form. Before the concrete hardens, insert a J-bolt into the center, leaving the threads above the concrete surface.

5 After the concrete sets, attach post-base hardware using washers and nuts. The post sits on a metal standoff that allows for drainage and keeps the bottom of the post dry.

Pier Anatomy

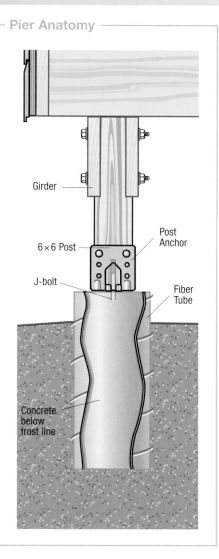

Girder

6×6 Post

Post Anchor

J-bolt

Fiber Tube

Concrete below frost line

Estimating Concrete for Piers

Piers generally don't require much concrete unless you're putting in a lot of them. It's easy to mix one batch at a time in a wheelbarrow or tub, working as you go.

Box forms: *To determine the cubic footage of a box, multiply the length times the width times the depth (all in inches), and divide the result by 1,728.*

(l × w × d) ÷ 1,728 = cu. ft.

Cylinder forms: *To determine the cubic feet in a cylinder, multiply the radius (half the diameter) by itself (square it), and then multiply by its height and 3.14. Divide the result by 1,728.*

(r × r × h × 3.14) ÷ 1,728 = cu. ft.

Setting Formless Piers

TOOLS & MATERIALS

- Posthole digger or power auger
- Measuring tape
- Shovel
- Wheelbarrow
- Spirit level
- Hammer

- Steel reinforcing bar
- Post hardware

1 Use a shovel and a posthole digger—or to save time, a rented power auger—to excavate a hole for a formless pier. The earthen walls of the hole serve as the formwork.

2 Measure the depth of the hole carefully to make sure that the base of the pier will rest on undisturbed or compacted soil that is below the minimum frost depth for your region.

4 Insert a metal base for a post or girder into the concrete when the mix is just firm enough to hold it but not yet hardened. This hardware will attach the framing to the pier.

3 Fill the hole with the required concrete mix and steel reinforcement bars. The bottom of the hole should be tamped down with a tamper or the end of a 2×4 or 4×4.

5 Adjust the hardware so that it is level, plumb, and properly oriented to support the structural post or beam, which will be installed later. Once the concrete has set, it can't be adjusted.

Wall Foundations

Full-wall foundations are generally only found on houses in colder climates. They are expensive to dig and build, and subject to an array of moisture problems. Other than a huge dairy barn, you'll rarely see a full-wall foundation on a utility building. However, a short-wall foundation with a small wall of either poured concrete or concrete block is a possibility for some designs. Permanent wood foundations built from pressure-treated lumber have become increasingly popular in cold regions.

Short-Wall Foundations

A short-wall foundation is a concrete block half-wall that sits on a concrete footing. Concrete blocks are stacked one on top of another until the wall's desired height is reached. On top of the last tier of blocks, you can install 4-inch cap blocks to close off the hollow cores or, more typically, fill the voids and add anchor bolts and a sill. If you want a crawl space, frame the floor on top of the half-wall. The minimum allowable floor-joist-to-ground space generally is 18 inches. If you use girders beneath the joists, the minimum distance between the outside bottom of the wood structure and the ground is usually 8 inches.

Footings beneath these foundations serve the same purpose wider sections of slabs serve: they spread the building's live and dead loads over a wider footprint, distributing the building's weight to the ground. Prepare the soil beneath the footing to ensure proper drainage, just as with a slab.

Permanent Wood Foundations

Permanent wood foundations use prefabricated sections of pressure-treated lumber and sheathing that are lowered onto a concrete slab or a stable bed of compacted gravel. The walls are braced before plastic sheeting or additional protection is applied outside the wood walls. You can also use pressure-treated joists in place of the slab, eliminating concrete entirely. The system (without concrete) can be installed even in subfreezing temperature.

Laying Concrete Block

TOOLS
- Trowel
- Brickset & hammer
- Jointing tool

MATERIALS
- Concrete blocks
- Mortar
- Mason's string

1 Once the footing is cured, use a string and a line level to keep the wall straight. Spread mortar with a trowel, and lay the courses of blocks, staggering the joints. Check that every course is level.

2 When the wall is at full height, you can finish the top of the wall with cap blocks. More often, voids are filled with concrete, and J-bolts are added to secure a building sill.

3 Use a jointing tool to smooth the mortar on the outside of the wall into a slightly concave shape. This shape sheds water and keeps the mortar from deteriorating.

Foundation Alternatives

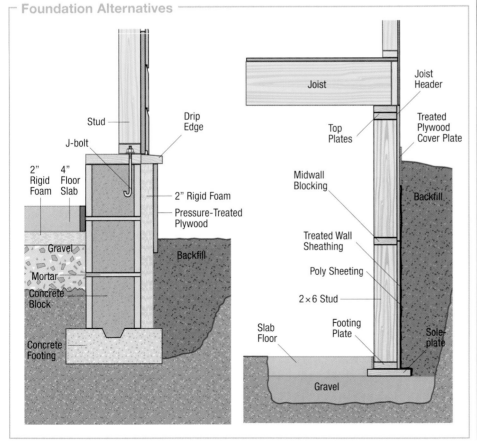

Stud
J-bolt
Drip Edge
2" Rigid Foam
4" Floor Slab
2" Rigid Foam
Pressure-Treated Plywood
Gravel
Backfill
Mortar
Concrete Block
Concrete Footing

Joist
Joist Header
Top Plates
Treated Plywood Cover Plate
Midwall Blocking
Backfill
Treated Wall Sheathing
Poly Sheeting
2×6 Stud
Slab Floor
Footing Plate
Sole plate
Gravel

Skid & Trench Foundations

A small shed—one of less than 100 square feet—can usually sit on a foundation constructed of pressure-treated 4×4 skids or concrete blocks that have been cut into the soil and set level. The use of this type of foundation is subject to local code restrictions.

Skids

Some jurisdictions may consider wooden skids to be nonpermanent foundations, and this may eliminate the need for a building permit. Check this with your local building department before you build. Make sure you use pressure-treated wood that has been rated for ground contact—at least 0.40 pound per cubic foot, 0.60 if it is available.

The key to a good skid foundation is to prepare a stable base with good drainage. Because slight movement will not affect the foundation's stability, you don't need to remove soil to the frost line. You will need to dig out 5 or 6 inches of soil for the shed's entire footprint, however, and replace it with gravel so that the runoff does not sit underneath the shed. A layer of 6-mil perforated polyethylene sheeting or landscape fabric under the gravel will aid in drainage as well.

Trenches

If there is minimal or no frost heave in your area, you can also make a rudimentary concrete perimeter foundation in a trench. Pour concrete into parallel trenches 8 to 10 inches wide and 12 inches deep. Depending on how firm your soil is, you may or may not need to use form boards. Lay rebar on chairs in the bottom of the trench for additional strength. Depending on the kind of shed you are building, you can add anchor bolts to the foundation to attach a sill or just build pressure-treated floor framing right on the concrete.

Skid Foundations

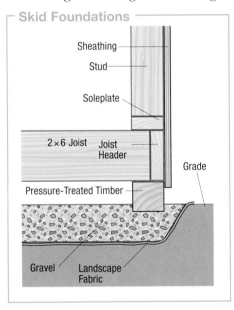

- Sheathing
- Stud
- Soleplate
- 2×6 Joist
- Joist Header
- Grade
- Pressure-Treated Timber
- Gravel
- Landscape Fabric

Trench Foundations

- J-bolt
- Soleplate
- Sill
- Concrete
- Rebar
- Chair

Building a Skid Foundation

TOOLS
- Shovel
- Circular saw
- Spirit level

MATERIALS
- Cloth or polyethylene sheeting
- Pea gravel
- 4×4 or 6×6 pressure-treated lumber

1 After laying out the outline of your shed on the ground, use a shovel to excavate out the first 4 or 5 in. of soil. Tamp the remaining subgrade firm with a hand tamper or the end of a 2×4.

2 Cover the hole with landscape fabric or 6-mil perforated polyethylene sheeting, and fill it in with gravel. This will help the drainage and keep the foundation timbers from rotting.

3 Place two 4×4 or 6×6 timbers, pressure-treated and rated for ground contact, parallel with each other. Align their outer edges with the outer edges of the shed.

4 Check the timbers for level, and add or subtract gravel as needed. Use a straight 2×4 longer than the width of the shed to make sure that the timbers are level with each other.

CHAPTER 4

Basic Framing

Framing walls is probably the most gratifying and enjoyable part of a major project such as building a barn or shed. The simplest method of framing is a straightforward process requiring only basic tools and carpentry skills. You have to measure and cut carefully, of course, but you don't need to make precise joints the way you do with trim. There are many ways to frame a utility building, and no matter which one you choose you'll need to have a set of plans approved by the local building department. The most basic system is building the structure stick by stick, generally with 2×4 studs in the walls, the way most houses are built. You can also use a grid of structural poles, or try the old-fashioned but challenging system of timber framing.

Framing Systems

You can construct a utility building with steel and concrete, adobe, or even straw bales and rebar. But in most areas—and for barns and other outbuildings—the most common way to build is by framing with wood. Small sheds are often built like houses, piece by piece, using a system known as stick framing. With this approach, you typically install a foundation or footing piers, build a platform of girders and floor joists, and cover the platform with plywood before raising walls.

The old-fashioned way of doing this, called post-and-beam building or timber framing, uses fewer but larger timbers in the structure. The heavy-timber system, which can require a crane or special rigging to set large beams, is practiced mainly by professional contractors. Another option, called pole framing, is often used on barns because it provides large clear-span areas inside the building. But poles for a large structure can be heavy and unwieldy, and they require professional installation.

A stick-frame structure has walls built from 2×4s or 2×6s set 16 or 24 in. on center. They are often built on the deck and tipped up into position. Floors and roofs are framed with heavier lumber.

Stick Framing

Stick framing refers to two types of construction. Platform framing consists of a skeletal web of milled two-by lumber that makes up the frame of the floor, walls, ceilings, and roof. Walls are often framed on the deck (made of floor joists and plywood), and then raised into place. An older method, called balloon framing, doesn't divide the stories into platforms but uses long studs to frame the entire structure. Mainly because of declining lumber quality, balloon framing is rarely used today.

Timber Framing

Traditional timber or post-and-beam frames require high-quality carpentry work involving classic skills such as shaping mortise-and-tenon joints that fit without play. There's also the considerable trouble of either obtaining and moving large timbers into position. But a well-built timber frame is stronger than a stick-framed structure. Also, this system has the authentic appeal of an old barn, which you can preserve by

Timber framing with a small number of large beams was the norm until the 20th century when it gave way to stick-framing systems that use two-by milled lumber, generally on 16-in. centers.

leaving the huge posts and beams exposed inside and cladding the structure with prefabricated roofing and siding panels. A post-and-beam frame may consist of only a hundred or so individual pieces that make an elegant frame. But making the complex joints and erecting the frame generally takes much more time and skill than conventional stick framing.

Pole Framing

A pole building is similar in many ways to a commercial building made with steel. A pole-framed structure doesn't rest on the ground with a full foundation but hangs from a grid of poles. Chemically treated poles (or square pressure-treated posts) are connected with large timbers or pairs of timbers that are bolted in place. These timbers serve to support floor joists, walls, and rafters, but all of the building loads travel down the poles. For small buildings, you might use 4×6 posts that are only 10 or 12 feet long. Larger barns can call for poles the size of telephone poles. Overall, pole framing is an economical system because it does not require a full foundation and allows for large, open areas with high ceilings. It is one of the best ways to build on a sloped site.

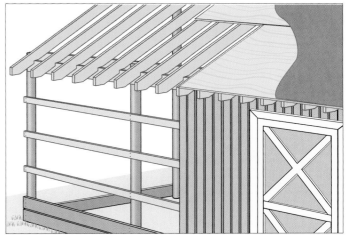

Pole framing is especially popular for livestock barns, which need a large, open central space. For smaller projects, pressure-treated posts can be substituted for heavy poles.

Building Loads

Your barn design must take building loads into account—the weight of the building itself, what goes inside it, and the elements outside, such as wind and snow.

A framing system is like a network of streams along which structural loads flow: from the roof, through the building and foundation, and ultimately into the ground. Like water, loads tend to take the path of least resistance to the lowest point, in accordance with the law of gravity. Just as water won't run uphill, structural loads from a rafter won't jump out into the attic to appear in the middle of the floor. They flow down the rafter to the support wall framing below.

Load Paths. Loads must be carried from the top of the structure to the foundation without interruption. If there is a break in the system—for example, if you fail to install an adequate header over a door—weight from above will cause deflection on top of the door frame, and the door will stick. Even minor structural weaknesses can pop nails in drywall or siding, bind windows, crack trim, and create other problems.

Load-bearing and Nonload-bearing Elements. Major structural elements such as floors, posts, columns, roof framing, and all exterior walls are load-bearing. They carry the weight of the structure and everything in it (such as people) or on it (such as shingles). Many interior walls are

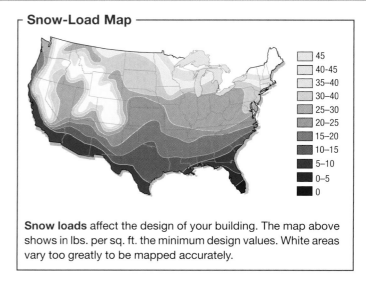

Snow-Load Map

☐	45
☐	40-45
☐	35–40
☐	30–40
☐	25–30
☐	20–25
☐	15–20
☐	10–15
■	5–10
■	0–5
■	0

Snow loads affect the design of your building. The map above shows in lbs. per sq. ft. the minimum design values. White areas vary too greatly to be mapped accurately.

not load-bearing. These partition walls simply divide up space. You can cut through a partition to create a doorway, or remove the wall altogether. But wherever you cut into a bearing wall, you need to account for the load it carries by installing a structural header.

Types of Loads

Structural loads consist of dead loads, such as the weight of the building materials and mechanical equipment, and live loads, such as the weight of people, furnishings, stored materials, and snow on the roof. Another type of load, shear load, is the force the building encounters when the wind gusts, the earth quakes, or the foundation shifts because of events like soil washout. A point load is the downward force exerted by a single heavy thing inside or on top of the structure, such as a fireplace, hot tub, or water heater. Lastly, there is the spread load, the outward force on walls caused by the downward-and-outward force of rafters, usually because of heavy snow pressing down on the roof.

The architect's or engineer's job is to anticipate all conditions that could reasonably be expected at the site. In residential design, potential loads and stresses are typically provided by local building codes. For example, floor systems are generally designed to support 40 pounds of live load per square foot. Because wood is resilient, the frame can absorb the extra strain as you move around or concentrate heavy furniture in one room.

In a wood frame there is bound to be some movement, particularly on the floor where joists span from one support to another. But the standard limit of movement, called deflection, is $\frac{1}{360}$ of the length of the span. That means if the floor joists were 360 inches long, they would have to be strong enough to deflect no more than 1 inch when loaded with people and furniture.

Although even a small shed has building loads, 2×4s generally are more than enough to handle them. In a large barn, however, your plans will have to conform to the guidelines on approved span tables and be checked by the local building department. Inspectors will check both the size and spacing of the girders, joists, and rafters.

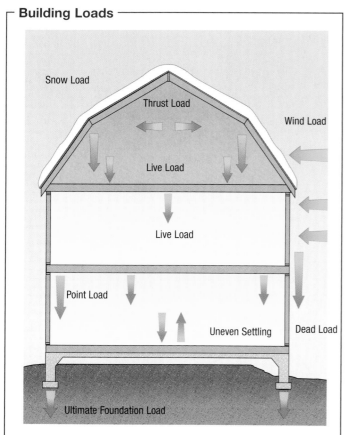

Building Loads

Snow Load
Thrust Load
Wind Load
Live Load
Live Load
Point Load
Uneven Settling
Dead Load
Ultimate Foundation Load

The total load includes the weight of materials, people, furnishings, and environmental loads, such as the forces of wind and snow. The structure must meet local codes for all loads.

Span Tables

The allowable spans for joists, rafters, girders, and other load-bearing elements of a building frame are all subject to local building codes. Codes specify the loads that framing members must bear in each location. For example, 40 pounds per square foot for floor joists in living space. They also set deflection limits, given as span in inches (L) over a given number. For example, an L/360 limit for joists means a 10-foot joist can bend a maximum of 120 inches divided by 360, or ⅓ inch, under the load.

Reading a Span Table. Span tables are organized by wood species and grade because they have different strengths. Different sizes for each grade are given different maximum span lengths in feet and inches for the most common on-center spacings. For example, looking at the table at top right, if you wanted to span 13 feet with southern pine 2×8s, you would need to use at least No. 1 grade at 16 inches on center. If No. 1 were unavailable, you would have the choice of using thicker lumber (such as 2×10s), or spacing No. 2 grade 2×8s at 12 inches on center.

Some codes use two tables. One gives the design values for each grade of wood—measurements of fiber strength in bending (Fb) and a ratio of stress to strain called the modulus of elasticity, or the E-value. Another gives span lengths according to these values. You first determine which size lumber will work for your span. Looking at the middle table, if you had a span of 14 feet, 6 inches, you'd need to use at least 2×10s—ones made from a wood with a minimum E-value of 1.2 (spaced at 16 inches on center) and an Fb of 1,036. The bottom table shows the design value for one type of wood (hemlock/fir) for this thickness. By matching the E-values and Fb ratings, you find that you can use No. 2 hemlock/fir (or any better grade).

It is possible for do-it-yourselfers to determine lumber sizes and spans. But final determinations are best left to an architect or engineer unless you use code-approved plans that pass muster at the local building department.

Floor Joist Span Ratings

Strength: For 40 psf live load 10 psf dead load.
Deflection: Limited in span in inches divided by 360 for live load only.

| Species | Grade | 2 × 8 | | | |
| | | Spacing On-Center | | | |
		12"	16"	19.2"	24"
Spruce/ pine/fir (southern)	Select structural	15'	13' 7"	12' 10"	11' 11"
	No. 1 and better	14' 8"	13' 4"	12' 7"	11' 8"
	No. 1	14' 5"	13' 1"	12' 4"	11' 0"
	No. 2	14' 2"	12' 9"	11' 8"	10' 5"
	No. 3	11' 3"	9' 9"	8' 11"	8'

Excerpted from Western Wood Products Association, Western Lumber Span tables

Floor Joist Span Ratings

With L/360 deflection limits. For 40 psf live load.

| Joist Size | On-Center Spacing | E-Value (in million psi) | | | |
		0.8	1.0	1.2	1.4
2×6	12"	8' 6"	9' 2"	9' 9"	10' 3"
	16"	7' 9"	8' 4"	8' 10"	9' 4"
	24"	7' 3"	7' 3"	7' 6"	8' 9"
2×8	12"	11' 3"	12' 1"	12' 10"	13' 6"
	16"	10' 2"	11' 0"	11' 8"	12' 3"
	24"	11' 8"	9' 7"	10' 2"	10' 9"
2×10	12"	14' 4"	15' 5"	16' 5"	17' 3"
	16"	13'	14'	14' 11"	15' 8"
	24"	11' 4"	12' 3"	13' 0"	13' 8"
Fb	12"	718	833	941	1,043
	16"	790	917	1,036	1,148
	24"	905	1,050	1,186	1,314

Excerpted from CABO's One- and Two-Family Dwelling Code

Design Values for Joists and Rafters

| Species & Grade | Size | Design Value in Bending (Fb) | | E-Value (in million psi) |
		Normal	Snow Loading	
Hemlock/fir	2 × 10			
Select structural		1,700	2,035	1.6
No. 1 and better		1,330	1,525	1.5
No. 1		1,200	1,380	1.5
No. 2		1,075	1,235	1.3
No. 3		635	725	1.2

Excerpted from CABO's One- and Two-Family Dwelling Code

Floor Framing

If your barn or shed will have a dirt or concrete-slab floor, you won't be building floor framing—the walls will be built right on top of the foundation. However, you will have to install a sill (sometimes called a sill plate) of pressure-treated wood around the perimeter of your foundation to make the transition between concrete and wood.

If you want your building to have a finished floor, however, a framework of floor joists, made from 2×6s or larger lumber set on end, will sit on top of the sill. You will then add a subfloor, generally made of plywood, on top of the joists. The subfloor will be used to support a finished floor or serve as the floor itself, as is in a work space such as a shop or potting shed.

Floor Frame Options

How you frame the floor depends on the type of foundation and the desired height of the floor above ground. Joists are spaced 16 or 24 inches on center, depending on their thickness and the load they support. They generally run parallel to the shortest side of the building, so that a 8 × 12-foot shed would have 8-foot-long joists.

For small buildings, 2×6 floor joists are often strong enough to run unsupported for 8 to 10 feet. If they will run more than 10 feet, you will need to use 2×8s or 2×10s, or support the joists midspan with a girder. It also helps to install bridging between joists. You may need to install tie-down hardware to prevent overturn; check local codes. Another option, generally reserved for houses, is to use

manufactured joists in the shape of an I-beam. They can span even greater lengths than a standard dimensional timber of the same thickness. In any case, you should consult a floor joist span table and the local building department to determine the type and size of wood you will need to span between supports.

Floor Framing on Pier Foundations

A structure built on piers doesn't have a continuous foundation on which to lay a sill. With piers, you generally attach the beams or joists to a framing connector sunk into the concrete. This keeps the floor as low as possible. If you want to elevate the floor more than a foot or so above the ground, such as when building on a sloping site, you can attach 4×4 posts to the piers using different metal connectors, and then attach the beams to the posts. Otherwise, you can use one of these two methods, adjusting sizes as required.

4×6 or Doubled 2×6 Header. Attach a 4×6 beam—or a rim joist made out of doubled 2×6s—to the pier blocks on each long side of the building. If you use precast concrete piers, you can bolt pressure-treated blocks to the piers and attach the beam to the blocks using 16d galvanized nails. For cast concrete piers, attach the beams to framing connectors. Once you attach the beams, hang intermediate joists between the beams with metal joist hangers. The two end joists (stringer joists) are nailed to the ends of 4×6 or doubled 2×6s at each corner with 16d galvanized nails. Some inspectors may require hardware on all floor frame connections.

Header on Beam. With this method, you still attach beams directly to the piers as above. Then you build the

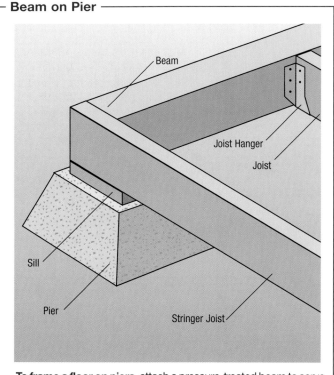

Beam on Pier

Beam

Joist Hanger

Joist

Sill

Pier

Stringer Joist

To frame a floor on piers, attach a pressure-treated beam to serve as both girder and header joist. You can hang your joists directly off the beam and nail stringer joists to the ends of the beam.

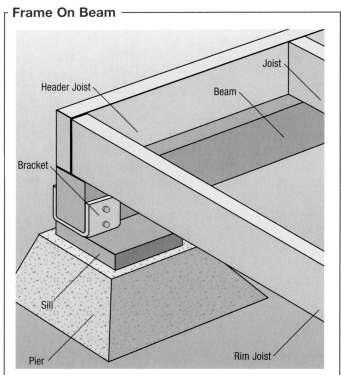

Frame On Beam

Joist

Header Joist

Beam

Bracket

Sill

Pier

Rim Joist

Another option is to set the joists on top of the girder, and in some cases, project them beyond the support. But this arrangement will increase the height of the floor.

grid of header joists and intermediate joists to the top of the beams. This will provide more ground clearance.

Attaching Sills to Concrete Foundations

You attach a pressure-treated 2×6 sill to a concrete slab or perimeter foundation using anchor bolts placed every 4 to 6 feet in concrete or concrete-filled voids of foundation block. In houses, a thin sealer strip of foam is installed under the sill mainly for energy efficiency, which may not be an issue in an unheated barn. In regions prone to termite damage, you may want to install a metal termite shield on top of the foundation before you install the sill.

Laying down the sill is your last chance to straighten a crooked foundation. When you set the sill over the anchor bolts, the outside edge of the sill should align with the outside edge of the slab or wall—unless the foundation is out of square. In that case, make small adjustments as needed to square up the sill on which the building will sit.

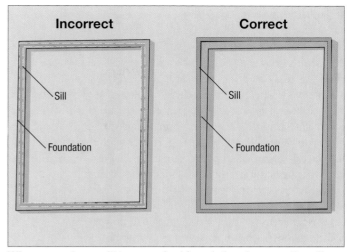

When squaring a sill to a crooked foundation, increase the sill size as needed to overhang the foundation up to ¹/₂ in. or water will collect on top of the foundation and leak into the building.

Installing a Sill

TOOLS & MATERIALS

- Circular saw • Combination square
- Pencil • Framing square
- Measuring tape • Power drill with ⅝" bit
- Wire brush • Socket wrench

- Pressure-treated two-by sill
- Sill sealer
- ½" anchor bolts, nuts, and washers
- Termite shield (optional)

SMART TIP:

Protect the threads of anchor bolts during construction by wrapping them with duct tape. You can brush away excess concrete, but it's sometimes impossible to repair damaged threads.

1 After sweeping the top of the foundation clean, set the sill—typically a pressure-treated 2×6—on the foundation, and use a combination square to mark the locations of anchor bolts.

2 Measure along your mark to duplicate the distance of the bolt from the outside of the foundation. Use a ⁵/₈-in. bit to drill a hole through the sill—this will make it easier to fit over the ¹/₂-in. bolts.

3 Thin sill sealer fills the slightly irregular space between the foundation and the sill if needed for energy efficiency. Local codes may call for a metal termite shield under the sill.

4 The threads of anchor bolts often become clogged with concrete. They need to be wire-brushed before you install the sill and try to tighten down the nuts.

5 Set the sill board onto the sealer, and leave the anchor bolts protruding. Slip a large washer on each one, make sure the sill is square, and tighten the nuts with a socket wrench.

Framing the Floor

After installing the sill and girders, the next step is to install the floor joists and cover them with sheets of plywood, called the subfloor or the deck.

Before placing joists on the sill, measure and mark your joist layout, generally spacing the joists 16 inches on center. This layout will allow the edges of the plywood sheets to fall along the middle of a joist—two edges of two sheets will share one joist. The exception is the first sheet in line along the edge of the building. You have to adjust the layout so that its edge covers the entire joist, which is an extra ¾ inch beyond the centerline of the outermost joist. If you are not very experienced with construction layout, it's wise to lay a starter sheet in position temporarily to be sure that you have the joists in the right places.

When determining joist length, deduct the thickness of the header, or rim, joists—the boards nailed across the ends of the floor joists. Header joists (with hardware) secure the floor joists upright. They also provide a clean edge for attaching subflooring. You can cut all the joists to size ahead of time, or let cantilevered joists run long, snap a line across the ends to create a perfectly straight line, and trim them in place.

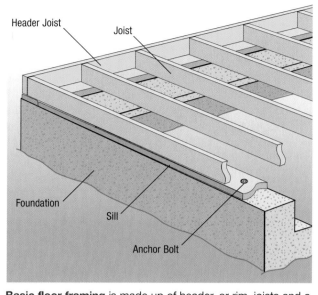

Frame On Foundation

Basic floor framing is made up of header, or rim, joists and a grid of floor joists set at 16 or 24 in. on center that rests on foundation sills. Long spans may require a girder at midspan.

Girders

Contemporary barn designs often call for big floor spans with no walls or columns to break up the space. In these cases, the entire floor load must be transferred to the perimeter walls and structural framing configurations have to be beefed up to accommodate longer spans.

Let's say you have a basement workshop that is 30 feet long and 20 feet wide. It would be easy to divide up this space by running a load-bearing wall across the room, making 15 feet the longest span (if joists were running lengthwise). Fifteen feet is a span that can easily be handled by readily available framing lumber. But if you want that space open, you won't want to divide it with a load-bearing wall down the center. Instead, you can install a beam, known as a girder, beneath the floor joists to split the span in half and carry a lot of the load. Each end of the girder can sit in a pocket in the foundation wall, on pilaster extensions, or the foundation itself. Steel I-beams are the strongest and can span greater distances. Wood girders—whether glue-laminated, made from two-bys, or manufactured wood I-beams—are easier to install and less expensive.

Girders on first floors are often supported in pockets cut or formed into opposite ends of the foundation. Most codes require these pockets to be a minimum of

4 inches deep to bear the load. You also need to guard against wood rot by setting the girder on a piece of steel baseplate and allowing ¹/₂ inch of space on both sides of the girder for ventilation. If pockets won't provide enough support for your design, you can raise girders to the sill or set them on masonry pilasters built onto the foundation.

On many girder designs, there is a point

of diminishing returns. You can keep adding boards to the girder to increase its width so that the girder can create an unsupported span. But once you get to the point of using three 2×12s, it's generally more economical to install a post. You can use wood or steel posts. Some steel columns have an adjustable cap that makes it possible to raise the girder should it sag.

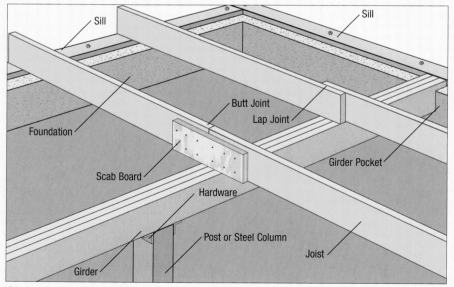

Girders support floor joists over long spans. You can butt joists where they meet over a girder, and add a scab board to keep them aligned, or lap them with each joist bearing fully on the girder. But this approach will offset your subfloor nailing pattern.

Framing The Floor

TOOLS & MATERIALS

- Circular saw or hand saw
- Framing square
- Framing hammer
- Measuring tape
- Combination square
- Bar clamp (if needed)

- Two-by lumber for joists and bridging
- 16d and 12d common nails
- Joist hangers and joist-hanger nails (optional)
- Carpenter's pencil

1 Place the rim joists on top of the sill (with both slab and wall foundations) or the beam (on pier foundations for a small shed as shown here). Square them up with a framing square.

2 Tack the joists in place, and stop to check the perimeter frame to make sure it's square. Use a framing square at the corners, and measure the overall diagonals, which should be equal.

3 End-nail the rim joists and end joist together with three 16d common nails. Check that they are tight against the sill. You may want to predrill nail holes near the ends to prevent splitting.

4 Mark your layout on opposite headers using 16-in. on-center marks, depending on the span and load. You may want to make duplicate layouts on both boards before installing them.

5 Set each joist in place at the marks. You can check the joists for square against the rim joist with a large framing square, and use a combination square to check vertical alignment.

6 Once they are square, you can end-nail the joists through the rim joist with three 12d common nails. Local codes generally require that you set joists into metal joist hangers.

7 If your code requires joist hangers, nail them through one pair of flanges to the header and through the other pair into the joist. Be sure that the top of the joist is flush with the rim joist.

8 To stiffen the floor overall and prevent exposed joists from twisting, add solid bridging made from floor joist material, or use premolded X-shaped metal bridging.

Subfloor

With the floor joists in place, it's time to put down the subfloor, or floor deck. In houses, the subfloor forms the base for floor coverings such as carpet or finished wood, and often is covered with another layer of material, called underlayment, before finish materials are installed. In sheds, barns, and other utility buildings, you'll probably leave the subfloor unfinished, if you install a floor at all.

Materials

Generally a subflooring is ½-inch CDX plywood. If codes permit, you may also use waferboard, oriented-strand board (OSB), or other sheet materials. But in an outbuilding that isn't heated or cooled, use an exterior-grade material that can stand up to moisture. If you plan to store heavy tools and machinery, use ¾-inch plywood or two layers of ½-inch plywood.

Installation

You can nail plywood decking, but for maximum strength apply a bead of construction adhesive to the tops of the joists, and fasten the sheets with screws. Lay down the subfloor by staggering panel edges so that the seams don't line up across the floor over one joist. If you start the first row with a full panel, start the second with a half panel. In an outbuilding where you anticipate a wet floor from tracking in and out, you might leave a ¹⁄₁₆-inch gap between panels to prevent the panels from buckling.

Nail or screw the subflooring every 12 inches along the edges and in the field of the plywood. If you don't use adhesive, nail or screw every 6 inches on the outside edges and 10 inches in the field. Remember that basic ½-inch sheets may satisfy local codes but bend under the weight of a heavy lawn mower or a stack of lumber. If you use ¾-inch panels, attach them with adhesive and screws.

Installing a Subfloor

TOOLS & MATERIALS

- Caulking gun
- Hammer or power drill with screwdriver bit
- Circular saw or table saw
- Measuring tape
- Chalk-line box
- 2-lb. sledgehammer

- Plywood or OSB panels
- Subfloor adhesive
- 8d ring-shank nails or 2" deck screws

1 Although it is not a requirement, gluing down the subfloor will increase the floor's stiffness and decrease nail popping. Run a ¼-in.-dia. bead of subfloor adhesive down each joist.

2 Nail panels to the joists with 8d nails, spaced every 6 in. along the edge and every 12 in. elsewhere. Install panels with the face-grain perpendicular to the joists and stagger panel joints.

3 If you're using ordinary square-ended panels instead of tongue-and-groove subflooring, leave about a ¹⁄₁₆-in. space between the panels to allow for expansion without buckling.

4 If you started with a half panel in your first course, start the second course with a full panel. This keeps the panel seams from aligning over one joist and makes for a stronger floor.

5 You can use a scrap board, such as a 2x4, to work a panel into position. But this technique is more often used to fit together sheets of interlocking tongue-and-groove plywood.

Rough Openings in Floors

Many framed floors have openings for stairways, chimneys, and other features. The basic idea is to install double headers at each end of the opening and double joists (a standard joist plus a trimmer) along the sides. This creates a strong box around the opening that can carry the loads normally carried by full-length joists. The extra framing should be the same size as the surrounding joists. In most regions, you need to use metal hangers on these connections.

Building the Opening

To make a rough opening in floor framing, first measure the dimensions of the opening on the plan, and then cut the lumber accordingly. Double up joists on both sides of the rough opening, anchor them at the ends, and face-nail the trimmers every 16 to 24 inches with three 12d nails. You also can use 16d nails (3½ inches long) driven at a slight angle to prevent the sharp points from protruding through the 3½ inches of lumber.

To install the header joists, mark the header positions on inside trimmer joists at both ends of the rough opening. Install the headers by running double thickness of joist lumber perpendicular to the floor joists. As you install the headers, check them to be sure they're square. Fasten them with joist hangers.

In most installations you'll need short joists called tail joists to span from the headers to the outer joists of the floor frame. Space the tail joists at the standard on-center spacing of regular floor joists to maintain nailing surfaces.

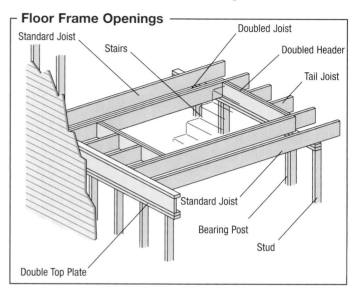

Floor Frame Openings

Standard Joist · Stairs · Doubled Joist · Doubled Header · Tail Joist · Standard Joist · Bearing Post · Stud · Double Top Plate

---

Framing Second Floors and Lofts

If your design calls for a second floor or a loft, you will need to add ceiling joists supported by the exterior and interior load-bearing walls. Ceiling joists are usually spaced 16 inches on center. If there's no second-floor living space, the joists can be smaller because they bear a smaller load—generally 30 pounds per square foot or less anticipating light storage, as compared to 40 pounds per square foot in living areas.

The loads they will carry and the length of the unsupported span determine the size of joists you must use. If the house will have a truss roof, the bottom chord of the truss will substitute for the ceiling joists. It may be small in size but is reinforced by the internal braces of the truss. Of course, many barn designs don't include a second-floor frame and leave the rafters open.

Most often, ceiling joists run parallel to the shorter side of the building and are toenailed to the tops of exterior and interior load-bearing walls. When the roof is framed, the roof rafters are face-nailed to the ceiling joists.

If room dimensions are too large for the length of normal ceiling joists, you will need to add a girder or bearing wall, generally at midspan, or use larger joists.

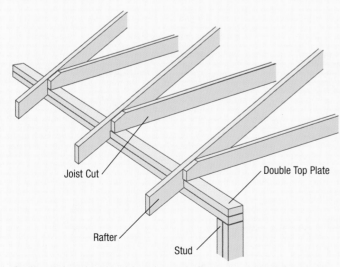

Joist Cut · Double Top Plate · Rafter · Stud

Ceiling joists *in a load-bearing attic floor should be laid out so that they rest against the rafters. You can toenail the joists to the double plate and also nail them to the rafters.*

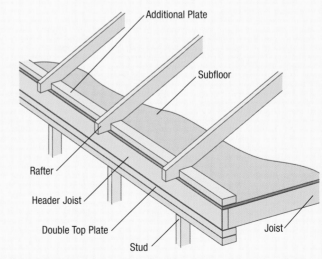

Additional Plate · Subfloor · Rafter · Header Joist · Double Top Plate · Stud · Joist

Another option *is to frame a new deck with header joists on top of the walls. This approach works well on mansard-style roofs with usable floor space along the eaves.*

Wall Framing

Stick-built walls are constructed on a modular system designed to provide a combination of structural strength and nailing surfaces for sheathing materials inside and out. Adding windows and doors generally requires extra studs because the openings don't normally fall exactly into the modular plan.

The base of the wall is a horizontal 2×4 (or a 2×6 in some cases) called a soleplate, or shoe. Studs sit on the shoe, generally every 16 inches on center. The top of the wall is capped with two more horizontal 2×4s called a top plate.

There are three kinds of studs in most walls. Full-height studs, sometimes called king studs, run from the soleplate to the top plate. Jack studs, also called trimmer studs, run from the shoe up alongside a full stud at rough openings. The top of the jack stud rests under the header over a window or door. Cripple studs are short 2×4s that fill in the spaces above and below a rough opening, for example, from the soleplate to the sill of a window. They are spaced to maintain the modular layout and provide nailing surfaces for siding and drywall or other surface materials.

The load-bearing walls in a frame are generally made of 2×4s or 2×6s, depending on structural and insulation demands. Although each 2×6 stud costs more than a comparable 2×4, the overall cost is only marginally different because fewer 2×6s are needed. (Building codes usually allow them to be placed 24 inches on center.) Wider studs also allow more space for insulation. For any framing jobs in uninsulated buildings, such as sheds, barns, and garages, 2×4 studs are the most economical.

Assembling the Wall

Start by marking the plate and shoe according to the wall layout in your plans. Then you can cut the studs. A power miter box makes this job go quickly. King studs will be full length—generally 91½ inches for 8-foot ceilings. Jack studs will be king-stud length minus the combined height of the header and cripples above. You can cut the cripples and sills to length after you put the jack studs and headers in place. Some builders prefer to build rough openings after the wall has been raised.

One efficient way to build walls is to assemble the components on the deck and tip them into position. On long walls you'll need some help raising the structure, and on all walls you have to plan the framing carefully before nailing through the shoe and first plate and into the ends of the studs.

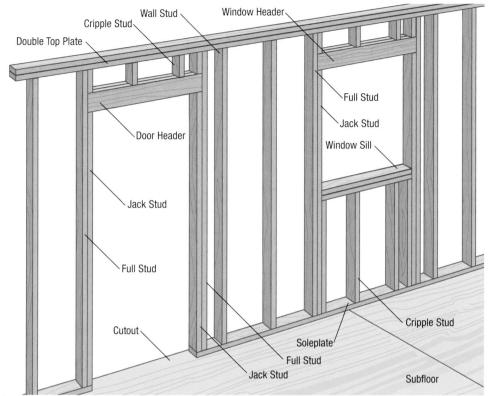

A stick-framed wall consists of studs—vertical 2×4s or 2×6s—between a single horizontal soleplate, often called a shoe, and a double top plate. Windows and doors have framed headers and extra jack and cripple studs to account for the missing full studs.

Squaring the Wall

Check walls to make sure they're square before you stand them in place, and again after you raise them. You can check the diagonals, which should be equal if the wall is square. It also helps to lock up the position by tacking diagonal braces along the wall. Some builders also install sheathing before raising, although this makes the wall even heavier.

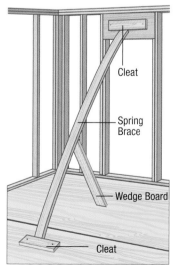

Apply a spring brace to fix a bow in a stud wall. Nail a flat brace (at least 8 ft. long) to cleats on the floor and wall, and force the wall into plumb.

To brace a corner, lock it in place with a 2×4. Leave the brace in place until the whole wall is finished—nail it outside the frame so it's out of the way.

Raising the Wall

Before erecting any wall, snap a chalk line along the subfloor or slab to establish a reference guide for positioning the inside edge of the wall soleplate. On a subfloor, also nail a few 2×4 cleats to the outside of the header joist to keep the wall from slipping off the deck as you raise it. With as many helpers as you need, slide the wall into position so that when you raise it, it will stand close to the guideline. Erect the wall, and align it to the chalk line.

Using a 4-foot spirit level, get the wall as close to plumb as possible. You'll fine-tune it for plumb when you install the adjacent wall. Run braces from studs to cleats that are nailed into the subfloor, or, on corners, to the outsides of the floor joists. When the wall is plumb, have a helper nail the braces to the cleats. With the bottom soleplate properly positioned, nail into the rim joists and floor joists with 16d nails. You can plumb a small wall by yourself. The trick is to nail an angled brace to a cleat on the deck and clamp it to the wall. Check with a level, adjust and reclamp as needed, and tack the brace to hold the wall plumb. On long walls of 20 feet or so, brace each corner and several interior studs.

To check for plumb, hold a 4-foot level against a straight 2×4. Pay particular attention to corners. If the wall is leaning in or out, release any braces and adjust the wall. Apply force to the braces to push the wall out. To bring the wall in, attach a flat brace between two cleats (one attached to the wall and one to the floor) and use a two-by as a kicker to bow the brace and force the wall inward. You can also apply braces staked outside the building. Retack the braces to hold the wall in its proper position.

Top Plates

When adjoining walls are in proper position you can add the second top plate and tie the walls together. The top plate on one wall overlaps the bottom plate of the adjoining wall. Where partitions join exterior bearing walls, the top plate of the partition should lap onto the top plate of the exterior wall. Secure all laps with at least two 16d nails.

Laying Out the Walls

To lay out the soleplate and top plates of a wall, first cut a pair of straight 2×4s (or 2×6s) to length. Tack the soleplate to the subfloor and set the top plate flush against it. Make your first mark ¾ inch short of your on-center spacing (15¼ inches), and make an X past that mark. This will place center of the first stud 16 inches from the corner. Measure down the length of the plates, and mark where the common, full-length studs will fall, every 16 or 24 inches, and mark each of these studs with an X. You can also measure and mark the locations of cripple studs (C) and jack studs (O).

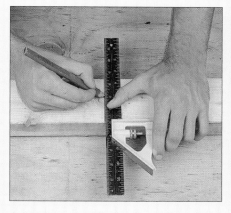

Avoid layout confusion by marking the shoe and the top plate the same way in a step-ahead system. You may want to mark the soleplate and top plate at the same time with a combination square.

Once the square line is drawn, step ahead of the line to mark the location of a stud with an X. You can also use the tongue of a framing square, which is 1½ inches wide, to mark the full width.

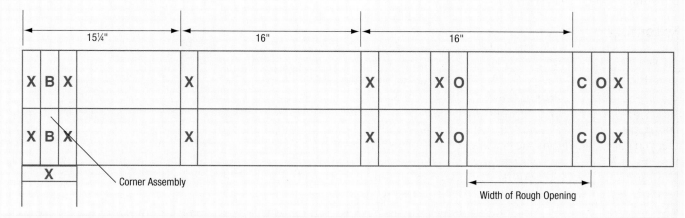

Lay out corners and rough openings on your plates as indicated on your plans. Mark all full-length studs with an X, jack studs (also called trimmers) with an O, blocking with a B, and cripples with a C.

Framing Walls

TOOLS & MATERIALS

- Carpenter's pencil
- Circular saw or table saw
- Combination square
- Framing square
- 4' spirit level
- Hammer
- Measuring tape
- Safety goggles and work gloves

- 2x4 or 2x6 lumber
- 16d and 12d common nails

1 Start by marking the layout on both the soleplate and one of the two top plates at the same time—this ensures that the studs will line up when the wall is erected and squared.

2 Work on the subfloor (or the surface of the slab) to assemble the frame. Position each stud, stand on it to prevent shifting, and nail through the soleplate with two 16d common nails.

3 When the soleplate is nailed on, shift to the top of the wall, and follow the same procedure to nail on one of the top plates. Before nailing, check the stud position for square.

4 Check the overall frame by comparing diagonal measurements. If the wall is square, the diagonals should be equal. Once the wall has been adjusted, you can nail on a temporary brace.

5 Small shed walls can be raised by one person; larger walls may require three or more. The wall components are nailed to the floor framing with 16d nails, and then braced.

6 Once the wall is braced, use a 4-ft. level to check several studs for plumb. It's easiest to assemble corner posts that may include short pieces of blocking on the deck and add them later.

7 With the walls straightened and the corner posts in place, you can install the second top plate, also called the cap plate. Stagger the joints over the corner in order to tie one wall to another.

8 Nail on the cap plate with 12d or 16d nails. Once all the exterior walls are in place, you can add sheathing and remove the temporary bracing as you nail on the sheets.

Installing Let-In Bracing

TOOLS & MATERIALS

- Chalk-line box • Circular saw
- Measuring tape
- Hammer

- Metal bracing or 1x4 lumber
- 6d common nails

SMART TIP:

If you plumb walls and install temporary wood braces, leave them on wherever possible as you install let-in bracing. Without wood braces, be sure to plumb the walls before nailing let-in braces in position.

1 Many do-it-yourselfers will find metal bracing easier to install than wood bracing. Start by snapping a chalk line from the top of the corner on a diagonal down and across several studs.

2 As with wood bracing, set your saw blade to cut only as deep as one side of the L-shaped metal brace. Then make one straight cut through the studs along the chalk line.

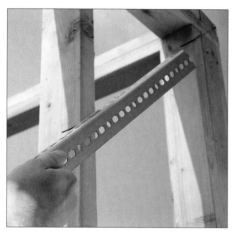

3 Metal let-in bracing is L-shaped. You simply set one edge into the straight line of cuts angled from the top of the corner to the sill. The cuts must form a straight line for the brace to fit.

4 The metal bracing is perforated, so it's easy to nail it in place at each stud. Installing braces (either metal or wood) strengthens walls and helps to keep them square.

5 To install wood 1×4 bracing instead of metal, you'll need to snap two chalk lines and cut two kerfs in the stud faces. Then use a hammer and chisel to make a $3/4 \times 3^{1}/_{2}$-in. channel.

Stud Configurations at Corners

You have several choices when it comes to framing corners. Stud-and-block corners use the most material, but they are the most rigid. The three-stud corner saves time and a little material *because you don't need the blocking. Both provide interior and exterior nailing surfaces. The two-stud corner may be fine for a small shed but does not provide for interior nailing on both walls.*

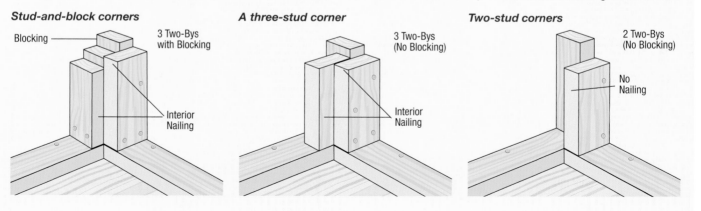

Stud-and-block corners — Blocking / 3 Two-Bys with Blocking / Interior Nailing

A three-stud corner — 3 Two-Bys (No Blocking) / Interior Nailing

Two-stud corners — 2 Two-Bys (No Blocking) / No Nailing

Rough Openings

Stud placement is crucial for rough openings in walls where you insert doors and windows. The rough opening size is listed in window and door catalogs, and generally allows ½ to ¾ inch of shimming space around the unit. This allows you to plumb and level the window or door even when the adjacent wall frame is out of kilter. Each side of the opening has a full-height stud. Inside that stud is a shorter jack stud. The distance jack to jack, allowing for shimming space, is the rough opening.

On windows, a short jack stud helps to support the sill. You add a jack stud that runs from the soleplate up to the header, and generally add a short piece in line above the header that runs to the plate. On doors, you need two long jack studs that run from the floor to the header, and filler studs above. You can rest the jacks on the soleplate, or run them down to the plywood deck. This covers the shoe end grain and on exterior doors will bear on the joist or rim joist below.

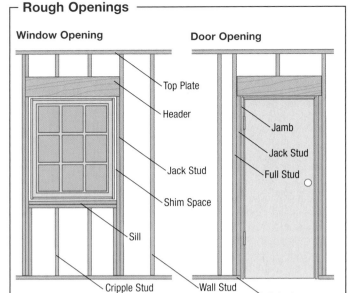

Rough Openings

Window Opening — Door Opening

Top Plate, Header, Jamb, Jack Stud, Full Stud, Jack Stud, Shim Space, Sill, Cripple Stud, Wall Stud, Soleplate

Building Rough Openings in a Wall

TOOLS & MATERIALS

- Circular saw • Combination square
- Hammer • 4' spirit level
- Measuring tape • Pencil
- Safety goggles

- 2x4 or 2x6 studs
- Two-by headers
- Common nails

SMART TIP:

Toenails will do in a pinch, but you can make a stronger frame by end-nailing at right angles through one board into another wherever possible.

1 At each side of the rough opening, nail a jack stud into the soleplate and adjacent full-height stud. In 2x4 walls, use two 10d nails every foot or so to create the structural equal of a 4x4 post.

2 A small window doesn't weigh enough to need a double sill, but it's wise to spike two 2x4s on the flat to jack studs and side studs anyway. You can end-nail through the full-height studs.

3 Continue additional jack stud sections along both sides of the window opening. These framing members will help to support the weight carried by the header across the opening.

4 Make up a header with two 2x6s, sandwiching a sheet of ½-in. plywood that packs out the header to the wall thickness. Wider openings will require larger headers.

5 Add cripple studs above the header and below the sill to maintain the on-center layout of the wall. You need the cripples for nailing surfaces (and strength) under surface materials.

Rib Construction for Sheds

This method of building small barn-style sheds (generally 10 feet wide or less) involves constructing complete framing units called ribs. These include not only roof members but studs and floor joists as well. Studs are added to the rear wall rib to provide a nailing surface for sheathing and siding, and a door is framed in the front rib. Plywood sheathing joins the ribs together, and the ribs themselves are reinforced at the joints with plywood gussets and galvanized hardware.

The drawings below show typical ribs for 8- or 10-foot-wide sheds. The length of the shed depends on the number of interior ribs. Ribs on small gable structures generally need no additional bracing. Gambrel designs may need bracing due to the built-in weak spot between rafter sections. Even small sheds must conform to building codes.

Bear in mind that the rib floor joists should be made of pressure-treated wood. It's best to elevate the structure on beams and concrete piers, or attach it to pressure-treated skids set into the ground, if code allows.

Installing Ribs

You can't nail up sheathing as you erect the ribs because you have to check and recheck that the ribs are plumb, are the same distance apart at either end, and are squared up to the foundation and to one another. It's better to follow the same installation technique used on roof trusses. Erect one rib, and temporarily nail up some 2×4 braces staked to the ground. As you erect the next rib, nail some strapping rib to rib as you bring it into plumb position to hold it in place.

To keep the ribs secure as you continue working, you should anchor the first rib with several braces. Be sure it is braced solidly side to side as well as end to end. And as you erect, plumb, and square up each rib in turn, leapfrog the strapping so that each strap spans two or three ribs with overlapping coverage.

Building individual ribs is a simple way to construct a small garden shed or toolshed. Each rib is a complete cross section of the building that is tied together with plywood sheathing.

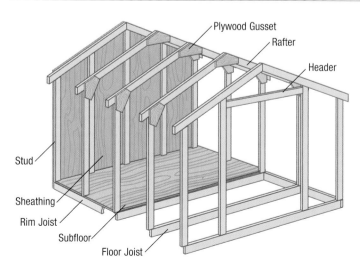

Framing ribs for a small gable-roofed shed is a simple project. Build one rib and use it as a template for others. Make simple jigs to help you mark and cut the lumber and gusset components. All non-gusset joints should be reinforced with hardware.

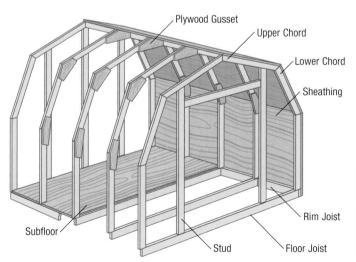

Building ribs for a small gambrel-roofed shed is a little more complicated because each rib has four rafters instead of two. Due to the two-part rafters, you may need extra pieces to reinforce the rafters and effectively turn part of the rib into a roof truss.

Pole Barn Design

Building on poles driven into the ground is one of the oldest construction techniques. It has endured because poles (in the form of unmilled trees) are everywhere, and the construction is highly practical. And by elevating a structure off the ground on poles, you avoid floods and vermin.

Furthermore, when you stick a quarter or even a third of a pole into the ground, the portion rising out of the ground has great stability and strength. Pole buildings generally have great resistance to racking, good wind resistance, and—when the poles are sized properly—excellent overall strength. Additionally, a well-engineered pole barn has structural components that interlock and absorb force and distribute loads across the entire frame—unlike stick-framed structures, where an isolated portion of the structure absorbs forces and has limited force-distribution paths. Pole barns are highly adaptable to most sites; they work much better for sloped sites than stick framing.

Parts of a Pole Barn

Vertical members can be either poles (round) or posts (square). Most of the horizontal members, which are usually dimensional lumber, are called girts. Depending on where a girt is positioned, it might be a floor girt (what a stick framer would call a header or rim joist), a siding girt (the horizontal

backing for siding), an eaves girt, or a ridge girt, both of which support rafters.

Once a pole frame is up, you can pour a slab for the floor, leave a dirt floor, or frame a floor suspended on the poles. Because you are not platform framing, with one floor depending on the floor beneath it, you can hang floors and ceilings off the poles at any elevation.

Choosing Poles

If you think that round poles don't live by the same rules as dimensional lumber, think again. Poles are subject to the laws of loads, spans, and stresses, just like timbers and beams. You will find, however, that poles are stronger than comparable dimensional timbers. This is because the tree, engineered by nature, naturally grows certain parts of its layers in compression and certain ones in tension. A pole that is simply a debarked tree, unmilled, is stronger than a timber milled to the same size because the timber loses these tension-compression relationships.

Poles are rated in classes by the American Wood Preservers Association. The different classes take into account the diameter and circumference at the top and the length of the pole in feet. (See the "Pole Classes" table at right.) Poles within classes are rated for their load-bearing capacity (for loads delivered on a vertical pole) and for span (for loads on a

Typical Pole Barn Construction

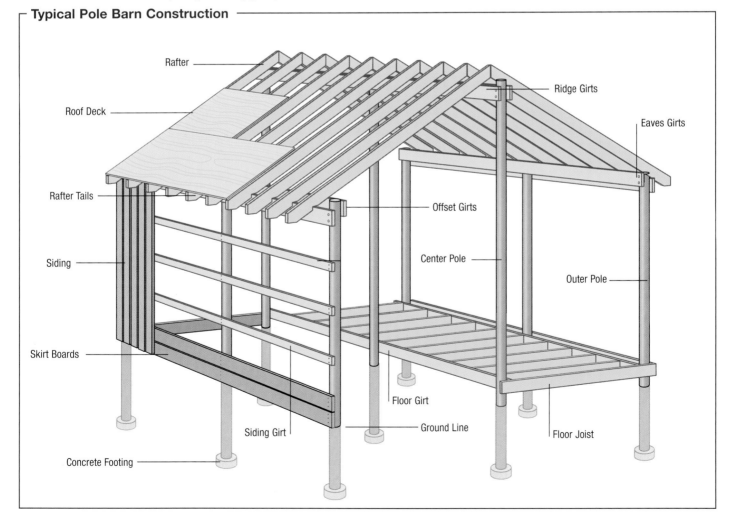

horizontal pole or girt). The upshot is that poles need to be engineered for your specific structure with careful consideration given to wind and snow loading, the dead load of the building (the weight of the material it is made from), and the live load of the building (weight of the things you put into the barn once it is built). If you're not working from code-approved plans, consult an architect, engineer, pole suppliers, or the trade associations that represent them.

Pole Treatments

Poles need to be treated with preservative just like any other wood that comes in sustained contact with the ground. The majority of pressure-treated wood has a recommended ground-contact concentration of preservatives. You need to be sure that the preservative is safe and approved by code. It's wise to check with the pole supplier and local inspectors to be sure that your poles are properly treated. Generally, building poles are treated with chromated copper arsenate (CCA) or less toxic alternatives. For lumber and timbers that are structural and in contact with soil or fresh water, look for a CCA concentration of 0.60. For aboveground use, a CCA concentration of 0.25 typically will do.

Using Posts

You probably won't find a local home center or even a big lumberyard that carries unmilled poles. Most likely you will need to special-order them from a lumberyard that specializes in pole buildings. (Cutting down trees and chemical-treating them yourself is dangerous and not recommended.)

However, in the absence of poles, 6×6 or 8×8 pressure-treated posts work well for most small projects. Many lumberyards carry 12- and 16-foot 6×6s, which would be long enough for a building with an 8-foot wall height and a 4-foot frost depth. In fact, it is much easier to attach girts to the square side of a post than the round edge of a pole. But oversize posts like this can be quite expensive.

Poles for construction are usually dark brown or green from chemical treatments that protect the wood from rotting.

Common Pole Classes

Class	1	2	3	4	5	6
Diameter at top	8½"	8"	7¼"	6¾"	6"	5½"
Minimum top circumference	27"	25"	23"	21"	19"	17"
Length of pole	Minimum circumference at 6 ft. from butt					
20'	—	—	—	—	—	21"
25'	—	—	—	—	—	23"
30'	—	34"	32"	29½"	27½"	25"
35'	—	36½"	34"	31½"	29"	27"
40'	41"	38½"	36"	33½"	31"	28½"
45'	43"	40½"	37½"	35"	32½"	—

Check classes and sizes with the local building department.

Floor Framing for Pole Barns

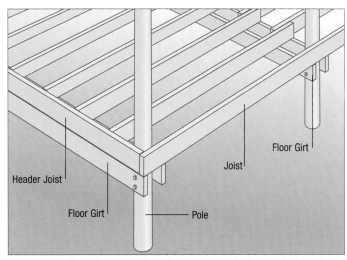

To frame a floor for a pole building, you can bolt double girts to the poles and frame your joist members on top of them the way you would add joists over a girder.

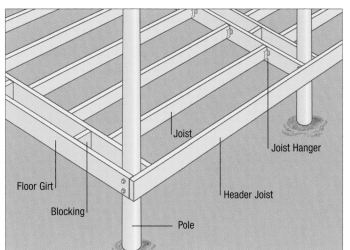

Another way to frame a pole building floor is to use the doubled girts as part of the finished floor frame, hanging joists between the girts on galvanized joist hangers.

Setting Poles

On small pole buildings, you may be able to tip up poles or posts with a few helpers. On most large barns you need a crane or a special setup called a gin pole, which is a type of site-built hand-powered crane held with guy wires on a hinged base. Similar systems using a tripod array and block and tackle are generally well beyond the scope of do-it-yourselfers. But on a large barn project, you might prepare the site, dig the holes, and have a professional crew set and brace the poles before continuing with sheathing and roofing on your own. Even on a modest project, you'll need one person to hold and brace the pole while another checks for plumb.

In loose or sandy soil, you can rent a two-person gasonline-power auger so that you (and a helper) can dig deep holes a lot faster than you can with a shovel and a posthole digger.

Preparing the Hole

The hole depth depends on your frost line and how you will set the pole. Whether you embed the pole in the ground, or use the common system of setting poles with hardware aboveground on piers, the base of the pole or pier needs to be set below the frost line. Otherwise, freezing subsurface water could cause shifting. The local building inspector can provide (and likely will check) the required depth.

The way you dig depends on the number of poles, their depth, and whether your soil is rocky. If you're building a small shed or workshop, a small number of 2-foot holes in sandy soil can be dug with a shovel and a posthole digger. Many deep holes call for a rented power auger. A narrow, 4-foot-deep hole will be almost impossible to dig without one. Extremely rocky soil will make digging tough, even with a handheld power auger. It's worth spending money to save time (and maybe spare you a few bruised ribs) by hiring someone to dig your holes with a tractor equipped with a

power-driven auger bit. If you don't have any willing farmers in your area, try a fencing company.

Raising the Pole

Before raising a pole, it helps to place a rough lumber plank on the side of the excavation that the pole will bear against on its way into the hole. This will keep the pole from caving in a lot of dirt. Once a pole is vertical, you need to hold it in place with at least two angled braces securely staked to the ground. Remember, poles are heavy. You can clamp the braces temporarily as you adjust for plumb and fine-tune the placement of the pole. Then nail the braces securely before you backfill the hole with soil or concrete.

Four Ways to Set Poles

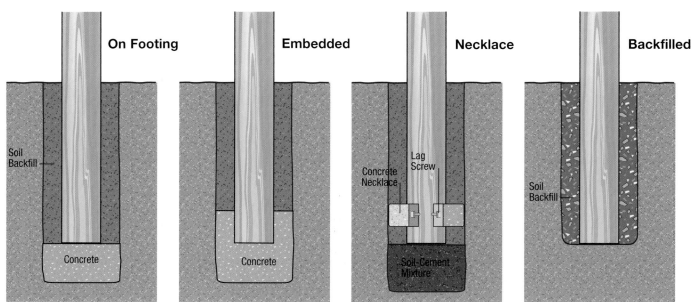

There are several ways to support a pole in the ground, including on a concrete footing, embedded in a concrete footing, on a soil-cement mixture with a concrete ring, called a necklace, poured around lag screws, and in a hole backfilled with soil or a soil-cement mixture. Poles also are commonly installed with hardware on aboveground concrete piers.

Raising, Setting & Bracing Poles

TOOLS & MATERIALS

- Shovel
- Posthole digger or power auger
- Power drill/driver
- 4' spirit level

- Poles or posts
- One-by boards
- Mason's twine
- 6" (or longer) bolts
- 2×4s for bracing
- Concrete

1 You'll need to dig a hole below the frost line for each pole. For small buildings, try digging with a posthole digger. For many poles, deep frost lines, or rocky soil, rent a power auger.

2 Place a few one-by boards on one side of the hole to keep the pole from dragging down dirt from the sides of the hole and making the hole shallower than it should be.

3 For greater stability (if you'll be pouring concrete into the hole), fasten a few large bolts or lag screws at the bottom of the pole (or post as shown here) so that they stick out a few inches.

4 A 12-ft. 6×6 post can easily be raised into position by two people; longer, heavier poles may require four or six people—or even a crane—to get them upright safely.

5 One or more persons should hold the pole or post in position while another checks it for plumb. Once it is straight, it can be secured in position with braces staked to the ground.

6 Use two sets of 2×4 braces and stakes to keep the post plumb while you pour the concrete or backfill the hole. Check it again as you work and readjust as needed.

7 Once all the poles are braced, fill the bottom of each hole with enough concrete to reach past the bolts. Other embedding systems use soil or a mix of soil and cement.

8 Once the concrete necklace has cured, you can backfill the hole with soil. Other systems use aboveground piers that keep the poles off the ground. Check local codes for preference.

Wall and Roof Framing

In most pole barn plans, poles or posts serve only as the vertical framing members that support dimensional lumber or rough-cut timbers. These pieces of lumber in turn support the siding and roofing. There are a number of different ways to fasten girts, joists, and rafters to the grid of vertical poles or posts. The best one depends on several factors, for example, whether you are using round poles or square posts, how large the timbers are, and what fasteners are favored by the local building department.

Lumber-to-Pole Connections

When connecting lumber to poles, you have four main choices: spikes, lag screws, machine bolts, and a spike grid. If you're using posts, it's easy to fasten the flat sides of girts against the flat surfaces of the posts. The two timbers rest against each other and provide more than enough bearing for a secure connection. But if you're using poles, only a narrow strip of a girt will rest against the pole because the pole is round. To improve this situation and gain more bearing in the connection, many builders recess the girts into the poles using a process called dapping.

The idea is to cut a shallow notch in the face of the pole and let in the girt, generally by about half its thickness. This way, the girt bears partially on the pole instead of hanging completely on the fasteners. Make the notch by setting the depth of cut on a circular saw and cutting several parallel

Spikes

Lag screws

Machine bolt

Spike grid

Attach girts to poles with one of these four types of connectors. Eight-inch ring-nail spikes can be used for smaller structures. Lag screws, machine bolts, and spike grids have more holding power. You can't rely on nails that are used on stick-built house frames.

Holding Up the Roof

Roof structures on pole barns are subject to the same stresses and loads as those built over a stick-framed structure. But in a pole building, the rafters (or trusses) are supported differently.

One option is to use double girts on the outer poles. This provides two points of support for conventional rafters and decreases the span somewhat. Another option is to use double girts bolted on the outside of the poles. The double-width top edge creates a support platform for rafters that is similar to the double top plate of a stick-built wall frame. And double girts can

be designed to support rafters between poles. On small structures, you can join rafters at a central ridgeboard. Depending on the slope of the roof and the rafter setup, you may also need the extra strength of collar ties.

On large structures with a line of poles at midspan, the upper ends of the rafters can rest on girts bolted to the center poles. (The central girts take the place of a ridgeboard.) If you plan to install roof trusses, you need a level platform for the bottom chord to rest on.

Two Girts Sandwich Pole

Two Girts on One Side

Truss on Two Girts

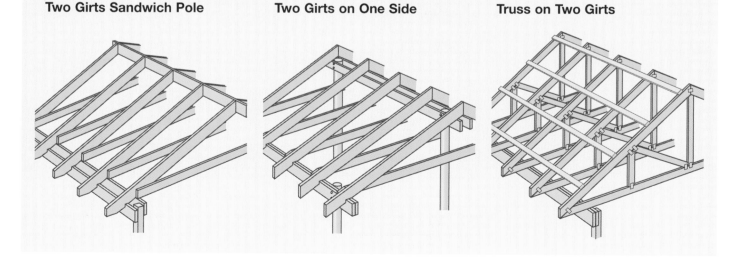

kerfs into the outer face of the post. Then knock out the wood between kerfs with a hammer or hatchet, and smooth out the surface with a chisel. The result is that the girt now nestles into the pole, creating a stronger connection.

The trick to this process is holding the saw flat even when you're cutting a pole that is round. It takes some practice to create an even series of kerfs that you can break out easily. You will find that it pays to make more cuts with kerfs closer together. This reduces the time needed to chip out and smooth the notch.

Four Ways to Make Connections

■ **Spikes.** You can attach lumber to a pole using 8-inch ring nails called pole spikes, generally four per connection. This connection won't support much load, around 2,500 pounds, and nails can loosen, so you should use this system only for small structures.

■ **Lag Screws.** Using two 4- to 6-inch-long rust-resistant lag screws can provide a connection that will support about 5,500 pounds. The screw threads won't loosen or pull out the way nails can.

■ **Machine or Carriage Bolts.** By predrilling the dimension lumber and pole and through-bolting the notched joint with stainless-steel machine or carriage bolts, washers, and nuts, you can achieve a solid structural connection capable of carrying about 8,000 pounds. Through-bolting, generally two bolts per girt connection, is often the best balance of efficiency and strength, and should meet local codes.

■ **Spike Grid.** Some builders use spike grids between poles and dimensional lumber instead of, or in addition to, through-bolting. There are several types, including shaped grids that fit between curved poles and squared lumber. But in every case be sure to check not only lumber sizes but lumber connections with the building inspector.

Attaching Siding and Eaves Girts to Posts

TOOLS & MATERIALS

- Measuring tape
- 4' spirit level
- Water level or line level and mason's twine
- Power drill/driver or framing hammer
- Bar clamps

- Pressure-treated 2×6s for skirt boards
- 2×4s for siding girts
- Nails or screws

1 Install skirt boards made of pressure-treated 2×6s. The bottom skirt board runs along the ground. Check for level, and then screw or nail them into the support poles or posts.

2 Horizontal girts provide a nailing surface for the siding. Most designs call for one every 24 in. Measure up from the top skirt board on the first post, and make a mark.

3 Mark all the posts for the siding girts using a line level, transit, or water level. Run the line along the posts, adjusting it to level all around the perimeter of the building.

4 A water level indicates level readings over large areas, even when the tube runs up and down across a construction site. The level at one end of the tube is level with the water at the other end.

5 Siding girts are usually 2×4s face-nailed (or screwed) to posts. For poles, they may be partially recessed into the face of the poles (a process called dapping) for extra support.

Attaching Rafter Girts

TOOLS & MATERIALS

- Measuring tape
- Power drill with screwdriver bit
- Extra-long spade bit or auger bit
- Wider spade or Forstner bit for countersink
- Bar clamps
- 4' spirit level
- Circular saw (or chain saw)
- Hatchet, 2" wood chisel
- Paintbrush
- Long-handled socket wrench
- Reciprocating saw, handsaw

- 2×10s or 2×12s for rafter girts
- 2×4 scraps for scab boards
- Wood preservative (such as linseed oil)
- ½" bolts or threaded rods (at least 8" long)
- Nuts and washers to fit bolts

1 The top of the rafter girts represent your wall height. Measure up on one pole from the level skirt boards, and then transfer this mark to the other poles using a line level or water level.

2 Make another mark below this, representing the bottom edge of the girt. Screw on a temporary scab board at this mark to hold the girts in place against the pole while you mark them.

6 After removing the girts, double-check the thickness. Although two-by lumber is usually 1½ in. thick, pressure-treated 2×10s and 2×12s may vary and are often thinner.

7 Set your circular saw blade to the depth of about one-half the girt thickness and make a series of closely spaced cuts across the face of the pole between the marks.

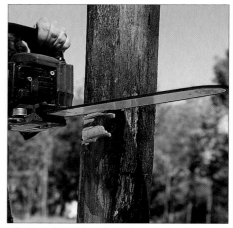

8 An alternative to using a circular saw is to make the kerfs with a chain saw. It's more difficult to control the depth of cut with a chain saw, which must be used with extreme caution.

12 Most rafter girts are held up by bolts centered on the pole about 2 to 3 in. from the edges. Drill a shallow hole with a bit the diameter of the bolt heads to countersink them.

13 Next, drill into the center of the countersinks all the way through the girt (or girts) and the pole. You'll probably need extra-long spade and auger bits for this job.

14 Once you drill all the holes, drive the bolts through (from the outside of the wall) with a hammer. Set them so that the top of the bolt head is flush with the surface of the wood.

3 Rest the rafter girts on the scab boards, and clamp them into place on the poles. Place one set of clamps at the end of each board; long girts should have a set in the center.

4 Once all the girts have been installed, check them for level with a 4-ft. (or longer) level. Make adjustments as needed by removing and replacing the scab boards one at a time.

5 Once all the girts are level, carefully mark the top and bottom of each with a pencil. These marks indicate the top and bottom of the dapping detail in the outer face of the pole.

9 When you've cut kerfs about ¹/₂ in. apart between the marks, chop out the wood between the cuts with a hammer or small hatchet. Then smooth the surface of the dap with a wood chisel.

10 Before resetting the girts, coat the notch with a wood preservative as a precautionary measure, even if the support pole or post is made of pressure-treated lumber.

11 Set the girts into the notches and clamp them. One clamp at each end should be enough to hold them. Be careful not to place the clamp where you'll be drilling the bolt holes.

15 For buildings with thick poles and two girts, there may not be a bolt long enough. In these cases, insert threaded rods and use nuts and washers at both ends.

16 Tighten the bolts with a socket wrench. Deep sockets are available for bolts where an inch or more protrudes from the girt. Trim excess length after the bolts are tightened.

17 Once the rafter girts are set, you can cut off the tops of the poles with a reciprocating saw. A chain saw is faster, but must be used very carefully from a safe and secure working position.

Timber-Framing Design

Timber framing is one of the oldest but most refined and durable forms of construction. In fact, you can travel the world and see straight and true timber-framed buildings dating back before the fifteenth century. Some archaeologists have dated timber-frame construction to 200 B.C.

Timber framing is not an easy trade; it will take some real practice before you can make timber-frame joints as tight and snug as they ought to be. There are several timber-framing schools where do-it-yourselfers can spend a few weeks learning the basics and actually erect a small timber-frame building.

You'll find that even modest projects often involve a lot of people. Tackling a timber-frame project on your own isn't practical unless you plan to build a very small structure with timbers you can handle by yourself. The upshot is that this section of the book is just a primer designed to help you get a running start when working with an experienced timber framer who is handling the construction.

Timber Framing versus Stick Framing

With a stick-built structure, you can raise one wall or even one stud at a time. Timber-framed walls generally are raised in complete cross sections of the building, called bents. They can be very heavy, and often have to be raised with a complicated system of ropes and pulleys, or even with a crane. In old-fashioned barn-raisings, large groups of people would hoist and push up the walls. But today that's a job for an experienced crew led by an even more experienced builder. And once heavy timber-framed sections are in place, you need heavy-duty bracing instead of simple furring strips that can hold stick-built rafters in position.

Also, unlike stick-framed structures, timber frames are not built with wood cut on-site. The frames often are measured and cut at a shop based on a detailed plan that includes complex (and sometimes machine-controlled) cuts for the array of joints. Sometimes the frame is assembled, marked, and only then transported to the building site and erected.

Basic Construction

Most connections in a timber frame are mortise-and-tenon joints. They have to be cut precisely and often are trimmed to final shape with large and extremely sharp chisels. When the tenon is in place, a wooden peg is driven through the joint to secure it. But most timber-frame joints also have shoulders that help to support the connection or other interlocking features that help to keep the joint tight.

Once the bents are constructed, one after another is raised. Then bracing is installed, and finally permanent cross timbers are installed on the walls and roof that tie the building together. The distance between each cross section,

Typical Timber-Frame Construction

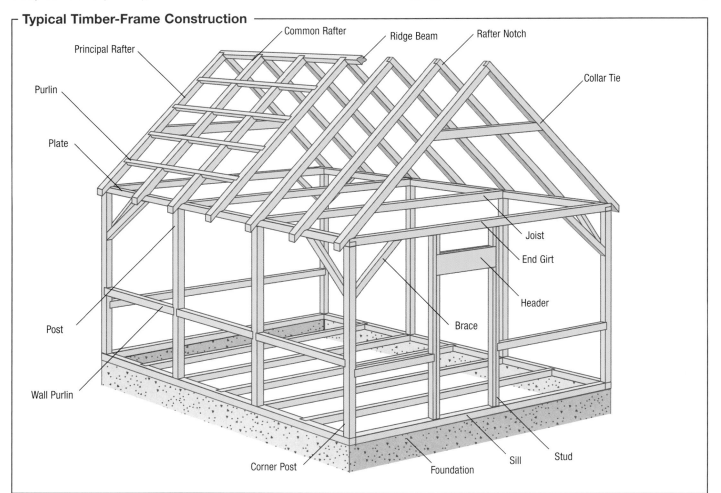

like the spacing between studs, is dictated by the size and strength of the lumber used in the frame itself.

Each bent has its own set of components, namely the diagonal braces; the plate, which spans the bent where the posts meet the rafters, the girts, which span from post to post; the posts, and the knee braces, which reinforce the girt-and-post joint. Timbers that span from rafter to rafter parallel to the ground are called purlins. Timber frames do share some common terms with stick-built structures. For example, the timbers that rest on the foundation are called sills. But you will find some variation in the nomenclature; there is no one way to name all the parts of a timber frame, and even some professional timber-frame builders use different terms.

Bent Configurations

The illustrations below show six common bent configurations. The design that you can use on your structure may vary depending on your region and the intended use of your building. In areas of heavy snow load, for example, it may be most efficient to use a queen post design instead of a king post with struts. Some designs allow for more headroom in second floors, while others increase the strength of a roof.

But these are only some of the options. The basic bent design for your structure can be any of a dozen or more configurations that tailor the space to your needs. Some, such as the hammer beam, require very complex joinery.

Timber-framed barns are built more like furniture than modern buildings. The heavy framing members are held together with fitted joints and pegs rather than nails or screws.

Common Bent Configurations

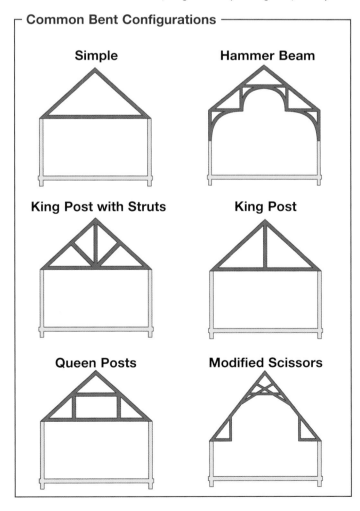

Simple

Hammer Beam

King Post with Struts

King Post

Queen Posts

Modified Scissors

The exposed timbers direct the load of the roof down to the posts. Some bents can be designed with additional cross members that allow you to add storage space above the plates.

Timber-Framing Joinery

When assembling the elements of a timber frame, you have to cut a tenon in the ends of many timbers and a corresponding mortise in adjoining timbers, for example, where a strut meets a plate or rafter.

When cutting any part of a timber-frame joint, keep in mind that the frame joinery in a timber-framed structure will be visible. Unlike stick-built structures, which have the frame concealed in the walls, timber-frame structures generally reveal the frame, at least on the inside. So when laying out and cutting joints, remember to face the timber's best sides toward the inside.

When laying out a timber for cutting, remember to figure the shoulder-to-shoulder distance, or clear span of the timber, and also the extra length needed for joints, such as tenons. The shoulder-to-shoulder distance is what establishes the distance between your bents, not the tenon-to-tenon distance. Also bear in mind that a sloppy shoulder cut or tenon cut too long will substantially compromise joint strength. These three-dimensional connections must fit snugly on all sides to create a strong joint.

Joint Variations

The mortise-and-tenon joint cut in the sequence at right is a square joint, which is the type of joint you would cut where a girt meets a post. Where a strut meets a rafter, a knee brace meets a post at an angle, or where you are cutting scarf joints, housed dovetails, or many of the joints called for in a timber frame, the joinery becomes considerably more complicated. To get a taste of the requirements, you may want to attempt a complex joint, such as a dovetail lap joint, in short scraps of 4×4 material.

Basic Timber-Framing Joints

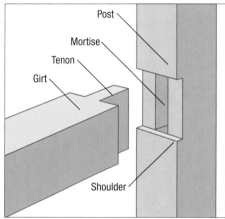

A housed mortise-and-tenon joint can be cut with the tenon extending into the post or extending all the way through so that the end grain of the tenon is visible. A shoulder helps to support the girt.

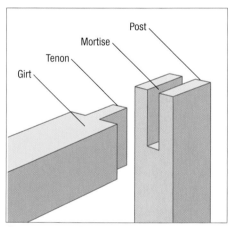

An open mortise-and-tenon joint is often found at the peaks of rafters that join together without a ridgeboard in between. This connection is not as strong as the shoulder joint but is more easily cut.

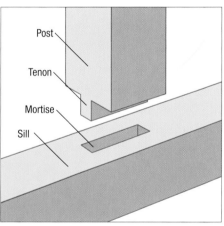

A stub mortise-and-tenon joint is found where posts are attached to sills. Here the mortise doesn't pass completely through the framing member. Gravity keeps the short tenon from pulling out of the mortise.

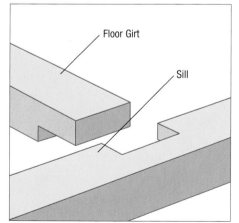

The lap joint—simpler to build than a mortise and tenon—is often used at sill beam corners and splices, or (as shown here) where floor girts meet the sill. It should be pegged particularly at corners.

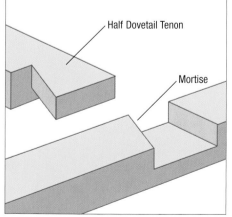

A dovetail lap joint is used to join timbers at right angles. It is harder to separate a dovetail lap joint than a standard lap. The half-dovetail shown above is easier to make than a full dovetail.

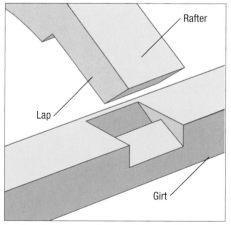

A step-lapped rafter seat is used to connect the rafter to the girt. This rather complicated joint does not need to be pegged, except at the ends of the plates to keep it from sliding off.

Cutting a Mortise and Tenon

TOOLS & MATERIALS

- Framing square • Combination square
- Measuring tape • Circular saw
- Heavy-duty framing chisels (min. 5" long and 1½" wide, with a 25° point)
- 30-oz. hardwood mallet
- Heavy-duty power drill and 1½" auger or Forstner bit
- Handsaw

- 2 rough-cut timbers
- Hardwood pegs

1 Always start with square ends to your timbers. Check the ends with a combination square, and cut away any excess with a circular saw set to maximum depth of cut.

2 Determine your shoulder-to-shoulder distance and the tenon length, and mark them on one of the timbers. Mark the tenon and an X on the wood to be removed around it.

3 Using a circular saw, cut away the waste wood, keeping the blade kerf to the waste side. If the saw blade isn't large enough to cut the full tenon, you can finish these cuts with a handsaw.

4 Clean the tenon with a chisel to make sure all the sides are flat and square. Then put a slight chamfer on the edges of the tenon using a block plane, chisel, or belt sander.

5 The mortise will be the same dimensions as the tenon. Mark its outline, drill out the bulk of the wood, and clean up the four sides of the mortise with a sharp chisel.

Mortise and Tenon Tips

Reduce chiseling work on a mortise by drilling out the bulk of the wood. For best results, use a Forstner bit (left) with a depth stop or depth mark to be sure that the floor of the mortise is flat. Then trim the corners and side walls with a sharp chisel.

After you cut the tenon and clean up the faces of the cut, use a chisel to shave a small chamfer along the edges. This helps the tenon slide into the mortise without compromising the strength of the joint.

Assembling a Bent

Working with a timber frame means handling large pieces of wood. Assembling timbers into a bent often includes using brute force to draw them together. You can gain a lot of mechanical advantage using a come-along, which has cables and a ratchet to pull on timbers with more force than you can

muster by hand. You may find that it's handy to use more than one come-along to pull together components of a bent from several directions at once. Check for square and plumb as you would with a stick-framed wall, and check diagonal measurements to see if the bent is square. Once the bent is assembled and the joints are snug, you can drill and peg the joints.

Assembling and Raising a Bent

TOOLS & MATERIALS

- Varies widely according to scale of job

- Timbers cut according to plan
- Hardwood pegs

SMART TIP:

In almost all cases, bents of even modest-sized barns are raised by a professional crew, and your main job is to prepare the site and make sure that the foundation is ready for the installation.

1 Once all the timbers and joints have been cut and delivered to the site, the components can be assembled into bents right on the deck or slab.

2 Bents are often assembled on top of one another to save space and to be sure that they match each other. The profiles have to be the same for the walls to be square.

3 Here, the final bent has been assembled and is being braced in preparation for being strapped to a hook and raised into place by a crane.

4 The first bent has been strapped to the crane and is raised into place. The stub tenons at the bottom of the posts need to be guided into the mortises by crew members.

5 When the second and third bents have been raised, the side girts and purlins are raised into place. The final step is the two-piece ridge beam.

Building a Shed from a Kit

If you don't need a custom shed, just a utilitarian box for storing tools and equipment, a shed kit is a cost-efficient alternative. Typical kits are simple buildings with gable roofs and 6 or 7 feet of clearance inside, sized anywhere from 5×4-foot to 10×17-foot for equipment sheds.

Wood kits generally come with all the lumber precut as well as enough fasteners to complete the project. Many styles are available. You can choose the cheapest, finished with T1-11 siding, or pick a kit with a similar siding to your house. Kits with metal siding and roof panels—usually steel with baked-on enamel finish—are also available in a variety of styles. There are even sheds that look like a miniature version of a typical red-and-white gambrel barn.

Metal kits are designed to be simple to assemble. Most parts snap together and are further strengthened with sheet-metal screws. The kits include prehung doors and other fixtures, but you still have to build the foundation. Because small metal buildings are light, they must be anchored to the foundation. In many regions these sheds are considered permanent structures, and you will need to check installation details with your building department.

Small tool shed kits can be purchased at many lumberyards and home centers. They include the entire shell, but generally don't include materials for building a foundation or interior floor.

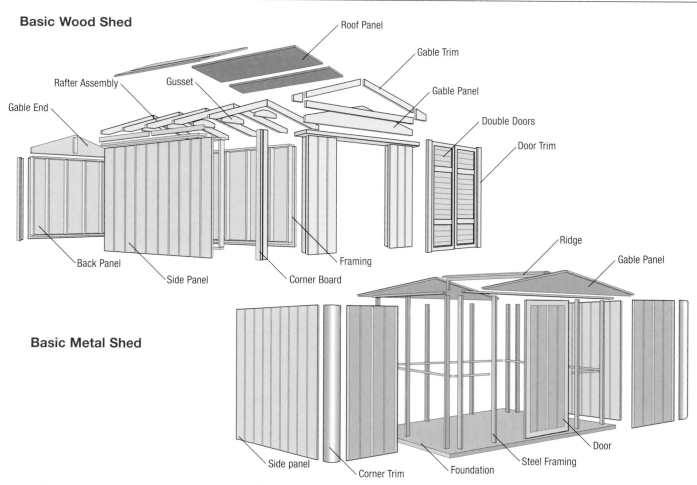

Basic Wood Shed

Roof Panel · Gable Trim · Rafter Assembly · Gusset · Gable Panel · Gable End · Double Doors · Door Trim · Back Panel · Side Panel · Corner Board · Framing · Ridge · Gable Panel

Basic Metal Shed

Side panel · Corner Trim · Foundation · Steel Framing · Door

Shed kits come in many styles. Some arrive as a pile of precut lumber and fasteners, while others are sold as preassembled frame wall panels with siding already attached. Metal kits often snap together and require only a few sheet-metal screws to fully assemble them. If you need only a small shed for a few garden tools, a kit may be the way to go.

Stairs

Depending on its design, your barn may need stairs on the inside to access a second floor, loft, or attic; or on the outside for an exterior door that's a few feet above grade.

The easiest staircase to build is a set of straight-run stairs with no turns or intermediate landings. In most circumstances, a straight-run design will be your first choice. For a barn, you will probably want to build open-riser stairs.

All the steps in a flight of stairs must be the same size. The most critical calculation is the ratio between unit rise and unit run and their consistency from one step to the next. Local building codes regulate the acceptable dimensions. For most people, a 7-inch rise and 11-inch run are the most comfortable. An 11-inch run also makes it easier to build the treads—it works out to two 2×6s or three 2×4s.

The maximum rise generally allowable is 7¾ inches; the minimum run is 9 inches. On the first riser, you need to subtract the thickness of the tread from the riser, so that the rise is uniform throughout the stairs.

Building codes also address landings and the room people need to get onto and off of the stairs safely. Headroom is another important issue. It's defined as the vertical distance measured from an imaginary line connecting the front edge on all of the treads up to overhead construction. Again, most codes establish a minimum (80 inches) from that line to any object above. This is required to prevent you from knocking your head against the ceiling or other obstruction.

Parts of a Staircase

Stringers are the diagonal elements that support the treads. You generally need to use 2×12s for your stringers. If your treads are more than 36 inches wide, you'll need a third

stringer, called a carriage, to support them in the middle. Stringers can be notched into a sawtooth pattern to support the treads, but it is easier to leave them uncut and support the treads on stair brackets. For a utility building, regular two-by boards are fine for the treads. If the stairs are going to be outside or near a dirt floor, use pressure-treated wood.

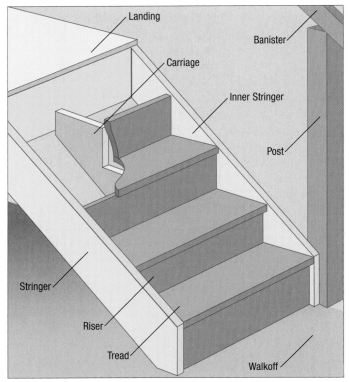

Utility stairs consist of the same parts as other stairs in your home. You may not need to include riser boards as you would inside. Treads can be made of dimensional lumber.

Calculating Stair Dimensions

■ *Measure the total rise from one finished floor surface to the other. Even if the finished floor hasn't been installed, you must include it in your calculations.*

■ *The maximum riser height is 7¾ inches. Divide your total rise by 7.75. This number, when rounded up to the nearest whole number, gives you the total number of risers you'll need. Then divide the total rise by this number to determine the actual unit rise.*

■ *The minimum tread depth (called the run) is 9 inches, however 10 or 11 inches is safer. Two simple formulas to match the tread depth to the riser height are rise + run = about 17 to 18, or, alternatively, rise × run = about 70 to 75. By the first formula, a riser of 7¼ inches can have a tread depth anywhere from 9¾ to 10¾ inches.*

■ *Calculate the total run by multiplying the number of steps by the tread depth. Check to make sure that you'll have sufficient head clearance for the entire run. Typical code requirements specify a minimum of 80 inches of headroom in all parts of a stairway.*

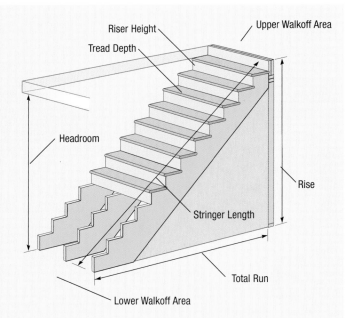

When planning a staircase, the total rise is the only given. The measurements of treads and risers must fall within parameters; the total run can be anything that won't cause an obstuction.

Building Utility Stairs

1 Start the layout at the top of the stringer using proportions listed on the framing square that match your layout. Slide the stops on the square along the stringer to repeat tread layout lines.

2 As an extra guide to your installation, also mark the thickness of the treads on the stringer. For a cut stringer, test the stringer in place before making any saw cuts.

3 Attach the top ends of your stringers with brackets and screws. Even when you have access to drive fasteners into the stringer end grain, brackets make a stronger connection.

4 Screw galvanized metal stair brackets to the insides of your stringers following your layout lines. Allow for the tread thickness and a slight overhang at the front of each step.

5 After you've installed all the stair brackets, measure the stair frame opening, and center the low end of the middle support. Double-check the position with a framing square.

6 Cut square ends on the stair tread boards. Treads mounted on brackets should be cut at least ⅛ in. short of the overall space to allow room for expansion and drainage.

7 Predrill treads to avoid splits, and nail or screw the boards to the brackets. For designs with a cut stringer or for landings (shown above), extend treads past the stringer or joist.

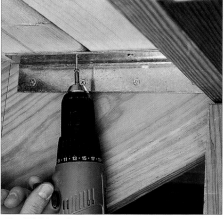

8 Hidden fasteners can reduce splits on treads. On low treads, you can fasten the brackets to the treads first, and then screw the assembly to the stringers with deck screws.

CHAPTER 5

Roof Framing

You can build a roof at almost any angle, from nearly flat to almost vertical, and select from an array of materials to cover it. The choices are mostly a matter of design and matching the roof style, such as a gable or mansard design, to the overall building style. But you have to consider the weather, too, and use a style that's suited to the site. For example, you generally want a steeper slope in regions of heavy snow. You also need to plan ahead for overhangs, which can be several feet deep on a big barn where you want more weather protection for windows and doors. The roof frame must account for weather protection, ventilation, and other important concerns.

Roof Types

The gable roof is perhaps the most common roof profile. It has two sloping sides (not necessarily the same size) that meet at a center ridge. On the eaves walls you get the protection of an overhang, and on the gable ends you can install windows or vents. If the roof pitch isn't too low, gable attics can be spacious. Steep-pitched gables are ideal in areas with heavy winter snows. There are several other roof shapes, including shed, gambrel, saltbox, and hip, and many variations on the basic configurations.

Choosing a Roof Type

The kind of roof you use will depend on your architectural taste, the climate, and the building's function. Shed roofs are often used on barns and wood sheds. These roofs are easy to build and the easiest type of roof to shingle.

Gambrel and mansard roofs also can be practical in the long run because their rafter configuration provides extra second-floor space, which can be handy for storage in a barn. But these roofs are more difficult to frame because they have more surfaces that meet at angles. The same goes for hip roofs, which are used more on houses than on barns. But this design allows a deep overhang on all four sides of the building, which offers the most weather protection.

In any case, consider the option of using trusses, which are available in almost every style. You can order these locally, erect them yourself on a small structure, or hire a contractor with a crane to set trusses on a large building.

Spans & Loads

Rafters must be able to span distances safely and according to code. Many factors bear on the allowable span, but the basic idea is that a large piece of lumber, such as a 2×10, has more strength and can span a greater distance than a 2×6, assuming the same type of wood species and grade of lumber. But at a low angle (one closer to level) there is more strain on a rafter than at a high angle (one closer to vertical). So a steep roof with a high angle creates less rafter load.

On-center framing distances also affect rafter span. Rafters placed 16 inches on center can take on a greater load than rafters of the same size set at 24 inches on center. That means you can use a smaller size (or a lesser grade of lumber in some cases) if you set rafters at 16 instead of 24 inches.

The grade of the lumber also affects allowable rafter span. No. 1 Douglas Fir will have a greater span than No. 2 Douglas Fir, for example, because the wood has more strength. That's why span tables used by architects, engineers, and building departments take wood species and grades into account.

When referring to tables, which are available from your local building department among other sources, make sure it's a rafter table and not a joist table. On a rafter table you'll notice that there are two categories of span, not a listing for every possible angle. The tables typically break down the slopes into steep-sloped roofs, with slopes of 4 in 12 or more, and low-sloped roofs, with slopes of 4 in 12 or less. Remember that the building department has the final say on the design and construction.

Roof Types

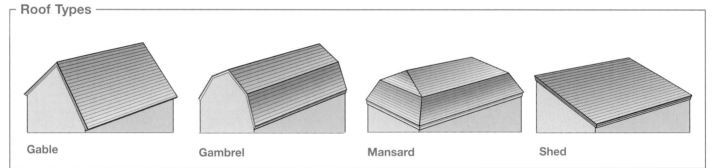

Gable   Gambrel   Mansard   Shed

Engineered Components

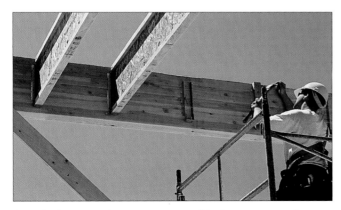

Metal stirrups, or hangers, are used to fasten composite joists and rafters, such as wood I-beams, to support beams.

Engineered wood framing often needs special fasteners, but this system offers benefits over conventional framing.

Roof Terminology

Rise is the height of the roof at its ridge measured from the top plate of the end wall below the ridge.

Span is the horizontal distance from wall to wall. A roof's span does not include the overhang at the eaves.

Run is the horizontal distance from one wall to a point under the ridge, or typically half the span.

Pitch is the angle of a roof as a ratio of the rise to the span. A 24-foot-wide structure, for example, with a gable roof that rises 10 feet from side wall to ridgeboard has a pitch of 10/24, or 5/12. A pitch of 1/4 or 1/3 is common for gable roofs. A Cape Cod–style roof might have a 1/2 pitch.

Slope is expressed as the rafter's vertical rise in inches, or unit rise, per 12 inches of horizontal run, or unit run. If a slope has a unit rise of 4 and a unit run of 12, the roof surface rises 4 inches for every 12 inches along the run line. This is expressed as 4:12 or 4 in 12. On most building plans, you'll notice a right triangle off to the side—for example, 4 in 12 with a 12 at the top of the triangle on one leg of the right angle and a 4 on the other leg. The hypotenuse of the triangle shows you the angle of slope. The higher the number of inches in unit rise, the steeper the roof. A 12-in-12 roof, common in Cape Cod-style roofs, rises a foot in elevation for every foot of run (a 45-degree angle).

Making Measurements

If you know the slope of a roof but don't know the total rise, you can determine that dimension using the total run on a symmetrical roof. First, divide the span in half to get the total run. Let's say your structure has a span of 20 feet. The total run is 10 feet. Now multiply the unit rise by the number of feet in the total run. An 8-in-12 roof with a total run of 10 feet means the total rise is 80 inches (8 × 10) or 6 feet 8 inches. If you increase the run, the slope doesn't change, but the total rise increases. For example, if you have a 12-foot run with an 8-in-12 roof, the total rise is 96 inches (8 × 12) or 8 feet.

When you determine rise, you use a measurement along a line from the cap plate's top outside edge to the ridge's centerline. The point at which the rafter measuring line and the ridgeboard centerline intersect is known as the theoretical ridgeboard height. The rise is the distance from the plate to the theoretical ridgeboard height.

But if math is not your strong point, there is another option (shown step by step on page 90). You erect braced posts at each end of the ridge, adjust the ridge up or down as needed with clamps, and test rafters for length, angle, and end cuts. This may be the best system for do-it-yourselfers working on an addition and trying to match an existing roof line.

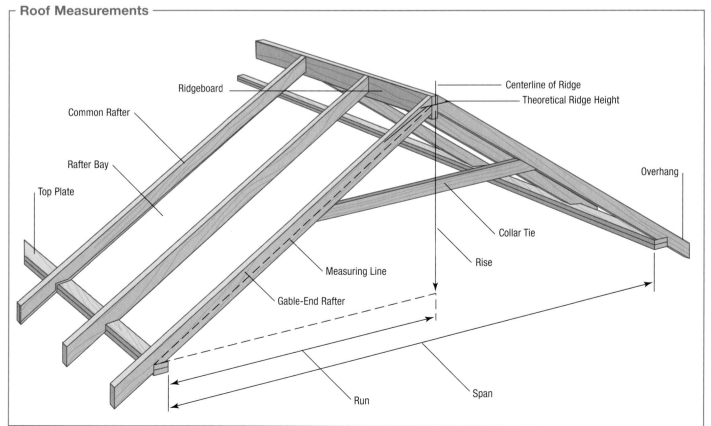

Roof Measurements

Ridgeboard

Common Rafter

Rafter Bay

Top Plate

Centerline of Ridge

Theoretical Ridge Height

Overhang

Collar Tie

Measuring Line

Rise

Gable-End Rafter

Span

Run

Three Ways to Calculate Rafter Length

There are three ways to calculate rafter length, aside from the trusted do-it-yourself method of holding a board in place and marking the cuts. The calculations used here are an example and are not meant for all rafters, but you can use the principles for any common gable rafter.

#1: Using the Pythagorean Theorem

Determine the roof slope. Here, assume a slope of 8 in 12, which means the roof rises 8 inches for every 12 inches it runs. Then determine the building width. For this example, assume the building is 30 feet wide. Next, determine the run. The run is one-half the building's width, in this case, 15 feet. Finally, determine the rise. Once you know the slope and run, you know the roof will rise 10 feet (8 x 15 = 120 inches, or 10 feet).

You're now ready to figure the rafter length for an 8-in-12 roof on a building 30 feet wide. If you think of half the roof as a right triangle, you already know the base (15) and altitude (10). You need to figure the hypotenuse of this right triangle, which represents the rafter length. Using the Pythagorean theorem:

RIGHT TRIANGLE

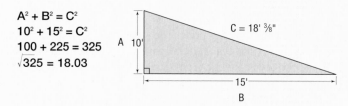

$$A^2 + B^2 = C^2$$
$$10^2 + 15^2 = C^2$$
$$100 + 225 = 325$$
$$\sqrt{325} = 18.03$$

The square root of 325 feet is 18.03 feet, which equals 18 feet ³⁄₈ inch. If your rise and/or run are not in whole feet but in feet and inches, then convert the whole figure to inches, do the math, and convert it back to feet. Use decimals of a foot rather than inches when you divide the resulting number of inches by 12 on a calculator to arrive at feet.

#2: Using a Rafter Table

The rafter table found on a framing square contains work-saving data and is useful for many calculations. You need only look at the first line of the table, which gives unit rafter length for common gable rafters. To find the unit length you need, look on the blade below the inch designation that corresponds to your slope. If, for example, you're framing a 6-in-12 roof, look at the number below the 6-inch mark on the framing square's blade. You'll find it reads 13.42. If your total run is 14, multiply 13.42 by 14 to get 187.88 inches. Divide 187.88 by 12 to get 15.656 feet, or 15 feet 7⁷⁄₈ inches.

#3: Stepping Off with a Framing Square

You can also accurately measure a rafter by stepping off dimensions with a framing square in 12-inch units of run.

Lay a straight piece of rafter stock across two sawhorses. Sight down the edge of the rafter, and position yourself on the crowned side, which will be the top of the rafter. To make accurate marking easier, attach adjustable stops called stair nuts or stair buttons to the square to set the rise and run positions.

Let's say you want to lay out a roof with an 8-in-12 slope. Lay the square on the left end of the stock. Hold the square's tongue in your left hand and its blade in your right. Pivot the square until the edge of the stock near you aligns with the unit rise mark (8 inches in this example) on the outside of the tongue and the 12-inch mark on the outside of the blade. Mark along the outside edge of the tongue for the ridge plumb line. You'll use this mark as the reference line for stepping off full 12-inch units.

If the span is an odd number of feet, say 25, with a run of 12½ feet, you'll have to include a half-step to accommodate the extra length. Mark off the partial step first, and then go on to step off full 12-inch units. Holding the square in the position in which you had it to mark the ridge cut, measure and mark the length of the odd unit along the blade.

Shift the square to your right along the edge of the stock until the tongue is even with the mark you just made. Mark off a plumb line along the tongue of the square. When you begin stepping off full units, remember to start from the new plumb line and not from the ridge cut line.

Testing a Template

Whatever system you use, take the time to test a rafter in place to be sure that the cuts are correct. Check the ridge cut, the overall length, and the overhang. Then you can use that rafter as a template to make others in the roof.

RAFTER TABLE

	2|3	2|2	2|1	2|0		4	3	2°	1
Length Common Rafters Per Foot Run						12 65	12 37	12 16	
Length Hip or Valley Per Foot Run						17 44	17 23	17 09	
Difference in Length of Jacks 16 Inches Centers						16 ⁷⁄₈	16 ¹⁄₄		
Difference in Length of Jacks 2 Feet Centers						25 ⁵⁄₁₆	24 ³⁄₄	24 ⁵⁄₁₆	
Side Cuts of Jacks Use						11 ⁷⁄₈	11 ⁵⁄₈	11 ¹³⁄₁₆	
Side Cuts of Hip or Valley Use						11 ¹¹⁄₁₆	11 ¹³⁄₁₆	11 ¹⁵⁄₁₆	
	2|2	2|1	2|0	1|9		3	2°	1	

Framing Square

Rafter Data

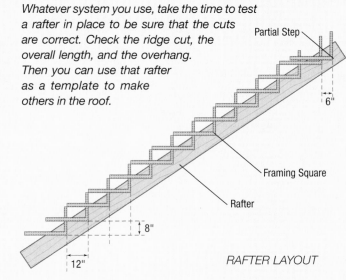

Partial Step

6"

Framing Square

Rafter

8"

12"

RAFTER LAYOUT

Basic Gable Framing

Calculating rafter length and the angles at the ridge and rafter tail is more complex than framing walls. But the job is doable using only basic math if you break down the task into smaller, more simple steps. On gable roofs, you can either run the rafters individually to a center ridgeboard or assemble gable-style trusses on the ground and lift them into position. Some lumberyards carry prefabricated trusses for several basic roof spans and pitches.

Measuring Gable Rafters

Because all common rafters in a gable roof are the same, you can mark and cut one, test the fit, and use it as a template.

Three Basic Cuts. Most common rafters get three cuts: a plumb cut at the ridge where the rafter rests against the ridgeboard, a plumb cut at the tail, which makes the shape of the bottom end, and a bird's-mouth cut where the rafter seats on the plate of the outside wall. Sometimes you need a fourth cut, a horizontal cut at the tail, which is often used with an overhang and soffit.

The simplest way to mark these cuts is to hold the lumber up to the ridgeboard, which you can temporarily install on vertical supports. Once the rafter is aligned with the top of the ridgeboard at one end and resting against the top plate at the other, you can scribe the ridge cut and the seat cut directly onto the rafter.

You can also measure these cut lines using a framing square. If you've stepped off the rafter, the first mark you make will be your plumb or ridge cut, the cut that rests against the ridgeboard.

Number of Rafters. If it's not included on your plans, you'll need to calculate the total number of rafters you'll need. For 16-inch-on-center framing, multiply the length of the building by three-quarters, and add 1 (L × 0.75 + 1 = X rafters). For 24-inch-on-center framing, multiply the building length by one-half and add 1 (L × 0.5 + 1 = Y rafters). If your plans include a gable-end overhang to match the eaves overhang, you'll need to add four pieces of lumber for the barge, or fly, rafters that extend beyond the gable-end walls.

Estimating the Size. Before you order rafter lumber, you must know what size boards to get. You can approximate the sizes using a framing square and measuring tape. To determine the exact rafter lengths, you can use any of three methods: work with rafter tables; use the Pythagorean theorem; or step off the rafters with a square.

To mark rafters, you have to find the roof slope indicated on the building plans. The rafter length will be determined by the roof slope and the building width. The rafter-length measurement will determine where you'll make the cuts on the rafters. The rafter length is the distance from the ridge to the edge of the building. Remember that the rafter size (and wood species and grade) will have to be approved by your local building department.

Subtracting the Ridgeboard Thickness. You start by calculating the length of the rafter to the center of the ridgeboard. Then you must shorten the rafter to accommodate the width of the board. Measure back from the center of the ridge line a distance of one-half the thickness of the ridgeboard. If you're using a two-by ridgeboard, the distance will be ¾ inch. Mark another plumb line at this point as the cut line.

Calculating the Overhang. The overhang (sometimes called projection) is the level distance from the edge of the building. But the actual rafter length is longer because of its slope. You can use the Pythagorean theorem to figure out the dimension you'll have to add to the rafter length for the overhang. If you want an 18-inch overhang on the same 8-in-12 roof, for example, you must envision the overhang area as a minia-

---

⌐ Rafter Cuts ────────────────

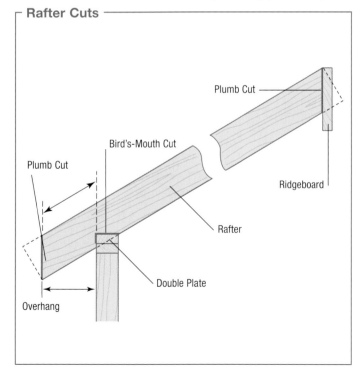

Plumb Cut

Bird's-Mouth Cut

Plumb Cut

Ridgeboard

Rafter

Double Plate

Overhang

⌐ Gable Rafter Layout ──────────

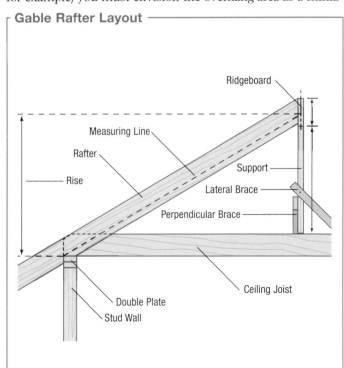

Ridgeboard

Measuring Line

Rafter

Rise

Support

Lateral Brace

Perpendicular Brace

Double Plate

Stud Wall

Ceiling Joist

ture roof. The run is 18 inches (the horizontal dimension of the overhang) and the rise is 12 inches ($8 \times 1.5 = 12$). Therefore,

$$12^2 + 18^2 = C^2$$
$$144 \text{ inches} + 324 \text{ inches} = 468 \text{ inches}$$

The square root of 468 inches is 21.63 inches, which is 1.80 feet, or 1 foot 9⅝ inches.

The gable end of a roof may also need an overhang to match the eaves overhang. You can create a slight overhang without adding extra rafters. You simply add blocking to the side wall, and add a trim board, often called a rake board. To build a deeper overhang, you can add fly rafters.

Framing a Gable Roof

After you lay out and cut the first rafter, use it as a template to lay out the second one. You can test the two rafters for fit on the ground by placing the bird's mouths over each end of a 2×4 you have cut to a length equal to the width of the building measured across the top plate. But it's best to test the rafter against the ridgeboard. If you're installing ceiling joists, nail these in place before erecting the rafters. This also stiffens the side walls against push-out as you install rafters and provides a working platform.

Cutting the Ridgeboard. Cut the ridgeboard to length, and mark the rafter positions on it and on the top plates. If the roof will overhang at the gable ends, allow for the overhang at each end when you cut the ridgeboard. In many cases, it pays to let the ridgeboard run long and trim it to exact length after the last rafters are installed and the layout is checked.

Preassembling End Rafters. On small sheds you may be able to assemble some components on the ground. For example, you might attach two end rafters to the ridgeboard, adjust the spread of the rafters, and nail a temporary cleat to hold them in position securely as you raise the assembly into place. In most cases, you need to fix the ridgeboard in its final position ahead of time and brace it very securely so that it doesn't move as you nail up rafters one at a time.

Adding the Remaining Rafters. Once the end rafters are nailed in place, you can add the remaining rafters. On most projects, you can face-nail through the ridge to set the first rafter only. You have to toenail the second rafter. Codes may require hangers.

Adding Strapping. Before you add any other framing, be sure that the

---

Marking Rafter Cuts

To mark plumb rafter cuts, such as the ridge cut and tail cut, set a framing square on the rafter with the blade and tongue measurements set at the rise and run of your roof.

Stepping Off Rafter Length

TOOLS & MATERIALS

- Framing square with stops
- Combination square
- Pencil

- Rafter (to serve as a template)

SMART TIP:

No matter how you lay out and cut rafters, always check the first one in place before using it as a template to make others.

1 Before marking a rafter, sight down its length to see which side is crowned or raised in a slight bow shape. Lay out and install all the rafters with the crowns facing up.

2 Pivot the square until the edge of the stock near you aligns with the unit rise mark on the tongue and the unit run mark on the blade. You can attach stops to capture the correct position.

3 Step along the rafter, laying out in 12-in. units of run. When the layout reaches the centerline of the ridgeboard, you need to deduct half its width from the overall rafter length.

rafter layout is correct. On all but small sheds, you should add strapping perpendicular to the rafters at midspan to keep the rafters square and prevent bowing. You can remove the strapping as you nail down roof decking.

Framing the Gable End. Now you can add studs along the gable-end walls. Each one gets two cuts to make a lap onto the rafter. The depth of the cut is equal to the thickness of the rafter so that the stud face is flush with the rafter face. The base cut in the lap has to be angled to match the angle of the rafter. At the bottom, toenail the base to the top plate of the first floor wall. At the top, nail through the rafter into the lapped portion of the stud.

Attaching Collar Ties. Some roof designs also require collar ties. These short horizontal timbers turn the inverted V-shape of raters into an A-shape. Collar ties hold opposite rafters so that they can't spread apart. To provide the extra strength where required by code, the collar ties generally should be installed in the lower one third of the rafter span.

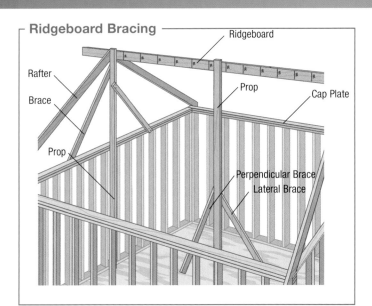

Ridgeboard Bracing

Ridgeboard
Rafter
Prop
Brace
Cap Plate
Prop
Perpendicular Brace
Lateral Brace

Installing the Ridgeboard & Rafters

TOOLS & MATERIALS

- Circular saw and handsaw
- T-bevel square and framing square
- 4-ft. level
- C-clamps and hammer
- Measuring tape, pencil, and safety goggles

- Two-by ridgeboards
- 2×4 post
- 2×4 bracing
- Common nails

1 For maximum safety, build a plumb post with a cleat extension to temporarily support the ridgeboard. Tack or clamp two braces at right angles, check the post for plumb, and nail the braces.

2 Set the ridgeboard on the brace post, leaning it temporarily on the 2×4 cleat. Then clamp it in position. A few screws will also work. Check to make sure that it is level and parallel with the building line.

3 You can use the supported and braced ridgeboard as a guide to mark the correct plumb-cut angle on your rafters. Use a sliding T-bevel to mark the rafter cut; then cut it using a circular saw.

Shed Roofs

Shed roofs are like one half of a gable roof. They are easy to design and build because they have only one shallow slope with basic rafters that notch over the low wall and the high wall in a straight run. Before cutting, be sure to sight each rafter, and make sure the crown edge is facing up.

If you're framing the building walls with 2×4s, the bird's-mouth seat cuts on the rafters should be 3½ inches wide. Using the framing square, line up the blade with the building line and move the square up or down until the 3½-inch mark on the tongue intersects the underside edge of the rafter. Draw the 3½-inch-long seat-cut line.

The bird's-mouth plumb-cut line runs from where the seat-cut line intersects the building line (inside line for the top of the rafter and outside line for the bottom of the rafter) down to the rafter edge. The depth of the bird's-mouth plumb cut should not exceed one-third the width of the rafter.

Shed Rafter Cuts

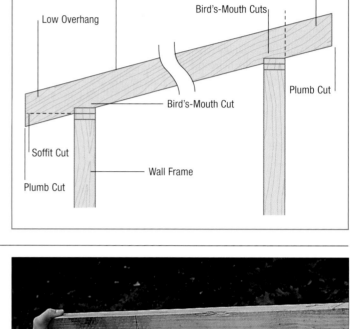

Marking & Cutting Shed Rafters

TOOLS & MATERIALS

- Framing square and measuring tape
- Circular saw
- Hammer or drill-driver with screwdriver bit

- Rafter lumber
- 12d nails or 2" galvanized deck screws

SMART TIP:

To use a fascia board the same size as your rafters, you need to make a heel cut parallel to the ground at the base of each rafter. This shortens the plumb cut at the rafter tail.

1 To mark the bird's-mouth cuts on the lower wall, have a helper hold the rafter at the roof peak. Typically, the cut will be at least 1½ in. deep. Outline the position of the cap plates with a pencil.

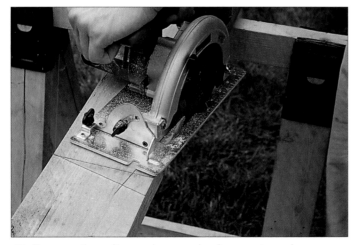

2 Remove the rafter, and use a circular saw to make a bird's-mouth cut at the marks. Don't overcut the marks, this will weaken the rafter. Instead, finish the cut with a hand-saw to make the notch area drop out.

3 Test-fit the shed rafter against the high- and low-wall top plates. If the rafter fits, use it as a template to mark and cut the rest. Then toenail the rafters at their on-center locations on the plates over the studs below.

Framing the Gable End

After you've framed the roof with common rafters, use a plumb bob (or level against a straight 2×4) to find the center of the gable-end plate under the ridgeboard. If you'll be installing a gable-end vent, measure one-half its width to each side of center and mark for the first full studs. Continue to mark along the plate at your stud spacing. Set a stud at a full stud position, plumb it, and mark where it intersects the end rafter. Set the stud at the next stud position, and mark it again. The difference in height is the common difference between studs. Cut notches 5 to 6 inches long and 1½ inches deep into the tops of several studs, matching the bottom of the notch to the rafter angle. Cut the studs to fit between the top plate and the end rafters, using the difference determined earlier, or one at a time if need be. Toenail the studs to the cap plate, and then nail through the rafters with 16d nails.

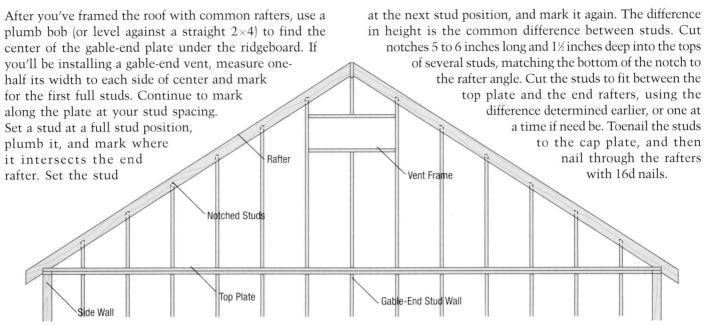

Rafter

Vent Frame

Notched Studs

Top Plate

Gable-End Stud Wall

Side Wall

Installing Gable-End Overhang Rafters

Aside from a hip roof, which allows for an overhang on all four sides, most roofs provide only two overhangs. If you want to match the eaves overhang at the gable ends, for example, you need to add a set of boards, called barge rafters or fly rafters.

There are two ways to attach them. As a general rule, for overhangs 12 inches wide or less, you can build a rake ladder made of two identical rafters attached to each other with two-by blocking. The inner side of the ladder is face-nailed to the end rafter, and the outer side is stabilized by nailing it to the extended ridgeboard. This system works best for roofs finished with relatively lightweight material, such as asphalt shingles.

The other method involves notching out the end rafter for lookouts. In some cases these boards sit on edge like rafters, but extend out past the gable-end wall at right angles to the main rafters. Another option is to recess lookouts on the flat into the end rafter and butt one end into a common rafter and the other into the barge rafter.

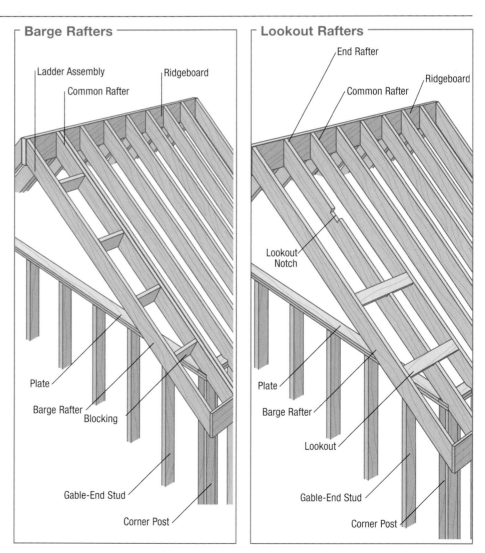

Barge Rafters

Ladder Assembly

Common Rafter

Ridgeboard

Plate

Barge Rafter

Blocking

Gable-End Stud

Corner Post

Lookout Rafters

End Rafter

Common Rafter

Ridgeboard

Lookout Notch

Plate

Barge Rafter

Lookout

Gable-End Stud

Corner Post

Finishing the Overhang

The eaves section of the roof generally is called the overhang, or cornice. There are a number of different ways to finish the area. You can take the simple approach and leave the overhang open for ventilation. The roof sheathing is left exposed between the rafter tails, and the siding stops below the rafters. You can add a fascia—a long board that covers the ends of the rafter tails. This addition is wise on any overhangs of more than a few inches because it keeps the rafter tails square, and provides a support surface for gutters, among other things.

Overhangs can also be soffited or boxed. In these types of designs, horizontal siding material or sheets of plywood (usually with some kind of ventilation added) is fastened in place between the fascia and the wall.

Installing the Fascia

Before installing a fascia, snap a chalk line across the ends of the rafter tails, and check the end of each with a framing square (for square-cut ends) or a level (for plumb-cut ends). Trim any rafter tails that are not even.

The simplest fascia is a continuous piece of two-by lumber. The fascia can be even with the top of the rafter; or be trimmed with a bevel cut along the top. This extra step creates continuous support for the roof sheathing. Some people prefer to install two-by lumber, called a subfascia, and finish its face with a one-by fascia that matches the trim on the rest of the building.

Soffited & Boxed Overhangs

A boxed cornice generally is blocked out slightly from the wall and doesn't use soffit joists. This detail is more than adequate on basic sheds where you want the look of an overhang or the chance to provide a narrow strip of ventilation.

A soffited cornice has additional framing that connects the facia to the shed wall. The framing creates a flat area, called a soffit, that generally is covered with plywood. Most soffits include vents to allow air to sweep up into the roof along the entire overhang on both sides of the building. You can use plug vents between rafters, strip-grill vents that extend along the overhang, or perforated panels instead of solid sheets of plywood.

Overhangs

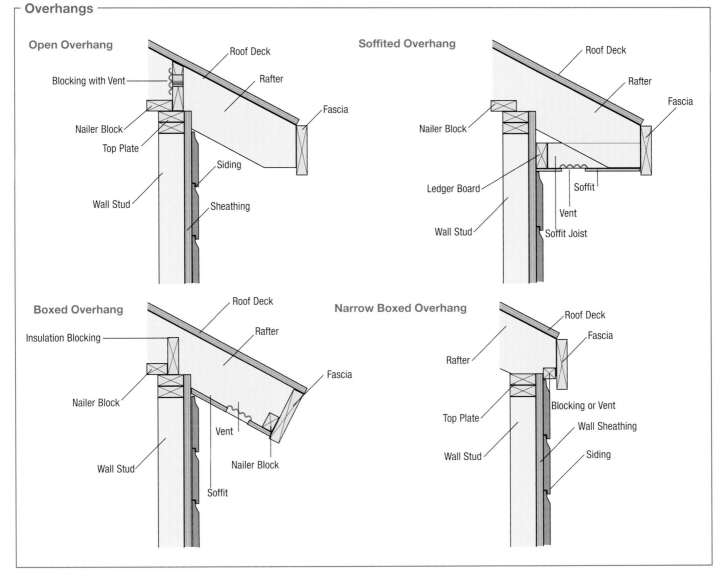

Open Overhang — Roof Deck, Rafter, Blocking with Vent, Nailer Block, Top Plate, Fascia, Siding, Wall Stud, Sheathing

Soffited Overhang — Roof Deck, Rafter, Fascia, Nailer Block, Ledger Board, Soffit, Vent, Wall Stud, Soffit Joist

Boxed Overhang — Roof Deck, Rafter, Insulation Blocking, Nailer Block, Fascia, Vent, Nailer Block, Wall Stud, Soffit

Narrow Boxed Overhang — Roof Deck, Fascia, Rafter, Blocking or Vent, Top Plate, Wall Sheathing, Wall Stud, Siding

Trusses

If you're nervous about cutting rafters from scratch and you don't mind losing the open attic space, roof trusses are a good option. On small sheds, trusses are usually 2×4s held together by gussets, which are flat metal or plywood plates that cover and reinforce the joints. The two top chords and one long bottom chord form the shape of a gable roof. Internal framing members called webs tie the chords together. Cutting any one of the members compromises the structural integrity of the entire truss, which means you can't chop out webs here and there to make storage space.

Roof trusses commonly come in two forms, the Fink and Howe truss. But there are many different configurations and sizes. End trusses often don't have the same webs as the trusses for the interior of the roof. Instead, the webs are vertical two-by studs installed at 16 or 24 inches on center.

Order trusses from a truss manufacturer by specifying the length of the bottom chord, which should include the span, wall thicknesses, and soffits. You may not have much control over ridge height, as trusses tend to come in low-angle pitches. In areas of the country where you need a steeper pitch, you may need to order custom trusses.

Setting Trusses

Lightweight 2×4 trusses for a small shed are easy to set up. The key is to add braces and strapping to trusses as you set them in position. But the only way to erect large trusses is with a crane, which is an expensive and potentially hazardous proposition best left to a professional.

The First Truss. Before lifting up the first truss, nail short two-by boards on the gable ends of the structure to act as stops so that the truss doesn't slip off the end of the plate. These can be removed when the sheathing is in place.

The best approach is to set the truss upside down, hanging from the wall plates peak down. Then walk it into place and

---

Erecting Trusses

TOOLS & MATERIALS

- Hammer
- Stepladders or scaffolding
- 4' spirit level
- Measuring tape

- Trusses
- 16d nails
- 2x4s for braces, blocking & strapping

SMART TIP:

Trusses make roof framing easy, but don't try to install trusses that are too large. Have a professional install larger trusses.

1 Place the first truss on one end of the building and its ends on the cap plate with the top pointing downward. Two or more people will be needed to raise it upright depending on its size.

2 Fasten the truss to the cap plate using 16d nails or metal anchor brackets. Plumb the truss with a level, and nail it off to 2x4s that brace it securely to stakes in the ground.

3 Mark the positions of all the trusses on the cap plates. Nailing 2x4 spacer blocks between the truss locations will make it easier to hold a truss straight while it is toenailed into place.

4 Set the second truss in place against its spacer, and toenail it to the cap plate with four 16d nails or fasteners specified by the truss manufacturer. Brace each truss in position.

5 With three trusses installed, tack strapping across the top on each side. Nail strapping on additional trusses as you set them in position to tie the trusses together.

turn it upright after calculating where the bottom chord will land on the plate. You need to work carefully.

Bracing the First Truss. Positioning the first truss is relatively easy on a small shed. It's more time consuming to brace it securely. You'll need several long 2×4s that reach down to the ground and lateral braces that pin the truss in place on the gable-end wall. Because the rest of the trusses will depend on the stability of this first truss, you should include at least two braces running from the truss down to cleats on the floor of the building.

Adding Strapping. With strapping passed up from below, tie trusses together with at least one line of strapping on each side of the ridge. Use a strong material, such as 2×4 boards or 5/4 furring. You can stagger the strapping temporarily and use short boards in a pinch to secure the next truss in line. Another option is to leave some strapping extended into the next bay before you tip up the truss. But after several trusses are installed you should go back to the end wall, double check for plumb, and install a continuous strip of strapping on each side of the ridge.

The Last Truss. Setting the last few trusses in place can be difficult if you do not have a crane because there isn't much room to maneuver them. You often have to raise them peak up. Set the last truss against two-by stops on the gable-end plate to keep it from slipping off during positioning. For safety, you need to have braces at the ready to lock the last truss securely in place.

Final Checking and Fastening. Go back and check for plumb on the trusses, and adjust them accordingly. It's wise to tack strapping so that you can easily pull the nails to make small adjustments. Then follow with nails into the plates, and add sheathing with staggered joints to cover the roof. If possible, sheath the trusses the same day you erect them.

Trusses for small buildings, such as this 12-ft. truss for a 4-in-12 gable-roofed barn, can easily be carried and raised into position by two strong people. Larger trusses will need special equipment.

Basic Truss Types

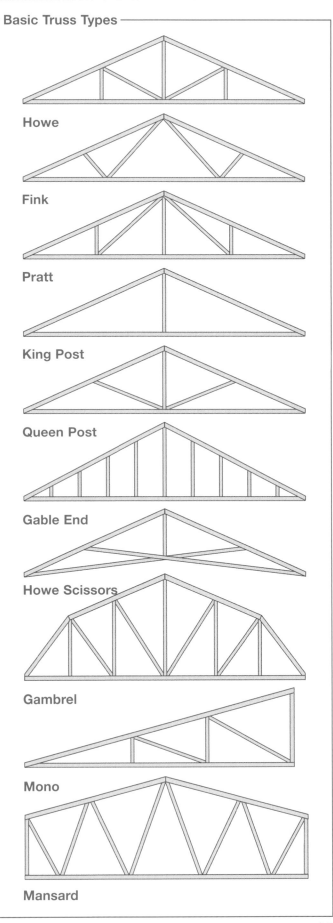

Howe

Fink

Pratt

King Post

Queen Post

Gable End

Howe Scissors

Gambrel

Mono

Mansard

Gambrel Roofs

Gambrel roofs are often found on barns and utility buildings because the design allows for more usable room on the topmost floor. Remember that you need to take this area into account when you plan the building. Adding second-floor joists suitable for heavy-duty storage can increase the load on exterior walls and foundations.

Basic Gambrel Design. A gambrel roof is really a combination of two gable roofs with varying slopes. The part of the gambrel roof that rises directly off the top plates—the first gable—tends to have a severe slope, such as 16 in 12, which is a $\frac{2}{3}$ pitch. The part of the gambrel roof that rises to the ridge—the second gable roof—has a less severe slope—often something like 8 in 12, which is a $\frac{1}{3}$ pitch.

With stick framing, you need a support such as a wall or a horizontal beam, possibly with posts, wherever the rafters on one slope meet the rafters on another. These cuts and joints can be tricky. In a true gambrel roof, the two parts of each side of the roof have rafters of the same length, and all four rafters describe chords of a semicircle. (See this type on the far right at the top of the next page.) Not all gambrel-style designs fit this pattern, however. A common layout—easier to calculate and measure—has the upper and lower roof angles at 30 and 60 degrees respectively. (See this type on the left at the top of the next page.)

Measuring for a Gambrel Roof

For measuring purposes, a gambrel roof is divided into two different roofs with two different rises and runs. The total run for the lower part of the gambrel roof is found by measuring the distance from the cap plate of the building wall to the center of the cap plate of a mid-pitch supporting wall. The total rise is the distance the roof section rises from the floor to the top of the wall. The total run for the top part of the gambrel roof is found by measuring from the cap plate of the mid-span supporting wall to the center of the ridge-board. The total upper-portion rise is the vertical distance from the support wall's cap plate to the center of the ridge.

It's important to plan for the wall or other support system where the two slopes meet, unless you use a code-approved truss design (generally only on small spans) that does not require additional support.

You can build standard gambrel rafters that join over the double plate of a support wall, buy gambrel roof trusses, or, for a small-scale project, build your own trusses on-site.

Making Gambrel Trusses

The easiest approach is to build trusses on the deck or slab before framing the walls. You need a flat surface to make an accurate assembly.

One option is to make what amounts to a full-scale drawing of the truss on the slab using a chalk-line box. Start by snapping a baseline across the short dimension of the floor so that you won't run into the anchor bolts that are sticking out of the concrete. Find the center of your baseline, and snap a perpendicular line. Measure and mark a point above the baseline to define the peak. Then snap diagonals running from the peak to each end of the baseline as if you were defining the bottom edge of two gable rafters.

Next, snap a mid-line that runs above and parallel with the baseline, and two lines running from the midpoint of the baseline through the intersections with the diagonals. There are no hard rules governing the offset of the two gambrel roof planes. Once the offset points are established, snap the bottom edges of the gambrel lines, running the chalk line from the peak to the offset point and from the offset point to the end of the baseline on both sides.

┌ Prefabricated Gambrel Truss ─────────────

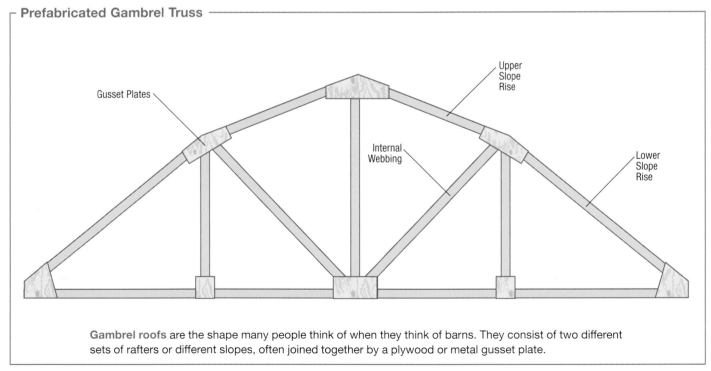

Gusset Plates

Upper Slope Rise

Internal Webbing

Lower Slope Rise

Gambrel roofs are the shape many people think of when they think of barns. They consist of two different sets of rafters or different slopes, often joined together by a plywood or metal gusset plate.

Laying Out a Gambrel Roof

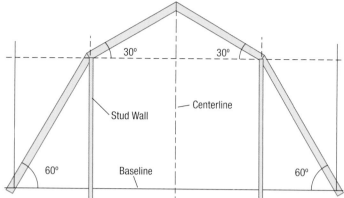

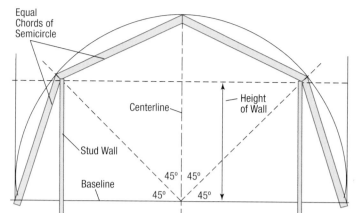

A simple layout for a gambrel roof has the first set of rafters at a 60° angle to the baseline and the second set of rafters at a 30° angle. In gambrel designs you need to support the joint at rafter segments with a beam (like a low-set ridgeboard) or a bearing wall.

A true gambrel roof—one that will give you more space in the second story—has rafters of equal lengths that describe chords of an imaginary semicircle. The intersections of the rafters and the peak of the roof will be the same distance from a central point.

Marking & Cutting Gambrel Trusses

TOOLS & MATERIALS

- Chalk-line box
- Pencil
- Sliding T-bevel
- Circular saw
- Power drill with screwdriver bit

- Two-by lumber for rafters and chord
- 1½" screws
- Plywood for gussets

SMART TIP:

Check gambrel truss plans with your local inspector. Very small spans may be allowable with gusset plates only. Due to the weak link at each two-part rafter, you may need internal webs.

1 Obtain the roof slope and run from the plans, and then determine the rise. Snap chalk lines on a concrete slab (or driveway) marking the roof outline, including an overhang at the eaves.

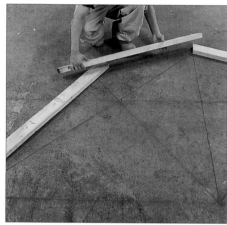

2 Estimate the length you will need for each of the four rafters in the truss, leaving a few inches extra. Lay them down with the horizontal bottom chord over your chalk lines.

3 Mark the cut lines onto the rafters with a sliding T-bevel. The two cuts should align with the radius line that intersects with the center of the layout. Cut the marks with a circular saw.

4 Lay the rafters back on the chalk-line layout to make sure they fit. If they do, trace a plywood gusset to fasten them together. The gusset needs to be cut flush with the tops of the rafters.

5 Before you attach the gussets, trace both gussets and all four rafters to assemble the next truss. Then fasten the gussets together with construction adhesive and 1½-in. screws.

CHAPTER 6

Closing In

Once the basic framing is finished, you will need to close in the barn or shed with roofing and siding as well as doors and windows. The roofing and siding not only determine the finished appearance of your structure, they also protect it and everything inside it from the elements. This chapter covers the most common types of siding and roofing used on outbuildings and explains how to install them. It also details different options for doors and windows. It will cover Z-braced barn doors you can build yourself, attach hinges to, and hang in rough openings or in homemade jambs, and how to install windows and doors purchased preassembled with jambs and hinges attached.

Sheathing Walls

With the exterior walls plumb, square, and braced, it's time to add sheathing. You can apply sheathing vertically or horizontally. Horizontal sheathing is generally a better choice, although some building codes require that you put 2×4 blocking behind the horizontal seams.

Vertical sheathing is a good choice on 8-foot-high walls where you have a nailing surface along all four edges of the plywood. But on walls where the inside height is 8 feet, the outside wall may be higher, and you will need to extend sheathing over ceiling joists (if there are any).

If you sheathed these walls vertically, you would need to fill in strips at the top. That could compromise the superb racking resistance of plywood or oriented-strand board. Installing fill strips between full horizontal sheathing panels in the middle of the wall is a better approach and maintains better racking resistance.

Also, most wall designs call for the bottom edge of sheathing to overlap the sill plate and cover some of the foundation or slab. This overlap provides the wall with shear resistance and helps to seal out drafts and insects.

When sheathing walls, it's often easiest to sheath right over the rough openings that you created within your stud framing. When you're finished sheathing, you can mark the openings from the inside and cut them out from the outside with a reciprocating saw or a circular saw.

Material Choices

Many types of sheathing materials are available—from gypsum and fiberboard nonstructural sheathing to oriented-strand board and conventional plywood— all in a variety of thicknesses. Your plans will probably specify the kind of sheathing to use. One-half-inch CDX plywood rated for use on exterior walls is the most common type of material for outbuildings that are sheathed.

Installing Sheathing

TOOLS & MATERIALS

- Measuring tape
- Hammer or drill-driver
- Screwdriver bit
- Chalk-line box
- Circular saw
- Handsaw or reciprocating saw

- Sheathing material (plywood or OSB)
- 6d or 8d common nails or 1½" screws
- 2x4s for blocking (if required by code)

SMART TIP:

To cut sheathing, set the depth of cut on a circular saw to just over the thickness of the material.

1 Vertical sheathing should be installed with its edges exactly at the studs' centers. It may be helpful for nailing to snap chalk lines that will line up with the studs every 16 or 24 in.

2 Screw or nail the sheathing panels into the studs, spacing the fasteners every 6 in. along the edge and every 12 in. in the interior. Leave a ⅟₁₆-in. gap between the panels for expansion.

3 In horizontal applications, if two sheathing panels don't reach the top of the wall, you'll need a filler strip of plywood. It's best to install this strip in the middle of the wall.

4 For each rough opening, drive a nail or drill small holes from inside through the sheathing at the four corners. Use these to snap chalk lines on the outside of the sheathing.

5 Cut the rough openings using a circular saw. Plunge-cut into the sheathing, and continue cutting to the corners of the box. Finish the cuts with a handsaw or reciprocating saw.

Vertical Siding

Several types of siding can be installed vertically, including board-and-batten siding and variations such as batten-and-board. Panel siding includes sheets of steel, fiberglass, and wood, including a popular variety called Texture 1-11, or T1-11, plywood, which is an exterior-rated plywood manufactured with grooves to simulate vertical siding joints.

Install most wood sheet panel siding just as you would plywood sheathing, with nails every 6 inches around the perimeter and every 12 inches in the interior of the panel. Metal or fiberglass panels typically have proprietary fasteners, such as nails or screws with gaskets. Check with the manufacturer for installation recommendations.

Vertical siding is ideal for barns—particularly pole barns and timber-framed barns that aren't sheathed with plywood but stand simply as framed walls. These are usually unheated, uninsulated structures. Vertical siding is typically installed on 1×3 or larger strapping set 24 inches on center or flush against the frame, nailed to the studs and to blocking installed between studs, 24 inches on center. The siding will stand out a bit from the frame. In the case of pole buildings, board siding can be installed on 2×4 girts and skirt boards spaced 24 inches apart.

Board-and-Batten Siding

Board-and-batten siding is the most popular vertical siding because it is economical and can be installed properly with basic skills and tools. Board widths come 1×6, 1×8, 1×10, and 1×12. Each board width gives a different look to the barn, so choose carefully. Most builders use the same width boards for the entire barn. Random widths generally look sloppy in board-and-batten siding, although you may have success with a repeating pattern of different sizes.

For the board stock, low-cost, rough-milled boards cut from spruce, pine, or fir are widely available, and they need not be kiln-dried before installation. In fact, board-and-batten siding, in theory at least, can be put up the same hour it is milled. The reason: the battens overlap the boards by ½ inch or more, so even severe shrinkage will not expose gaps.

Board Siding Types

Board on Board

Board and Batten

Batten and Board

Installing Board & Batten Siding

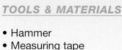

TOOLS & MATERIALS

- Hammer
- Measuring tape
- 4' spirit level
- Circular saw or power miter saw

- One-by boards (optimally the full height of the wall)
- 1×2 battens (optimally the full height of the wall)
- Two-by blocking (same dimension as stud lumber)
- 10d galvanized nails
- A ½ " wide board to use as a spacer

1 Install nailers across studs or horizontal blocking between studs to provide a nailing surface for the boards and battens. Be sure nailers are level as you fasten them in place.

2 Start at one end of the frame, and nail a board onto the face of the corner studs. Leave about ½ in. between boards. (Use a full-board spacer to maintain this margin.)

3 Cover the gaps between the wide boards with 1½-in. wide battens the same length as the boards beneath. Drive nails through each batten to penetrate into the blocking or strapping.

But the shrinkage could pull nails and cause other problems. Although board siding is usually installed with thinner 1×2s nailed on top of the seams between wider boards, other variations include those shown in the illustration opposite left, "Board Siding Types."

Metal Siding

Although not as common as the metal roofing panels often used on barns, metal siding is becoming a popular covering for utility buildings. Steel panels are generally available in widths from 24 to 36 inches. They come in a variety of baked-enamel finishes, including barn red, of course. Most siding panels are galvanized, or covered with a coating of zinc to prevent them from rusting.

Metal siding needs to be ordered directly from the manufacturer. Most manufacturers will deliver panels cut to a specific length to minimize the amount of cutting you will have to do. The manufacturer will also provide you with their minimum requirements for support. Keep in mind that barn animals can and will dent metal siding, as will normal activity around the barn. Dented metal panels are unsightly and difficult to replace, especially if they were custom sized.

Board siding—such as the weathered tongue-and-groove boards pictured here—are charactertistic of old farm buildings. Recycled siding similar to this may be available from some suppliers.

Metal Siding Types

Many metal siding panels come 38 inches wide. After lapping at least one rib or corrugation, this yields 36 inches of coverage. Panels are usually ribbed along the face to add strength.

A high-quality metal siding will have ribs every 9 inches or so, and they will be ¾ inch high. (Metal siding panels are designed to interlock.) The ribs act as a stiffener, which adds durability, but they also keep the siding from crumpling during transportation and installation. The ideal thickness range is 24 to 26 gauge in galvanized steel.

There is a wide range of accessories you can buy with metal siding. It may be best if you choose a single metal siding manufacturer because they have attachments, caps, corners, and other fittings that are designed for use with their particular siding. Using compatible parts makes trimming out windows and doors much easier.

Metal buildings don't need to look like commercial storage facilities. Until you see the siding close up, you may not realize that the barn is sided in enamel-coated steel instead of wood.

Box Rib

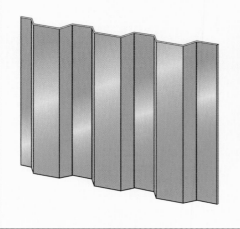

Corrugated

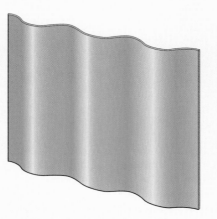

Bold Rib

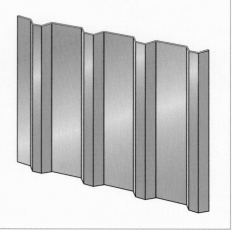

Wood Panel Siding

Many lumberyards carry Texture 1-11 panels. These 4×8-foot sheets have grooves cut into their face 4, 8, or 12 inches apart to simulate the look of separate planks. But many other styles and surface treatments of wood panel siding are available. Not all plywood can be used for siding—only sheets rated for exterior use, which are assembled with special glue that can withstand the exposure.

Panel siding can be particularly economical because it sometimes can serve as wall sheathing and siding (check local codes), and be attached directly to the studs. In those cases it's wise to add diagonal let-in bracing for extra support.

Panels are usually installed vertically and stacked as needed to cover high walls. If you install them horizontally, blocking between the studs may be required by local codes where the panel edges meet. This blocking provides a continuous nailing surface along the edges, which is important for siding that doubles as sheathing.

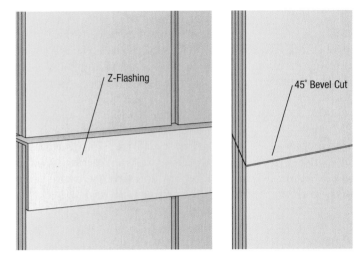

The joints between stacked wood siding panels can be protected from water with a piece of Z-flashing, left. If you don't want to see a metal strip, join panels with a 45-deg. cut.

Installing Panel Siding

TOOLS & MATERIALS

- Circular saw or saber saw
- Chalk-line box
- Sawhorses and ladders
- Drill-driver
- Combination square
- 4' level and plumb bob
- Hammer and C-clamps
- Work gloves and eye protection

- Plywood siding panels
- 2×4 ledger boards and corner boards
- Z-flashing
- Galvanized nails or screws

1 Establish a level line on the foundation, and snap a chalk line to mark it. Then nail a 2×4 ledger in place to support heavy siding panels as you plumb them and nail them.

2 Start at an inside or outside corner, and hold the sheet up to the framing, making sure the sheet is plumb. Nail it into the studs using fasteners specified by the manufacturer.

3 On panels with shiplap edges, tack the edge of the last panel; then install the next sheet, aligning it so that the groove has the same width as the others. Nail through the lapped section.

4 To install corner boards over siding panels, mount the first board flush and the second board lapping the first to cover its edge. If you prefer, you can also miter corner boards.

5 To accommodate protrusions, such as hose bibcocks, measure out from the corner and up from the level baseline to mark your cutout. Then carefully cut the siding using a saber saw.

Protecting the Joints. While the wood-panel surface will be coated with stain or paint for appearance and protection against the weather, panel edges often are not coated. They are the weak links because layers of thin plywood laminations are exposed along the edges. If the layers soak up water, the panel is likely to delaminate, which can pop nails and create an array of repair problems.

You can protect against this deterioration by brushing a primer coat on the edges prior to installation or by concealing the edges with trim, such as vertical corner boards. It's also important to caulk or flash seams around windows and doors and on two-story projects where one sheet rests on top of another.

On horizontal joints between sheets of siding on high-wall or two-story jobs, there are two good ways to protect the seams from the weather. (See the illustration opposite right.) One method is to cut 45-degree angles along the mating edges and apply a bead of caulk to the seam. Water would have to run uphill to get behind the siding. But this kind of joint is difficult to make on panel siding without the use of a table saw.

The other method calls for a piece of Z-flashing tucked up behind the top panel and extended onto the face of the bottom panel. No 45-degree cuts are needed, but you will see the flashing. Do not be tempted to simply caulk a butt seam on vertically stacked panels.

Siding Supports

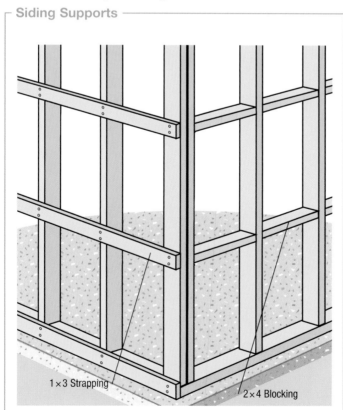

1×3 Strapping

2×4 Blocking

Vertical siding always needs strapping or blocking for support between studs. Strapping consists of furring strips (such as 1×3s and sometimes 2x4s, depending on the span between studs) nailed across the studs every 24 in. Blocking consists of 2×4s cut to fit between the studs every 24 in. and toenailed.

Wood Panel Types

Surfaced panels come in a variety of styles. The final appearance is mainly a product of the wood species, of course, but also depends on how the wood is sawed. The surface texture can be smooth, rough-sawn, striated, or brushed. These panels are often stained or covered with clear sealer for a rustic look, and their mating edges are covered with trim.

Composite panels are engineered for extra strength by combining and gluing together sawdust, wood chips, and other waste materials. Without a natural grain to twist one way or another, the panels are very stable. Many manufacturers sell either solid-wood or engineered trim pieces matched to the panels to finish off the job.

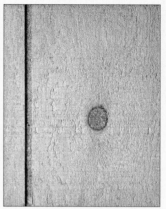

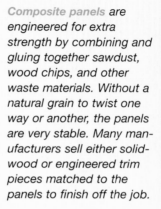

Grooved panels offer a variety of looks, depending on the groove profile. A wide spacing between grooves generally looks best on a big wall, while narrower spacing fits the scale on smaller buildings. These panels are built to join at a lap at the last groove so that seams between the panels aren't noticeable.

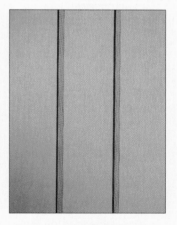

Board-and-batten panels have a wide, flat groove cut at regular intervals along the panel length. This configuration is designed to resemble a somewhat unusual twist on the typical board-and-batten design, called a reverse batten or batten-and-board, where a narrow board is set behind the simulated planks.

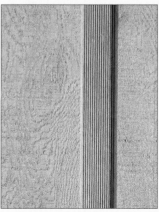

Horizontal Siding

Horizontal siding—the broadest category of all siding—includes clapboards, tongue-and-groove, log cabin, shiplap, and channel rustic boards, among other types.

Clapboard Siding

If you install clapboards instead of panels, you take a step up in material price, workload, skill level, and sheathing requirements. Clapboards are installed over sheathing because they generally cannot span studs and blocking as board-and-batten siding can. House wrap, felt paper, or some other protective backing is used underneath.

Choices vary widely among grades of siding, from premium products like clear vertical-grain all-heart cedar to spruce. You get what you pay for, though spruce, with proper caulking and careful attention to painting, can last a long time.

Clapboards typically range from 4 to 10 inches, generally with 1 inch covered by the course above. Most clapboards are around ½ inch thick at the bottom. Some types also take two nails per course, so be sure to check nailing specs with the manufacturer and local building inspector.

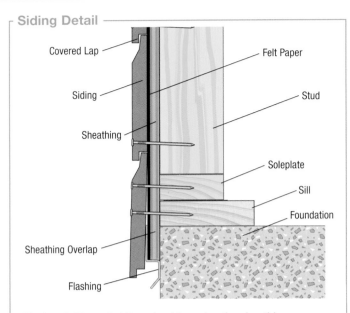

Siding Detail

Covered Lap · Siding · Sheathing · Sheathing Overlap · Flashing · Felt Paper · Stud · Soleplate · Sill · Foundation

Horizontal board siding should overlap the sheathing. Flashing will further protect the sheathing and framing from moisture and insects. You may also need a termite shield.

Horizontal Siding Styles

Rabbeted-edge siding has a lap between each board, dictated by the way the edge is milled. Fasten it with 8d nails.

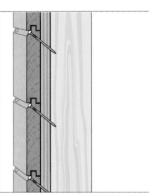

Tongue-and-groove siding should be set with the tongues firmly in the grooves. It also can be set vertically. Use 8d nails.

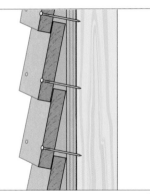

Board-on-board siding needs to be lapped so that the top board covers about 1 in. of the bottom board. Use 10d nails.

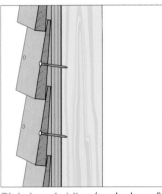

Plain bevel siding (or clapboard) has a wedge shaped profile that dictates a 1-in.-minimum lap. Use 6d nails to attach it.

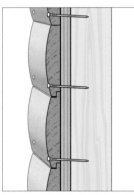

Log-cabin–style siding looks similar to the exterior of a log home. It usually has no revealed lap. Attach it with 10d nails.

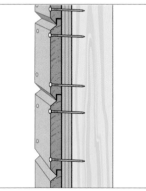

Shiplap siding has a reveal dictated by the profile, though extra space may be left. Use 8d nails to fasten it.

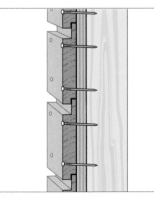

Channel rustic siding usually has a ½-in. lap. Fasten the siding with 8d nails. It may also be hung vertically.

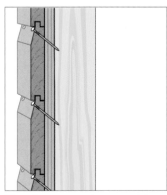

Drop tongue-and-groove (also called novelty siding) is available with cupped, beveled, or beaded upper edges. Use 8d nails.

Corner Options

Corner boards protect leak-prone siding joints at the corners of a building. Mitered joints look neat and elegant but aren't as durable as other options, and the technique requires laborious hand-fitting. Butted outside corner boards are easier to install. You nail them in place and simply cut the siding to butt against them. On outside corners you must account for the thickness of the adjoining boards, which means that one will be narrower. At inside corners one square board will do.

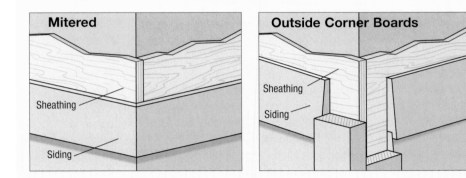

Mitered

Sheathing

Siding

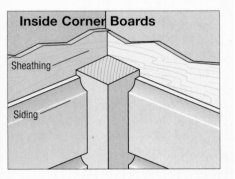

Outside Corner Boards

Sheathing

Siding

Inside Corner Boards

Sheathing

Siding

Installing Clapboards

TOOLS & MATERIALS

- Circular saw
- Drill-driver
- Spacing jig
- Ladder
- 4' level
- Hammer
- Measuring tape

- Clapboards
- House wrap
- Corner boards
- 6d nails

1 Install prefinished inside and outside corner boards to provide square edges against which the siding can butt. Using lumber that has been primed will save you time finishing later on.

2 Snap a level line for the base course, and nail a starter strip along the bottom edge of the sheathing. This will give the bottom of the first row of siding the proper pitch.

3 Overlap the starter strip with the first board, and drive nails high enough to be covered by the next course. Be careful not to split the thin top edge of the clapboard when you nail.

4 Stagger joints between siding lengths at every course. Place joints at random intervals spaced a minimum of 16 in. apart. This will prevent water from seeping into the joints.

5 Cut around any obstructions as you come to them. Always overlap boards and fittings so that any rainwater will run off of the siding. Caulk around vents and electrical boxes.

Metal Roofing

Metal standing-seam roofs look good, and are often guaranteed for 30 years or more. But they are expensive and generally installed by pros using special tools required to bend adjoining seams. Creating watertight valleys in these roofs can be difficult. But some modern systems simply snap together, are held to the roof with clips, and are easy to install for savvy do-it-yourselfers.

Agricultural-panel roofs, commonly called ag-panel, also can be installed by someone with average building skills. Ag-panels have ribs pressed into the panels to give them strength. Most ag-panels are galvanized steel, and they can easily last 15 years or more, though in wet climates or on low-sloped roofs where snow can build up, rust can form in as little as five years. They are an excellent low-cost roofing choice for most barns.

Ag-panels come in various lengths, typically from 8 to 16 feet in 2-foot increments, and are between 32 and 38 inches wide. Be sure to buy the required nails or screws (and sealing washers) at the same time. Attributes to look for in quality ag-panel roofing panel include the following.

- 26-gauge thickness.
- Factory-applied enamel coating. When choosing color, note that you will get the largest lateral thermal movement with darker colored roofs, which absorb the most solar heat.
- Flexible washers. These keep the fastener holes sealed. Because metal panels expand and contract with heat and cold, fasteners can shift and admit water.
- Watertight fittings. Practical designs accommodate watertight ridge caps, drip flashing, closure strips at the eaves, and sometimes a sealant or tape that seals the ag-panel overlaps along their lengths. These features will give you a watertight roof as opposed to a water-shedding roof, although that is not always needed in a barn.

Installation Techniques

Ag-panel roofs are installed over purlins, typically 2×4s, that run on edge across the rafters, normally every 2 feet on center. (See page 108.) The first row of purlins should be at the outermost eaves end of the rafters. Purlins can overhang the gable ends if you want the roof to overhang the walls.

Because ag-panels overlap, figure that the net coverage of your ag-panel will be between 30 and 36 inches. Multiply the net width of the ag-panel coverage in feet by the length of the rafter bay in feet, and then count the rafter bays. For instance, if your ag-panel's net coverage is 36 inches and your rafters are 12 feet long, each rafter bay will require 36 square feet of ag-panel. Of course, remember to order for both sides of the roof.

Metal Roofing Types

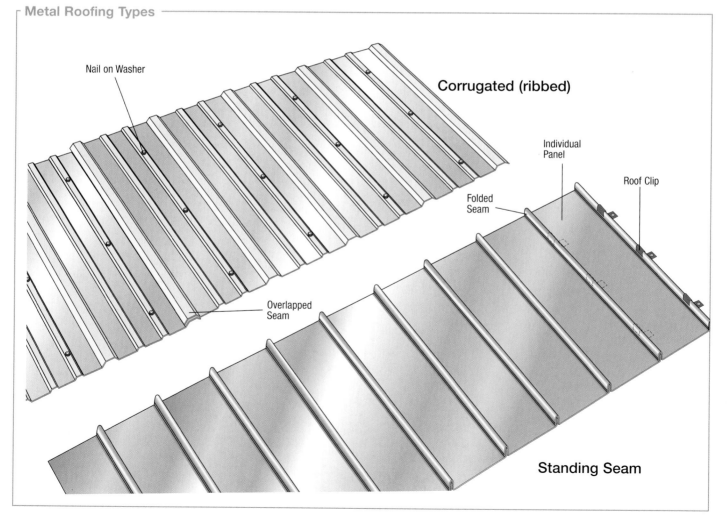

Nail on Washer

Corrugated (ribbed)

Individual Panel

Roof Clip

Folded Seam

Overlapped Seam

Standing Seam

Typical Components of Metal Roofing & Siding

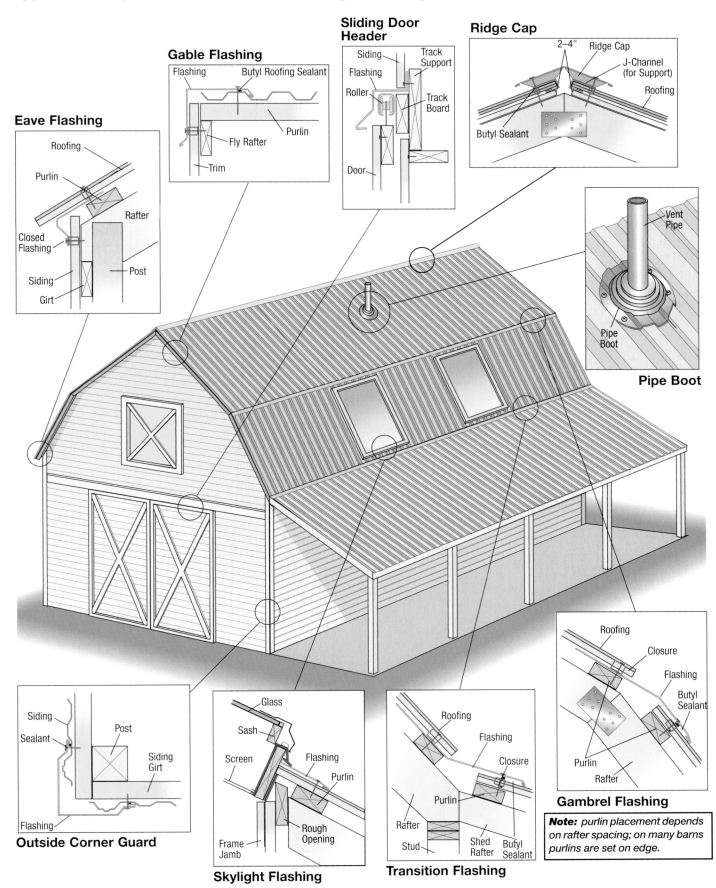

Gable Flashing

Flashing Butyl Roofing Sealant

Fly Rafter

Purlin

Trim

Sliding Door Header

Siding

Flashing

Roller

Track Support

Track Board

Door

Ridge Cap

2–4" Ridge Cap

J-Channel (for Support)

Roofing

Butyl Sealant

Eave Flashing

Roofing

Purlin

Rafter

Closed Flashing

Siding

Post

Girt

Pipe Boot

Vent Pipe

Pipe Boot

Outside Corner Guard

Siding

Sealant

Post

Siding Girt

Flashing

Skylight Flashing

Glass

Sash

Screen

Flashing

Purlin

Frame Jamb

Rough Opening

Transition Flashing

Roofing

Flashing

Closure

Purlin

Rafter

Stud

Shed Rafter

Butyl Sealant

Gambrel Flashing

Roofing

Closure

Flashing

Butyl Sealant

Purlin

Rafter

Note: *purlin placement depends on rafter spacing; on many barns purlins are set on edge.*

Plastic Roofing Panels

Corrugated panels made of plastic or fiberglass can provide a watertight yet translucent covering for part of the roof. If you're installing a corrugated metal roof, you can add a few panels between the metal ones to admit light into your barn. Panels are typically sold along with manufacturer-specific nails, filler strips, and caulk. The filler strips fit the contours of the panel and are installed along the eaves. The nails are compatible with metal panels (aluminum or steel). Use panels that interlock with the solid metal panel. To prevent leaks at the nailholes, every nail is set with a rubberized washer. The trick is to set nails just firmly enough to seat the washer without deforming it and causing a leak. At least one curve of the corrugation along the edge of a panel is covered by the next panel in line to prevent leaks at the seams.

Panel Roofing

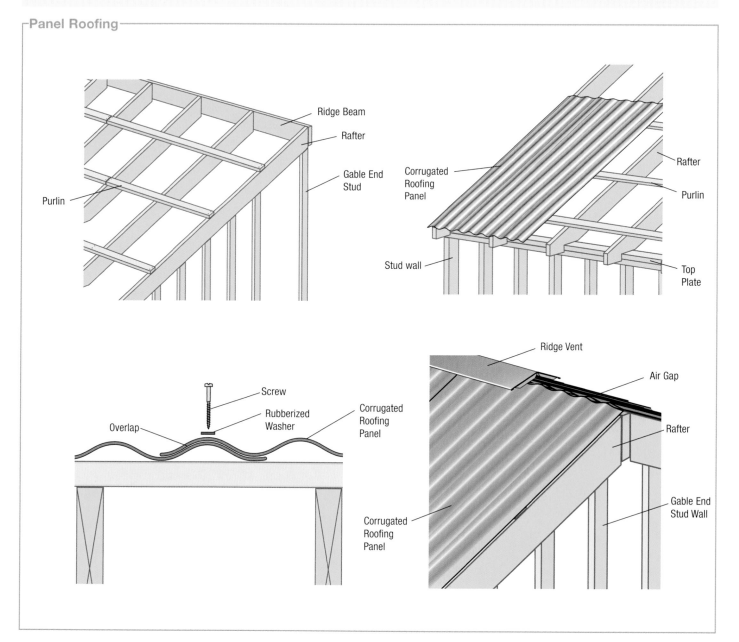

Roof Sheathing

If you don't install a metal roof attached to purlins, you need to install plywood decking. The sheets stabilize the rafters and provide a nailing surface for shingles or other roofing. Most areas require ½-inch-thick plywood rated for exterior use, although some codes allow less-expensive materials such as oriented-strand board (OSB).

When you install sheathing over rafters, stagger the end joints so that the seams don't line up. If you start with a full 4×8 sheet along the eaves, use a half sheet to start the next course. Prolonged exposure to the weather can damage the framing, so waterproof the roof sheathing as soon as possible.

Plan any panel cutting so that you can use the cutoff portions on the opposite side. You can start at the eaves with a full 4-foot-wide panel, provided you don't end up at the top having to use a strip less than 16 inches wide. A narrow strip may be too weak to support a person or provide a solid backing for the roofing. Trim the panels of the first row as needed to adjust the width of the last row. Also plan to stagger panels in succeeding rows so that the ends fall on different framing members.

In general, roof slope dictates the method of felt paper installation. In temperate climates, apply one layer of 15-pound felt on roofs having a 4-in-12 or greater slope. Lap the felt at least 2 inches horizontally and 6 inches vertically to shed water. Overlap the ridge by at least 6 inches. On roofs having less than a 4-in-12 slope, start with a 19-inch-wide sheet along the eaves. Lay a 36-inch-wide sheet over that, and then lap each subsequent sheet 19 inches horizontally and at least 12 inches vertically. Double coverage offers extra protection on any installation.

Use caution working on the roof at all times. Remember, the greater the roof slope, the more hazardous the job. On steep roofs, nail down 2×4 cleats for footing support as you work up the roof and always use appropriate safety gear.

Sheathing the Roof

TOOLS & MATERIALS

- Hammer
- Measuring tape
- Circular saw
- Chalk-line box
- Sawhorses

- Plywood sheathing
- 8d nails or power stapler
- Panel clips (for 24-inch-on-center framing)
- Drip edge
- 15-pound asphalt-impregnated roofing felt
- ⅞" roofing nails

1 To allow for a fascia to be nailed across the rafter tails, the bottommost course of roof sheathing should be installed so that its top edge does not protrude past the rafter's tail cut.

2 Begin installation at a bottom corner, placing the long side perpendicular to the rafters, with the end joint over the center of a rafter. Use 8d nails every 6 in. along the edges and 12 in. in the field.

3 To support the panel seams where they fall between rafters, use plywood panel clips in the center of the joint. Insert one end onto an installed sheet, and slide the next sheet onto the support.

4 Start the second course with a half (4 x 4-ft.) panel so that the seams will not fall in the same places. Stagger the panel ends on several different rafters as you work up the roof.

5 Mark the plywood at the eaves and ridge, and snap a chalk line to help guide nailing into the centers of the rafters. If you miss a rafter, pull the nail so that it won't work up into the singles.

Flashing

To keep the roof watertight you need to install flashing at many seams. Place it around vent pipes, chimneys and skylights, in open-style valleys that connect two sections of roof, where the roof meets a side of the building, and on the ends of eaves and rakes.

Flashing can be made from galvanized sheet steel, aluminum, copper, or flexible plastic in some cases. Generally you need to use nails made of the same material as the flashing. Copper nails may be hard to find, but you should use them if you are going to be installing copper flashing. Other metals may cause chemical reactions which might undermine the strength of the copper and eventually cause leaks.

In some cases you can cut and bend flashing yourself. Step flashing, for example, is simply a small sheet of aluminum bent in half. But for most applications you can use preformed flashing, sometimes with a complex series of bends, to fit the particular installation.

Drip Edge

Drip edge covers the ends of eaves and rakes, which often need to be protected by more than just the overhang of the roofing material. Install preformed drip flashing along the eaves of the

Types of Flashing

Nail drip edge along the rakes and eaves before installing your first course of shingles.

Vents are best sealed with formed flashing. A rubber vent collar seals the pipe.

Step flashing is short angled pieces of flashing that seal between shingles and walls.

Counterflashing is sealed into mortar to cover the top edge of standard flashing below.

roof before you place the underlayment (generally felt paper) and along rakes on each side after the underlayment is down.

Cut the corners carefully with metal-cutting shears, both for the sake of appearance and for better coverage. Work carefully and wear gloves, as cut sheet metal is extremely sharp. Nail the drip edge to the roof sheathing every 8 to 10 inches. Do not nail the drip edge to the fascia.

Vent Collars

Projections through the roof, such as plumbing vent pipes, are best sealed with flashing sleeves. These sleeves are available in a variety of styles and materials, including lead, sheet metal, rubber, and plastic. The most modern type (it's also the easiest to install) has a flexible rubber collar that makes a tight seal around the pipe. Below the collar, a piece of metal flashing makes the watertight connections to the roof. On the high side, the flashing tucks under shingles. On the low side it rests on top of them. You can trim shingles to make a neat fit around the flashing.

Step Flashing

Step flashing joins shingles to the sloping side of a wall or a chimney. Step flashing requires that each piece of flashing overlaps the one below it. The flashing is interlaced with the shingles as well. You can purchase step flashing precut, or you can cut the flashing into shingle-like pieces 10 inches long and 2 inches wider than the exposure of the roofing. You have to remember to insert a piece at the end of every course of shingles. You nail the high side against the adjacent structure, such as a dormer where it will be covered by siding, but do not nail the low side on the roof.

Valley Flashing

Valley flashing is installed on top of the sheathing and felt paper but beneath the roofing. The two basic types of valley treatments are called open and closed. If the flashing material is visible after the roof is finished, it is considered open. If the roofing material covers or even replaces the flashing, it is considered closed.

Open flashing works for all types of roofs. On the other hand, closed flashing is used only with asphalt shingles that are flexible enough to be woven together across the angle created by a valley. Open valleys are essential for wooden shingles, slate, and tile because the materials will not bend and overlap to make a closed valley. Open valleys also are commonly used with asphalt shingles because the design provides greater protection, especially from torrential downpours and the slow melt of heavy snow.

Valley flashing should extend 6 inches or more on each side of the valley centerline. (For low-sloped roofs, make that 10 inches.) Valley flashing can be galvanized steel or aluminum, center-crimped or painted. (If you crimp the flashing after it is painted, retouch the paint at the crimp line.) When you are using cedar roofing, underlay valley metal with 15-pound builder's felt (minimum). Double-coverage with a strip of felt paper or heavier roll roofing is a good idea for backup protection under all open valleys.

Typical Flashing for Roofing and Siding

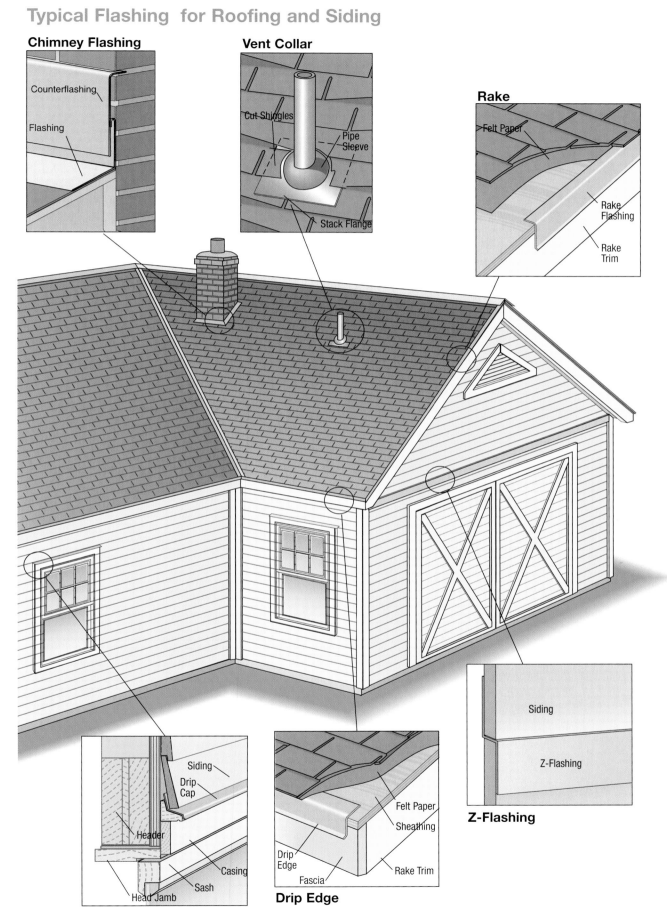

Chimney Flashing

Counterflashing

Flashing

Vent Collar

Cut Shingles

Pipe Sleeve

Stack Flange

Rake

Felt Paper

Rake Flashing

Rake Trim

Drip Cap

Siding

Drip Cap

Header

Casing

Sash

Head Jamb

Drip Edge

Felt Paper

Sheathing

Drip Edge

Fascia

Rake Trim

Z-Flashing

Siding

Z-Flashing

Finishing the Roof

There are many materials you can use to finish a roof aside from ag-panels and other traditional barn coverings.

■ **Asphalt-based shingles** are relatively simple to apply, last 15 to 20 years or more depending on their rating, and come in a variety of colors and shapes. These shingles, which are by far the most common roofing material in North America, are asphalt based, although these days the shingles have a fiberglass mat impregnated with asphalt and coated with mineral granules. Most suppliers offer only these fiberglass-based shingles.

Most shingles have adhesive beneath the tabs to keep them from curling or blowing back. They are suitable for every climate and can be applied to any roof that has a slope of 4 in 12 (4 inches of vertical rise for every 12 inches of horizontal run) or more. With double felt underlayment, they generally can be applied to a roof with a slope as low as 2 in 12 if shingle tabs are sealed down.

■ **Roll roofing** is ideal for utility buildings where appearance isn't crucial. It is the least expensive option for low-slope roofs. Roll roofing is not as attractive as composite shingles, but roofs with very shallow pitches are not visible from the ground anyway. Different types of roll roofing are made to be installed with different amounts of overlap. Single-coverage rolls are overlapped only a few inches. With double-coverage rolls, half of each course is covered by the next course. By increasing coverage, you can use rolls on slopes as low as 1 in 12 (1 inch rise per 12 inches of run). Roll roofing is 36 inches wide and is available in a variety of colors. Surface granules may be dark or light.

■ **Wood shingles and shakes** have twice the insulation value of asphalt shingles, are lighter in weight than most other roofing materials, and are very resistant to hail damage. They are also well suited to withstand the freeze-thaw conditions of variable climates. Wood shingles are machine-cut and smoothed on both sides. Shakes are thicker and rough on at least one side because they are split on one face and machine smoothed on the other. They vary in thickness and have a rustic appearance. A layer of felt paper sometimes is used between each course.

Both shingles and shakes require 1×4 strapping, often called skip sheathing, spaced to suit the desired exposure. Some modern wood roofs are laid over a mesh mat (instead of skip sheathing) that allows air to circulate under the wood and reduces the chance of rot and other problems. Pressure-injected fire retardant, as indicated by the industry designation "Certi-Guard," conforms to all state and local building codes for use in fire hazard regions. Given periodic coatings of wood preservative, shingles and shakes may serve for as long as 50 years. The drawbacks of using them include their high cost and slow application time.

■ **Hardboard shingle panels** are suitable for roofs with a 4-in-12 slope. With scored nailing and alignment lines, these shingles are installed in half the time it takes to apply cedar shakes. The panels do not crack with age, and they weather to a light gray. Shingle panels generally are 12 × 48 inches.

Installing Composition Shingles

Roofers often have their own methods of applying strip shingles, but in most cases all applications follow a few key guidelines. One of the most important guidelines is to double up the first row with a starter course. These starter shingles are set with the keys up instead of keys down. Some roofers also install an extra layer running lengthwise along the gable ends to reduce drips and help channel water back into the main roof and down to the gutters.

Roofers also sometimes stay in one place on the roof and install a few shingles stacked with overlaps for many courses. Do-it-yourselfers generally are better off installing only a few courses all the way across the roof, regularly checking straightness with a string line and measuring up from the starter course to keep the courses even.

It's also important to be safe during roof work. In that regard, the best guideline is to work only on walkable roofs, and even then only wearing nonslip shoes in good weather. If you have any misgivings about working on the roof, you should leave the job to a professional.

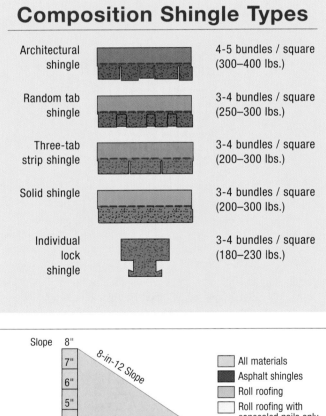

Composition Shingle Types

Architectural shingle		4-5 bundles / square (300–400 lbs.)
Random tab shingle		3-4 bundles / square (250–300 lbs.)
Three-tab strip shingle		3-4 bundles / square (200–300 lbs.)
Solid shingle		3-4 bundles / square (200–300 lbs.)
Individual lock shingle		3-4 bundles / square (180–230 lbs.)

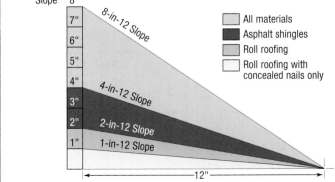

How you finish the roof depends on its slope. Wood or slate shouldn't be used at slopes shallower than 4 in 12. Anything shallower than 2 in 12 should have roll roofing or modified bitumen.

Installing Shingles

TOOLS & MATERIALS

- Hammer
- Chalk-line box
- Shears and utility knife
- Work gloves

- Metal drip edge
- Roofing nails
- Roofing felt and shingles
- Roofing cement

SMART TIP:

While some pros still use hammers with a hatchet end, most now use pneumatic nailers. Do-it-yourselfers will be safer using conventional hammers with a nail-pulling claw.

1 Nail on a metal drip edge at the edge of the eaves and the rake (on top of felt) with galvanized roofing nails. This helps keep water from the fascia boards and rake boards, preventing rot.

2 Roll out roofing felt on top of the roof decking, nailing it around the perimeter every 10 to 12 in., 3 in. from the felt's edge. Overlap adjacent rows by several inches.

3 For the starter course of shingles, snap a chalk line and lay the shingles with the tabs pointing toward the peak. Put one galvanized roofing nail through each tab.

4 The first visible course covers the starter course, with the tabs pointing away from the peak. Each shingle should be nailed just above the top of each key slot.

5 Start each new course at a 6-in. offset to stagger the seams in adjacent courses in a water-shedding layout. Make sure that the black adhesive strip is covered by the next course.

6 To shingle around a vent stack, trim to overlap only the upper half of the vent collar. Add roofing cement underneath this shingle. Do not drive nails through the shingles into the vent collar.

7 To shingle the ridge, cut single, slightly tapered tabs from whole shingles and wrap them across the ridge, nailing them on both sides in the area that will be covered by the next shingle.

8 To save time, you can let full shingles extend past the roof overhang. Come back later, and trim all of them at once with shears. This is much easier than cutting each to a specific length.

Installing Roll Roofing

Roll roofing, built-up roofing, and seam-sealed modified bitumen are the most common materials used to cover very low-slope roofs. Most roofs that appear flat actually have some slope to encourage drainage. While some types of roll roofing may be suitable, the material of choice today for flat roofs is a rubbery sheet material generally called modified bitumen or single-ply. Its seams are sealed with heat to form watertight seals. Single-ply also is widely used today instead of old fashioned built-up roofs that involve multiple layers of roofing material and hot tar. Both single-ply and built-up roofs should be installed by contractors.

On appropriate slopes, you can install roll roofing quickly. But the life of roll roofing is typically only 5 to 10 years. Given its plain appearance and short life, single-layer roll roofing is best used on sheds or in places where the roof is not visible. It may be used on slopes that are less angled than those normally covered by shingles, especially if a concealed nail application is used. Double-coverage roll roofing is best for roofs with a very low slope.

Roll roofing is more fragile than other roofing options. In temperatures below 45 degrees F, the material may crack, although you can work in colder conditions if you warm the rolls first. The roofing cement used at seams must be kept at a temperature above 45 degrees F, so store it indoors if you are working in cold weather.

Make sure the roofing has not curled at the edges or puckered in the middle. If it has, cut it into pieces 12 to 18 feet long and stack the pieces on a flat surface. Depending on the air temperature, they will take an hour to one full day to flatten. Felt paper may not be required, but is commonly installed over sheathing because it is inexpensive and worth the extra effort. Even small pebbles can eventually poke through roll roofing, so sweep the surface carefully.

Installing Roll Roofing

TOOLS & MATERIALS

- Chalk-line box
- Broom
- Hammer
- Mason's trowel
- Work gloves

- Builder's felt
- Roll roofing
- Roofing nails
- Roofing cement

1 Use a chalk-line box to snap a guideline 35½ in. from the eaves. Roll out the first layer of roofing on top of the felt paper, and nail it to the decking at 12-in. intervals.

2 After you install the first layer, spread roofing cement on it. This will help the second layer stick to this one. It's a messy job. Wear gloves, and keep the cement off of your shoes.

3 Roll out the second layer in a straight line, nailing it in place every 12 in. with roofing nails. Don't overdrive these nails, as this will puncture the roofing and could cause leaks.

4 Trowel on roof cement at course overlaps. Some roll roofing is designed to overlap up to half the previous layer. Be sure to read the instructions for the product you're using.

5 Cover each strip of roof cement with successive courses. Many brands of roll roofing are available with light-colored granules. Be sure your color matches roll for roll.

Roofing with Wood

Wood shingles and shakes are usually made of western red cedar, a long-lasting straight-grained wood. Even after years of weathering, wood does a much better job of shedding water than might be expected. In addition, wood shingles and shakes resist heat transmission twice as well as composition shingles. However, wood shingles often require more maintenance than other roofing materials, especially if you live in a harsh climate. In such areas it is advisable to treat wood shingles and shakes with a preservative every five years or so. Regular cleaning is also recommended to clear away debris that traps moisture and breeds fungus, mildew, rot, and insect borers.

Wood shingles and shakes are not fire resistant, and some local codes may require that the wood be treated with fire retardant. Some localities have banned wood roofing altogether, so be sure to check your local codes before deciding to use wood shingles or shakes. In addition, check with your insurance company to see whether your insurance premiums will be affected.

Shingles and shakes are not recommended for roofs with less than a 4-in-12 slope and exposure must also be limited for low slopes. For example, with a 4-in-12 slope, 16-inch shingles have a maximum of 5-inch exposure (6¾ inches on 5-in-12 slope). Shingles that are 24 inches long can have the greatest exposure (7½ inches on a 4-in-12 slope and 9¼ inches on a 5-in-12 slope).

Synthetic-fiber panels are an alternative to shingles. They are embossed with deep shadow lines and random-cut grooves to look like shakes. These 12×48-inch panels are applied lengthwise across the roof. They overlap with a shiplap joint between courses and a lap joint between shingles in the same course. The panels can be set over sheathing or old roofing if a layer of roofing felt is added first.

Installing Wood Roofing

TOOLS & MATERIALS

- Chalk-line box
- Hammer
- Carpenter's pencil
- Spacing jig
- Staple gun

- Roofing nails
- Heavy-duty staples
- Skip sheathing or roofing felt (over decking)
- Plastic mesh
- Drip edge
- Step flashing
- Shingles or shakes

1 Today, most wood roofing is laid over decking with a layer of builder's felt and a layer of plastic mesh that helps provide air circulation. Use a staple gun to attach the plastic mesh.

2 Install two layers of shingles at the eaves. Be sure to stagger their seams so that water can't penetrate to the roof beneath. Drive nails so that they will be covered by the next course.

3 Nail on step flashing in any seams where roofs meet walls. Apply a length of flashing under each shingle at these joints as you go along. Also install a drip edge at the rakes and eaves.

4 As you add courses, keep about ¼ in. of space between shakes by holding a pencil between them. This will help channel water off the surface and allow for expansion and contraction.

5 Build a T-shape jig to provide consistant distance between the bottoms of each course. This will help make the process move a lot faster because you won't have to keep measuring.

Doors

Buried beneath the finished wall and the trim around a door is the framing that forms the door's rough opening. It is composed of vertical 2×4s and a built-up horizontal piece called a header. The header is needed for extra support over doorways in load-bearing walls because some wall studs have been removed to make room for the door.

The doorjambs—two side jambs and the head jamb across the top—form the finished opening for the door, as well as the mounting points for the hinges and part of the lockset. The door sill, or threshold, lies below the door, and the door stops—narrow strips of wood nailed to the jambs—keep the door from swinging beyond the closed position. Trim, also called casing, covers gaps between the rough opening and the jambs. The gaps provide room to level and plumb the door and jambs.

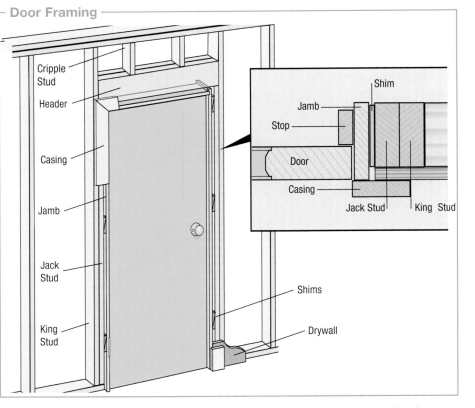

Door Framing

Cripple Stud
Header
Casing
Jamb
Jack Stud
King Stud
Shims
Drywall
Shim
Jamb
Stop
Door
Casing
Jack Stud
King Stud

Making Your Own Door

If you need a door to fit an odd-size opening or simply want to save money, you can build your own door from rough-cut boards or plywood. Some of the possibilities are shown in the drawing at top right, opposite. Doors up to 3 feet wide by 6 feet 8 inches tall can be made of ½- to ⅝-inch plywood reinforced with a surface-mounted frame and braces made of

1×4s. You can use the same one-by stock to make the trim to frame the opening. Because you install these somewhat rough looking doors with surface-mounted hinges, no jamb is needed. For taller or wider doors, you often need firmer bracing. To install large doors, it's wise to prop them up slightly during installation to account for a bit of sagging, even after mounting three hinges to carry the weight.

Types of Doors

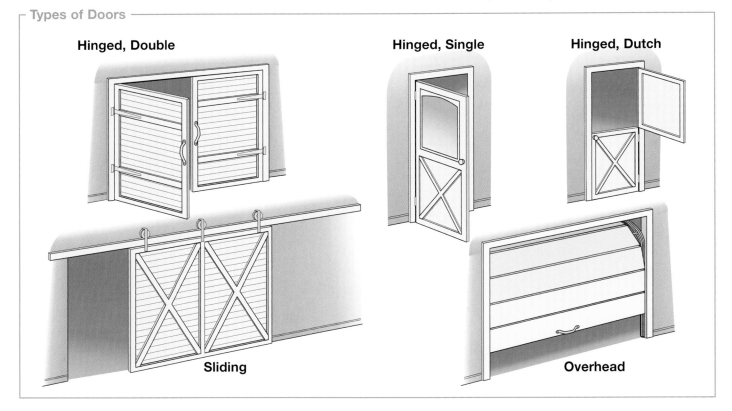

Hinged, Double

Hinged, Single

Hinged, Dutch

Sliding

Overhead

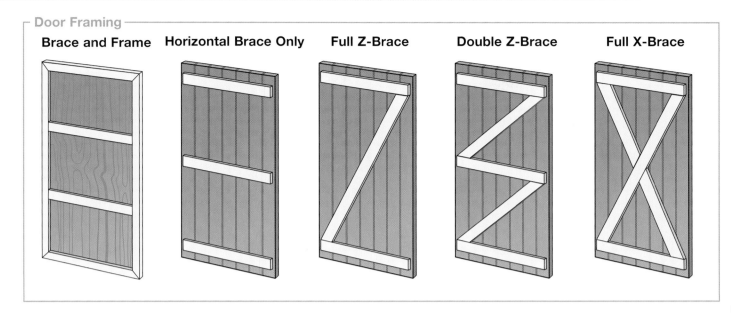

Brace and Frame **Horizontal Brace Only** **Full Z-Brace** **Double Z-Brace** **Full X-Brace**

Building a Z-Brace Door

TOOLS & MATERIALS

- Circular saw
- Drill-driver
- Screwdriver bit
- Combination square
- Sliding T-bevel
- Clamps

- File or sandpaper
- 1×4 or 1×6 boards
- 1¼" deck screws
- Carpenter's glue

1 Use a circular saw to cut 1x4 or 1x6 boards to length. If full-width boards won't fit the width of your rough opening, rip two boards to identical widths, and use those boards at the sides.

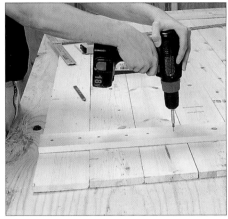

2 Align the boards on a worktable, and attach them with two lengths of 1x4 strapping near the top and bottom. Make sure that the fasteners don't poke through to the other side.

3 Lay a 1x4 for the Z-brace between the two straps. Use a sliding T-bevel to determine the angle at which to cut the brace to make it flush with the top and bottom straps.

4 Make the angled cuts in the Z-brace using a circular saw. Test-fit the cut, and trim it using a plane or file as needed for a tight fit. Don't force an oversized piece.

5 After applying some carpenter's glue, fasten the Z-brace between the straps. Put one or more screws through the Z-brace into each of the boards that make up the door.

Hanging a Door

A variety of hinge and latch styles are available for hanging exterior doors. Some of the most common are surface-mounted butt hinges, strap hinges, and T-hinges. On utility buildings, three factors are key to making a sturdy installation. First, make sure the hinges are large enough to support the weight of the door. Second, use galvanized or other rust-resistant hinges and hardware. Third, use screws long enough to reach well into the wall framing.

For most utility buildings, a homemade door will be surface-mounted to the siding, and the hinges will be left exposed. You can install the hinges on the door first and have a helper hold it in position. It's helpful to use shims to position the door with the proper spacing, including a slight rise on the opening side against sagging. If the door doesn't fit perfectly into the opening, you can use a block plane to shave down edges that scrape.

If you want to have the hinges on the inside of the door (as with a prehung exterior door), you generally have to install a doorjamb into the rough opening and mortise the hinges. Although there are exterior-mounted hinges with one-way screws and sealed pins that are difficult to remove, conventional leaf hinges are completely concealed from the outside and generally more secure.

Installing a doorjamb into the rough opening is not a difficult task, although it's easier to buy a prehung door. The process involves nailing jamb materials to the studs while using shims to make the jamb plumb and straight. Be sure to insert shims directly beneath all hinge locations. Hinges are attached directly to the jamb, generally in mortises.

Once the door is properly mounted and swinging freely, close the door with the exterior face flush with the building, and install 1×2 stops directly to the header and jack studs inside the rough opening. If you're installing double doors, you can install a door stop at the bottom of the opening, or use hardware to keep the doors flush.

Surface-Mounting a Homemade Door

TOOLS & MATERIALS

- Drill-driver
- Screwdriver bit
- Block plane
- Level

- Galvanized steel hinges
- Galvanized screws
- Shims

1 Attach the hinges to the outside of the door about 8 in. from the top and bottom. A heavy door may require three or more hinges. Align them with the barrel of the hinge just outside the door.

2 Set the door into the rough opening, and check its fit. If it is too large, plane one or more edges. Jack studs at the sides of the opening provide a nailing surface for the hinges.

3 As a helper holds the door in place, mark the holes where the hinges fall. You can also work by yourself and prop up the door on wood blocks or shims so that it won't scrape on it's hinges.

4 Fasten the hinges to the siding and jack studs using 2 in. or longer galvanized flathead screws. Screws must be long enough to reach well into the studs to support a heavy door.

5 If the door binds on the rough opening, mark the area with chalk to highlight contact points, and use a sharp block plane to shave down that section of the door.

Hanging a Door with Jambs

TOOLS & MATERIALS

- Hammer
- Measuring tape
- Pencil
- 1/2" wood chisel
- Rubber mallet
- Drill-driver

- One-by jamb stock
- Hinges
- Galvanized screws
- Shims

1 Assemble the side and top jambs for the rough opening. Precut jamb stock is available at lumberyards. Jambs should be the same width as the framing lumber plus surface materials.

2 Tip the assembled jamb into the rough opening, and shim it so that it is plumb and level with square corners. The jamb should be flush with the finished surface around the opening.

3 Use finishing nails to nail the jamb to the jack studs through the shims. This will hold the shims in place and fasten the jamb to the wall. Use screws to help support a heavy door.

4 Attach the hinges to the door, oriented so that the leaves of the hinge are on the inside and the pins are outside of the building. Set the door into the jambs to check its fit.

5 Temporarily attach the hinge to the jamb with one screw, if need be. Be sure the door is in the correct position. Then trace the hinge outline onto the jamb for mortising.

6 Use a sharp wood chisel to cut a shallow mortise in the jamb for each of the hinges so that they will sit flush with the surface of the jamb. This will allow the door to close smoothly.

7 Set the hinges into the mortises, and screw the hinges into the jambs and the studs. Reset the shims as needed so that the door is plumb and level with the floor as you work.

8 Add a stop to the latch side of the door to keep it from swinging through. Then add interior and exterior door casing to cover the jamb, shims, and jack studs.

Installing a Prehung Door

Most prehung doors come squared up and braced. It's wise to leave the braces on as long as you can during the installation to keep the door from racking. Most interior prehung doors are built to allow for thick carpeting, so you may need to cut both jamb legs if the bottom of the door is too high off of an uncarpeted floor.

Center the unit in the opening, and check that the top is level. Insert shims in the gaps between the doorjambs and rough framing to square and plumb the unit. Use prepackaged shims sold for this purpose, tapered wood shingles, or homemade shims. Set a pair of shims with opposing tapers between the frame and stud at each hinge location—and if there are only two hinges, in the middle. Increase or decrease the overlap of the shims to adjust the frame until it is plumb. Drive a finishing nail through the jamb, each shim set, and partially into the stud. Then install three sets of shims on the other side jamb and one set above the head jamb. When all shims are in place, the frame should be plumb and square, and there should be a uniform gap between the door and the jamb unless the framing is askew. Add a second nail at each shim, and drive all nails home.

After installing an exterior door in an insulated structure, stuff fiberglass insulation behind and above the jamb before installing the casing. Another option is to use a spray-in foam insulation. This is a simple and more thorough method of insulating between a doorjamb and framing, but there are some drawbacks. Foam can expand dramatically and deform your jamb if it is not securely attached. To avoid this, use low-expansion foam. Also, the process can be fairly messy. Polyurethane foam is difficult to remove; so wear disposable gloves to avoid getting it on your hands. Allow any excess to dry, and then scrape or cut it away with a sharp blade.

Hanging a Prehung Interior Door

TOOLS & MATERIALS

- Drill-driver
- Hammer
- Framing square
- Spirit level

- Prehung interior door
- Cross brace
- Shims
- Nails
- Trim

1 Although a prehung door is hinged in its frame, it pays to check to be sure it's square using a framing square. Once it's squared up, lock it into position with a cross brace if it doesn't have one.

2 Set the prehung unit on the sill and tip it into place. You can hold it in position temporarily with wood shims. Cross braces will keep the frame flush with the wall surface as you work.

3 Working from the inside of the wall, use more wood shims and a level to adjust the door until it is exactly plumb in the rough opening. Check both sides of the door.

4 When the door is plumb, drive 10d finishing nails through both the jamb and wood shims into the 2x4 wall framing. It's wise to double check for plumb and level as you work.

5 To use standard interior trim, cut mitered corners for a finished look, and install the pieces with glue and finishing nails. You can also use more rustic trim with butt joints.

Installing a Prehung Exterior Door

6 CLOSING IN

TOOLS & MATERIALS

- Utility knife
- Staple gun
- Spirit level
- Drill
- Hammer
- Putty knife
- Caulking gun

- Prehung door & lockset
- Caulk or flashing
- 2×4 brace
- Shims
- Nails
- Glue
- Wood putty

1 You can install flashing under the sill, although many manufacturers suggest using a waterproof caulk instead. Apply caulk liberally to the floor where the door sill will rest.

2 Set the prehung exterior door from the outside of the building. The door already has exterior molding attached to the frame. The molding around the door should fit tightly against the exterior wall.

3 Tack a brace across the outside to keep the door from falling out of the opening. Don't fasten the frame to the wall yet. Working from the inside, use a level to plumb the door.

4 As you plumb the door, insert wooden shims in the gaps between the frame and the 2x4 studs. The shims will not go through to the outside because the door molding is in the way.

5 When the door is in the correct position, predrill holes through the door frame and nail through the frame (and hidden shims) into the wall framing. Then you can remove the braces.

6 Also drive finishing nails through the face of the door's exterior molding well into the wall framing. Set the nailheads, and fill the holes with exterior-grade putty.

7 You can order most prehung doors with locks already installed or with the holes predrilled so that you can install your own. Follow the directions provided for installation.

8 A lockset plus dead bolt provides extra security. Use long screws in the strike plates that reach through to the house framing to improve the overall security of the opening.

Installing Windows

The most popular types of residential windows, double-hungs and casements, are suitable on more finished utility buildings. More rustic barns often have what amounts to one half of a double-hung—a large single sash, called a barn sash, that swings out awning style for ventilation.

Windows usually come with specific installation instructions, including a rough opening size. Generally, the rough opening is ½ to ¾ of an inch larger than the unit itself. This allows room for plumbing and leveling the window even if the frame is out of square.

Some windows come with an exterior casing, called brick molding, on the outside. You have to install this type from the outside, nailing through the brick molding into the siding and framing. Whatever type of window you use, always shim the windows plumb and level before nailing.

Many modern windows come with a nailing flange around the frame. Nail these windows to the outside of the framing or sheathing. Depending on the look you want, you can cover the flange with casing and bring the siding to the casing, or cover the flange with siding, using no casing at all.

Insulating and Sealing a Window

Stuff fiberglass insulation into the gaps between the window and framing (or fill it with foam insulation from a pressure can). Patch the vapor barrier (if one exists) with 6-mil polyethylene sheet. Seal the polyethylene to the existing vapor barrier with polyurethane caulk. Then apply a bead of caulking around the inside edge of the window, and staple the polyethylene patch into the bead.

On any window installation you need to protect the top seams from the weather with flashing. This drip cap, generally made from either aluminum or plastic, must be

Basic Window Types

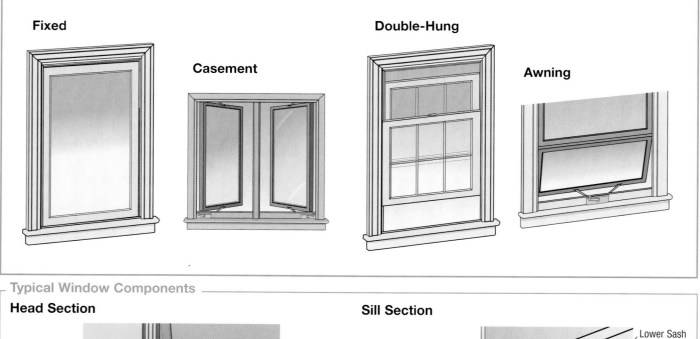

Fixed

Casement

Double-Hung

Awning

Typical Window Components

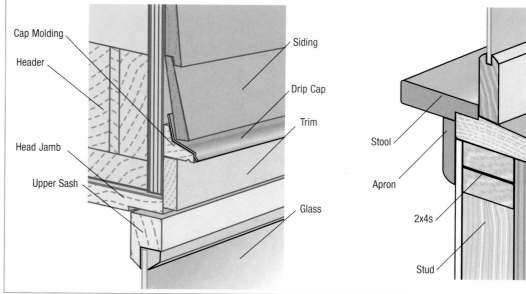

Head Section

Cap Molding

Header

Head Jamb

Upper Sash

Siding

Drip Cap

Trim

Glass

Sill Section

Lower Sash

Sill

Siding

Stool

Apron

2x4s

Stud

Installing New Windows

TOOLS & MATERIALS

- Measuring tape
- Circular saw
- Staple gun
- Caulking gun
- Level
- Hammer
- Safety glasses

- New window
- Exterior-grade caulk
- Nails
- Shims
- Insulation
- Trim

1 After laying out and marking the rough opening, set a circular saw slightly deeper than the depth of your sheathing (typically ½ in.). Plunge the blade into the surface to begin the cuts.

2 When you install felt paper or an air-infiltration barrier, make sure to leave enough excess to tuck back and staple onto the sides of the framed opening of the window.

3 To make a weathertight seal, add a bead of exterior-grade caulk to the back of the nailing flange before you install the unit. This will reduce the likelihood of moisture penetration.

4 Set the window unit into place, resting it on the sill so that you can tip the top into place. Temporarily tack a nail through the nailing flange to secure it while you adjust it.

5 Use pairs of tapered shingle shims to adjust the window on all sides in the opening. Next, use a level to check for plumb and level. This process should go quickly if the opening is properly framed.

6 Stuff insulation into gaps between the studs and the window frame. This will help eliminate drafts and improve energy efficiency. You can instead spray polyurethane foam also into the spaces.

7 Once you have plumbed and leveled the window, fasten it to the wall by nailing all sides through the holes in the perforated flange into the rough window framing. Use nails with large heads.

8 With the window fastened, you can add caulk and trim, J-channel for vinyl siding, or a variety of wood trim for clapboards or shakes. Using 1x4 pine works well for barns and sheds.

installed to form a barrier between the window and the sheathing to prevent water from seeping inside the wall.

The upper flange of the L-shaped flashing is installed underneath the siding above the window. The other side extends over the window frame. Install the drip cap with a downward slope to deflect rainwater. Be sure not to crimp or stress the flashing when you install siding or trim.

You can also install drip molding or cap molding above a window. This type of molding forms a projection past the casing and can add decorative detail as well as water-shedding protection.

It helps to seal the gaps between the window casing and the sheathing with an exterior-grade caulk. This bead of caulk will prevent water from seeping between the window and the wall, where it can cause rot. After you've installed the window trim, run a second bead of caulk between the trim and the siding. Check the caulk around the windows periodically and replace it as needed.

Trimming and Finishing Windows

For most barns and outbuildings, 1×4 pine makes a good rustic casing. Fasten it with galvanized casing nails long enough to extend well into the framing. You can take the time to miter corner joints, creating a tight fit by slightly undercutting the edges. This allows the visible surfaces of the boards to meet and close tightly before the full depth of the boards make contact.

But on barns and other outbuildings it usually looks fine to use a rougher style. For example, you can mount the lower and side casings with square-edged butt joints, and let the head casing run long. On unfinished interiors you can use the same approach. If you plan to finish the interior, nail the trim around the window after the drywall is in place.

Prime and paint (or stain) the trim to protect it from the weather and prevent excessive shifting. If you want the trim to have a contrasting color, coat the edges ahead of time to save yourself the trouble of cutting in a second color.

Installing Window Trim

TOOLS & MATERIALS

- Power miter saw
- Saber saw
- Power drill
- Hammer

- Stool, casing, and apron trim
- Wood glue

1 Cut the top and side pieces of trim at 45-deg. angles to make mitered joints. Test the fit, and nail the top trim with finishing nails. Add glue to the miters and nail the side pieces.

2 Use a saber saw to cut the deep, interior sill, called a stool, where it extends beyond the window frame. The extensions of the stool will provide a base for the vertical trim pieces.

3 Add glue to mating edges, and drive finishing nails at an angle through the stool into the window frame. To avoid splitting the stool near the edge, you can predrill for nailholes.

4 Add an apron under the stool for support and architectural decoration by cutting 45-deg. angles at the ends (to install small returns), and predrilling before nailing in place.

5 Cut complementary 45-deg. angles on short return pieces. Cut them on a power saw from a long piece to be safe. Glue these pieces in place, as they are too small to nail without splitting.

Ventilation

If your utility building is not going to be finished for use as living space, proper ventilation may seem like an unnecessary worry. That's true if you're building a wood shed or a small equipment barn. But even an uninsulated potting shed is going to need some ventilation to make it comfortable and safe to work in.

If you're building a barn to house animals, proper ventilation is extremely important. You should check special agricultural requirements for venting and other livestock matters with local code agencies.

Even if your building has operating windows (which are generally essential to satisfy health and safety codes), you may need to provide additional ventilation to keep the interior cool and dry during hot and humid weather. You may want to install screened eave or gable vents, roof turbine vents, ridge vents, or even a louvered cupola on the roof peak to exhaust air.

Vents should generally be used in a balanced combination of inlets and outlets. Intakes, such as plug and strip vents at the eaves, let air in, and outlets, such as a gable-end vent or a ridge vent, let air out. If your building has few (or no) windows, you may want to install wall vents at floor level.

To create good cross ventilation (either horizontally, vertically, or both) you need about the same amount of vent square footage to let air in as you do to let air out. If the mix is out of balance—for example, with large vents along both eaves but only a small gable-end vent at one end of a barn—fresh air won't flow freely into the building because there won't be enough vent area to exhaust it. It's also important to install combinations of vents that keep air moving in all parts of the building, and do not leave stagnant areas.

Types of Ventilation

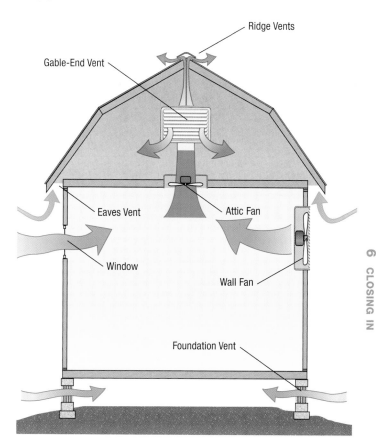

Ridge Vents

Gable-End Vent

Eaves Vent

Attic Fan

Window

Wall Fan

Foundation Vent

Adding a Cupola

Barn roofs are often ventilated with cupolas—small structures on the roof with louvered sides to allow for airflow and a shingled roof to keep out the weather. Some companies sell ready-to-assemble cupolas, or you can design and make your own.

A typical cupola has four side panels, consisting of two miter-cut 2×4 corner boards and 1×2 louvers glued into routed mortises in the corner boards. Louvers should be spaced close enough together to block light when viewed straight on.

To mount a cupola you cut a hole in the roof and join the two structures with frame hardware. Some may require flashing to close seams between the cupola and the shingles. When installed on finished barn structures, you can staple screening to the back of the side pieces to keep insects from entering.

Ready-made cupolas *in kit form are available through many specialty and lumber supply stores.*

A cupola *can be used to ventilate a building, or it can be installed as a purely decorative element.*

Roof Vents

A well-vented roof keeps a structure from becoming too hot in the summer, helps to prevent the formation of ice dams and condensation in the winter, and prolongs the life span of asphalt shingles.

One of the most practical barn vents is a continuous ridge vent. This waterproof cap along the building peak helps to create a natural flow of air up through the building and out the roof. It is effective in venting an open-plan utility building without leaving any hot spots. The ridge vent covers a slit that runs along the ridge. It caps the opening with screening and a small roof of plastic that keeps rain from entering. Many types can be covered with shingles to blend in with the roof.

Install a ridge vent by snapping a chalk line a few inches from the top of the ridge on each side of the roof, as specified by the manufacturer. Cut out the sections with a circular saw set to the depth of the roof sheathing. Attach the ridge vent with caulking and roofing nails. On new construction you can anticipate the installation and install sheathing a few inches short of the ridge on both sides.

Gable Vents

Other common types of vents include fixed grilles (usually installed high on the wall near the ridge), which allow air to pass through louvers, and a variety of power fans. The venting ability of these systems depends on the size of the opening and on the capacity of the fan. Building codes usually require the area of attic vent openings to equal at least 1/300 of the total square feet of attic space being ventilated, and 1/150 with no vapor barrier in the ceiling.

Soffit Vents

Soffit vents come in three basic configurations: round, rectangular, and perforated panels. The round variety, called plug vents, are easier to install than the other types. You need only a power drill and a bit or hole saw to cut the hole for plug vents, whereas continuous vents require a circular saw to cut the opening. It is easier and safer to drill an overhanging section than it is to cut it with an upside-down circular saw—especially if you're working on a ladder.

Another option for installing soffit vents is to remove the plywood, cut the holes (circular or rectangular) while the plywood is secured to a worktable, insert the vents, and reinstall the panels. This is a viable option if the soffit is delaminated and is in need of replacing anyway. If you're planning to install rectangular strip-grille vents, this approach is probably the most practical.

Continuous perforated soffits are manufactured in preformed sheets of vinyl or aluminum, and can be installed once the old soffits have been ripped out. Perforated soffits eliminate the need for cutting plywood, but they may not come in the size or color that you require. However, perforated panels let in air all along the overhang. Home centers usually have manufacturers' catalogs listing the sizes and colors of their products.

Requirements of Livestock

A barn housing livestock needs to have an efficient ventilation system to replenish the air supply and remove heat, moisture, and odors. A mature dairy cow, for example, may exhale 4 to 5 gallons of water vapor a day and produce over 2,000 Btu of heat per hour.

It helps to locate the building on high ground with the long axis perpendicular to prevailing summer winds, and to keep the building at least 50 feet from other buildings or windbreaks. Any building housing livestock should have continuous ridge vents, as well as eaves or sidewall vents that can be closed to keep in heat in the cold weather. Also, a roof slope of 4 in 12 to 6 in 12 is recommended for good air mixing.

Whether or not you will need electric exhaust fans to properly ventilate a barn will depend on your climate and the animals you are keeping. The table below, "Exhaust Fan Performance," will give you an idea of the fan size and horsepower you will need for your space. Ventilation systems may operate under positive or negative static pressure, which is measured in "inches of water." For the purposes of this table, a static pressure of 1/8 inch of water is assumed. Fans don't work in closed spaces. A fan must work in conjunction with properly sized vents leading to and from the outdoors.

Exhaust Fan Performance

Fan Diameter (in.)	Fan Speed (rpm)	Motor Size (hp)	Airflow (cubic ft./min. at normal static pressure*)
8	1,650	1/50	289
8	3,500	1/15	509
10	1,550	1/50	413
10	3,416	1/6	1,209
12	1,600	1/12	1,035
16	1,140	1/12	1,374
16	1,670	1/4	2,854
18	1,140	1/6	2,395
18	1,648	1/3	4,003
24	855	1/3	4,180
24	1,140	7/8	5,920
36	460	1/2	7,850
36	851	1/2	8,533
48	363	1	15,892
48	495	1	16,758

*Assuming a static pressure measured at 1/8 inch of water. Actual results will vary.

Adapted from "Fan Performance and Efficiency for Animal Systems" (University of Minnesota Extension Service).

Roof Vent

TOOLS
- Caulk-line box
- Circular saw
- Hammer
- Utility Knife

MATERIALS
- Ridge vent
- Asphalt roofing
- 8d galvanized nails

1 Use a chalk line to mark a straight line across the sides of the ridge. Cut along both lines using a circular saw. Set the blade to the depth of the plywood decking to avoid cutting the framing.

2 Nail the ridge vent to the roof using 8d nails. Some ridge vents come in sections, and others roll out across the ridge. Nail the vent about every 8 in. using nailing holes if they are provided.

3 Cut full shingles into thirds, separating the three tabs. Install them over the ridge vent, lapping each over the previous one. Set one nail into each shingle on each side of the ridge.

Soffit Vent

TOOLS
- Circular saw
- Hammer
- Chisel
- Drill-driver

MATERIALS
- Soffit vent
- 1" Galvanized screws

1 Mark the outline of the vent on the soffit. Begin the cuts by plunging the circular saw with the front of the saw base against the soffit. Set the blade depth to the soffit thickness.

2 After you make the long side cuts with the saw, use a hammer and chisel to cut across the grain between the two saw cuts, and remove the piece of wood in the middle.

3 Insert the vent into the opening. Use galvanized screws to secure the vent to the soffit. Fastener holes are usually provided. Caulk around the edges of the vent if needed.

Gable Vent

TOOLS
- Hammer
- Circular saw
- Drill-driver

MATERIALS
- 10d nails
- 2" Galvanized screws
- Gable vent

1 Frame the opening for the vent in the gable. This may require you to remove and relocate studs. They are not load bearing, so you don't have to worry about installing structural headers.

2 Nail into the sheathing at each corner of the opening to provide reference for the cut lines you will draw on the outside. Plunge a circular saw to begin your cuts.

3 Install the vent in the opening. Secure it using a drill with a screwdriver bit and galvanized screws. Apply a bead of exterior caulk around the vent after you have attached it.

CHAPTER 7

Wiring & Plumbing

Whoever said, "A little knowledge is a dangerous thing," must have been talking about wiring, a skill that must be learned from an experienced licensed electrician. It's not a standard do-it-yourself job, which means that if you decide to wire your barn, you should do so only under the close supervision of an experienced electrician. In many areas, codes require licensed work. There are fewer drawbacks to plumbing your barn. However, if you are installing a full septic system, soil pipe, toilets, sinks, and shower, you should consult and work with a licensed plumber. Much of the information in this chapter, therefore, is only a guide that you can use to plan the project.

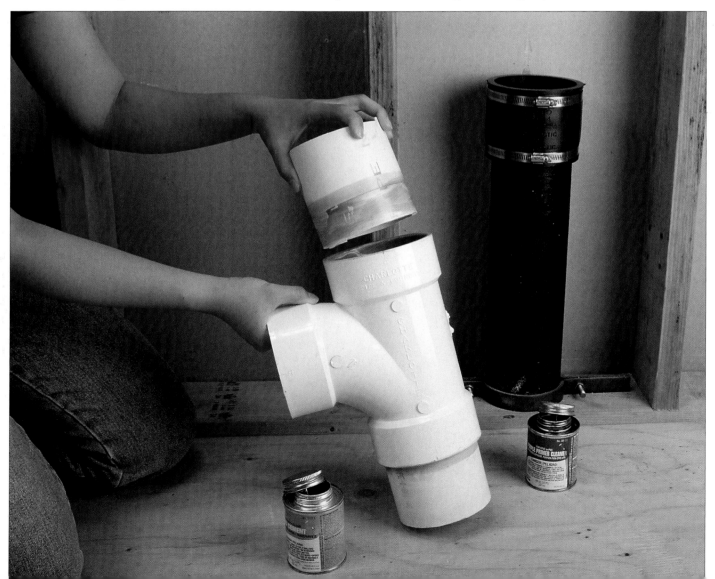

Wiring Basics

Electricity can be dangerous, but if you use common sense, you can work with it safely. The most important things to remember are to always, without fail, turn off the power at the main service panel before working on a circuit, only use one hand to disconnect or reactivate a fuse or circuit breaker, and before starting work, check the circuit with a voltage tester to make sure that the power is off.

All electrical procedures and materials are governed by local building or electrical codes. Some municipalities won't let anyone but a licensed electrician do any wiring work. Some will allow DIYers to rough-in their wiring as long as an electrician inspects it and makes the final hookup to the service panel. You need to check.

Local codes may also prohibit the use of a certain type of cable or may require a particular size of wire or minimum number of circuits. Codes governing barns may also present special requirements—for example, that 15- and 20-amp, 120-volt receptacles are protected by a ground fault circuit iterruptor. Always consult with the local building inspector.

Understanding Electricity

Electricity enters your home through overhead or underground wires, where it passes through a meter before entering the main service panel. The meter measures how much electricity you use. At the main service panel, the electricity is divided into branch circuits, each of which is protected by a fuse or circuit breaker. Power travels in a closed loop through the circuit's hot wires to outlets or fixtures and returns to the service panel via neutral wires, unless it is interrupted by an open switch or short circuit. The fuses or breakers protect these circuits from overloading (drawing more power than the wires can handle).

For an outbuilding, you have the choice of running wiring from your house or having it served by separate power lines. The option you choose depends on how much electricity you will consume, the capacity of the existing service panel at the house, and to some extent the distance from your house to the outbuilding.

Basic Electrical Terms

- **Amperes** or amps, measure current flow. The amp rating is marked on many appliances. The rating for your house's circuits will be marked on the circuit breaker or fuse—generally 15 or 20 amps for most room circuits and 30 amps or more for heavy-duty circuits supplying large appliances.
- **Volts** measure the force of electrical pressure that keeps the current flowing through the wires. Products are marked with a voltage capacity, usually 120 or 240 volts. You can't hook up a product designed to operate at 120 volts to a 240-volt electrical outlet. It's dangerous, and the product will burn out.
- **Watts** equal volts multiplied by amps. The wattage rating of a circuit is the amount of power the circuit can deliver safely, determined by the current-carrying capacity of the wires. Wattage also indicates the amount of power that a fixture or appliance needs to work properly.

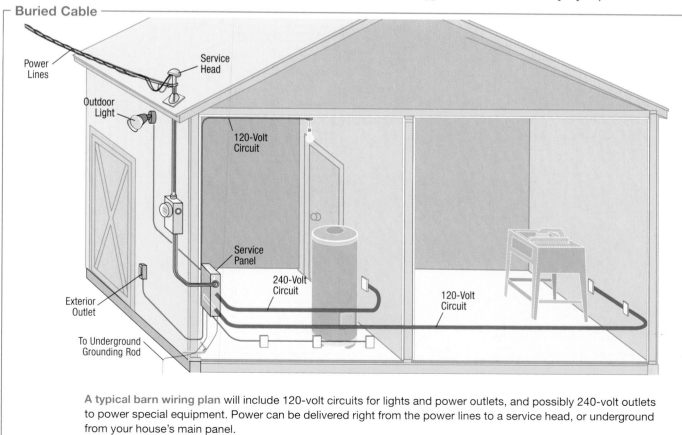

Buried Cable

Power Lines

Service Head

Outdoor Light

120-Volt Circuit

Service Panel

240-Volt Circuit

120-Volt Circuit

Exterior Outlet

To Underground Grounding Rod

A typical barn wiring plan will include 120-volt circuits for lights and power outlets, and possibly 240-volt outlets to power special equipment. Power can be delivered right from the power lines to a service head, or underground from your house's main panel.

Grounding

Electricity always seeks to return to a point of zero voltage (the ground) along the easiest path open to it. If you touch an electric fence, electricity will flow from the fence through your body to the ground, and the electrical path is grounded through you. A short circuit in wiring is a similar situation. Electricity is able to leave the closed loop of the circuit—maybe because a hot wire is off its terminal and touches the metal box of a light fixture—and return to the source by some other means. If the system is properly grounded, this short would be a fault to ground and pose no hazard. If it's improperly grounded, the electricity will seek to ground itself through your body.

To guard against this, your house's electrical system has grounding wires, which give the electricity a permanent alternative path for its return to the source. Each receptacle and fixture has its own grounding wires that return electricity to the main panel. The entire system is also grounded to your metal cold-water pipes or (if you have plastic plumbing) to one or more grounding rods buried underground next to your foundation—or to both.

Another way to protect against the danger of shock is by using a ground-fault circuit interrupter, or GFCI. This device detects minute amounts of current leakage in a circuit. If the amperage flowing through the black and white wires is equal, then the circuit is operating properly. But if there is as little as a 0.005-amp difference detected between the two wires, then the circuit is internally broken fast enough to prevent a severe shock. Codes often require GFCI outlets in outbuildings or in any spot less than 6 feet away from a source of water, such as a faucet or a sink.

Making a Wiring Plan

Before you make your plan, you need to estimate the overall demand on your system to determine the size of the service entrance cable and the individual circuits. A 100-amp service is considered the minimum for even moderate sized buildings. If you're building a workshop that will hold a lot of high-powered tools, or if you want to install electric heat, you might want to consider 150- or 200-amp service.

There are three options for setting up service in an outbuilding. If your house's service panel has the capacity and room for new circuits, you can run them directly from the panel. If it has the capacity but not the room, you need to install a subpanel for your outbuilding. Otherwise, the outbuilding will need a main service panel of its own. This is also a good idea if your building will be for a business and you want to keep the bills separate for tax purposes.

Basic Electrical Needs

The National Electrical Code (NEC) requires that houses have a base of 3 watts per square foot of living area for lighting. Use this as a guide. A good rule of thumb would be at least one light fixture (of 40–100 watts) and one outlet for every 100 square feet of floor space. This means you need at least one 15-amp circuit for every 600 square feet (which can supply up to 10 outlets) or a 20-amp circuit every 800 square feet (which can supply up to 13).

Ordinary power tools that you plug into the wall can be run off these standard 120-volt, 20-amp outlets. Larger equipment may require separate 120- or 240-volt circuits. For motorized appliances, you should supply 125 percent of the ampere rating on the nameplate for your estimate.

Lights should be controlled by switches. It's less important for outlets but can be a convenience in some circumstances. A basic outbuilding wiring plan will include one circuit for overhead lighting, switch-controlled from one or more locations, and at least one circuit for power receptacles.

Note that the number and location of outlets is controlled by codes. You should draw up a wiring plan before starting work. Mark where you want lights, outlets, switches, and other fixtures, and where each room's wiring is connected to the cable coming from the main service panel. This will provide a rough estimate of the materials that you will need for the project.

Circuit Breakers & Fuses

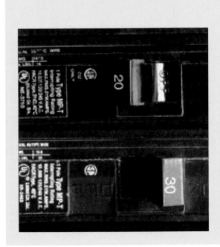

When a short circuit or ground fault occurs, a massive amount of current will surge through a circuit breaker, causing it to trip. You can reset it once. But if it trips again, call in a licensed electrician.

Overloads in older systems with fuses cause the metal strip to melt and create a break. Short circuits cause the metal element to vaporize, which leaves a distinctive sooty cloud on the fuse window.

Working with Wire & Cable

Single wires are insulated to carry electricity or bare for grounding. Most household wiring is contained in cable, inside flexible metal (such as BX) or plastic insulation (such as NM). Individual wires have size numbers based on the American wire gauge (AWG) system, which expresses wire diameter as a whole number. For example, No. 14 wire is 0.0064 inch in diameter; No. 12 is 0.081 inch. Smaller numbers indicate larger diameters that can carry more power. The National Electrical Code requires a minimum of No. 14 wire for most house wiring.

Wires have color-coded plastic insulation to indicate their function in your house's wiring system. Hot wires carrying current at full voltage are usually black or red but can be other colors. Neutral wires are white or gray. Grounding wires can be bare copper or in green plastic insulation. But you should always use a tester to confirm wire applications. Don't rely on color codes, particularly in older buildings.

Conduit

Insulated wires are sometimes run through metal or plastic pipe called conduit. Metal conduit comes in three types: rigid (preferred for outdoor applications), intermediate, and EMT (electrical metal tubing). Plastic conduit (preferred for underground locations) comes in two types. They are schedule 40 and schedule 80. Standard conduit diameters are ½, ¾, 1, and 1¼ inches. There are fittings to join conduit for straight runs and at 45-degree angles, and a special tool (called a hickey) for making more gradual bends in metal tubing. You may be required by code to use conduit for wires run underground or in open, unfinished walls. Even if you aren't, it's a good idea if you're running cable in areas where they can be damaged, such as a horse barn.

Both metal and plastic conduit can be cut with a pipe cutter or a hacksaw. A pipe cutter is the best tool—the shoulders of the cutter keep the pipe square in the device and ensure an even cut. When cutting with a hacksaw, remove any burring, which can damage the wires' insulation when they are pulled through.

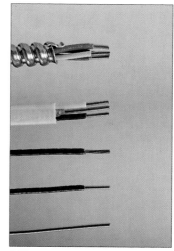

Different wires are used for different purposes. Most homes are wired with the second cable from the top. It is called NM, or nonmetallic sheath.

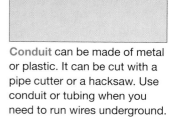

Conduit can be made of metal or plastic. It can be cut with a pipe cutter or a hacksaw. Use conduit or tubing when you need to run wires underground.

Estimating Wire Needs

To estimate the amount of wire or cable you will need, add an extra foot for every run you will make, and add about 20 percent to this figure. This will give you plenty of cable to make connections. For example, if you measure 12 feet between a new and existing receptacle, add another 2 feet for the two connections, and then add 20 percent (about 3 feet) to the total. To do the job, start working with 17 feet of cable.

American Wire Gauges

Wire Gauge	Current Capacity (amps)	Typical Use
No. 6	60	large appliances (240V), service ground wires
No. 8	40	large appliances (120V–240V)
No. 10	30	large appliances (120V–240V)
No. 12	20	small appliance branch circuits
No. 14	15	general-purpose house wiring
No. 16	10	extension/fixture cords
No. 18	7	low-voltage systems

Typical Electrical Loads

Appliance	Watts
Air conditioner, central	2500–6000
Air conditioner, room	800–2500
Clothes dryer (electric)	4000–5800
Clothes dryer (gas)`	500
Clothes washer	600–1000
Electric heat	250/baseboard foot
Fan, attic	400–500
Fan, ceiling	50
Fan, window	275
Freezer	500
Heater, portable	1000–1500
Motor, 1/4 hp	600
Motor, 1/2 hp	840
Motor, 1 hp	1140
Motor, 2 hp	2400
Motor, 3hp	3360
Refrigerator	300–600
Water heater	4500/element

Stripping Cable Sheathing 🔧

TOOLS
- Cable ripper

MATERIALS
- Cable

Attaching Wires 🔧

TOOLS
- Combination tool
- Needle-nose pliers
- Insulated screwdriver

MATERIALS
- Wire
- Switch or outlet

Capping Wires 🔧

TOOLS
- Needle-nose pliers
- Combination tool

MATERIALS
- Wire
- Wire connector

1 Slide the blade of the cable ripper onto the cable, and squeeze it 8 to 10 in. from the end. Squeeze the tool until the point penetrates through the plastic sheath covering the cable.

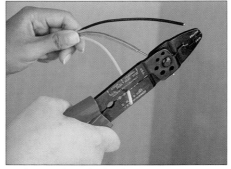

1 Insert the wire in the proper gauge slot of a combination tool, and clamp the jaws onto the wire. Strip ¾ in. of insulation from the end of each wire by pulling the tool away from the wire.

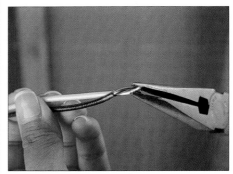

1 To join wires, strip ½ in. of insulation from the wires using a combination tool. Hold the wires parallel, and twist them together with pliers. Turn the pliers in a clockwise fashion.

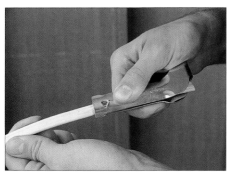

2 Grip the cable ripper in one hand and the cable in the other, and pull your hands apart so that the cable ripper moves toward the end of the cable, leaving a split in the plastic sheath.

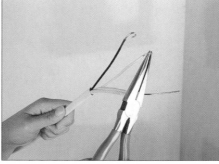

2 Use a pair of needle-nose pliers to form a tight clockwise half-loop at the exposed end of each wire. Avoid making nicks in the surface of the wire that could weaken it.

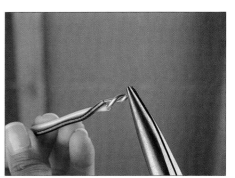

2 The twisted part should be long enough to engage the wire connector, and short enough to be covered completely by the wire connector when the wires are inserted into it.

3 Expose the wires by peeling back the plastic sheathing and paper wrapping. These can be cut off so that they don't get in the way. A cable ripper won't damage individual wires.

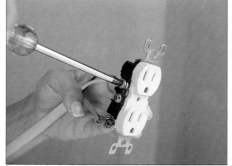

3 Hook each of the looped wire ends onto the correct screw terminal so that the wire goes around the screw in a clockwise direction. The wire loop will close as you tighten the screw.

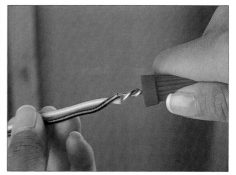

3 Screw the wire connector onto the wires until it feels tight and the exposed wires are covered completely. Use hand pressure only. Do not use pliers to tighten the connector.

Receptacles & Switches

A receptacle is a device into which you plug appliances and lamps. It's housed in a metal or plastic box attached to the framing. Behind a faceplate, the receptacle is held by two screws to the box. When these screws are removed, the receptacle may be pulled from the box.

Some receptacles are designed exclusively for use outside. Some are made to handle heavy-duty appliances such as air conditioners, dryers, and ranges, and have distinctive faces that won't accept ordinary two- or three-prong plugs. The most common receptacle is a duplex receptacle rated at 15 amps and 120 volts. Ground-fault circuit interrupter (GFCI) receptacles, code-required for outbuildings, have a safety device that compares the amount of current flowing in the black and white wires of the circuit and breaks the circuit if it detects as little as a 0.005-amp difference.

All receptacles must be properly grounded to prevent short circuits. Metal receptacle boxes require that a grounding wire is pigtailed to the grounding screws of the receptacle and to the box. With plastic boxes, the cable grounding wire attaches directly to the receptacle's grounding screw. Wiring configurations differ from receptacle to receptacle, however, and you should always follow local codes.

Installing Receptacle Boxes

Cable running to outlet boxes must be anchored to the framing within 12 inches of the box. Also, on a 120-volt circuit, you should have at least one junction box to accommodate the circuit wiring, as there will be a different number of wires going to and from the outlet boxes. A $4 \times 4 \times 2\frac{1}{8}$-inch box provides enough space for these additional wires.

Connect wires to terminals by looping the end around the terminal screw in the direction the screw tightens. The best way to loop the wire for terminal screws is with needle-nose pliers. Strip about $\frac{1}{2}$ to $\frac{3}{4}$ inch of insulation off the end of the wire, and bend the bare wire around the jaws of the pliers. Then hook the loop onto the terminals in the direction the screws turn down, and tighten the screws. As the terminals are tightened, the wire is forced under the screwheads and clamped.

To install a receptacle with the lower outlet always on but the upper outlet controlled by a switch, you must break off the metal link between the terminal screws. This system makes it possible to control table lamps from a wall switch, which is practical in a room that has no overhead fixture. Use a screwdriver to pry the link up; then break it off with pliers. Connect the incoming hot (black) wire and one switch wire to the lower outlet terminal. Connect the white wire and other switch wire to the upper outlet terminal.

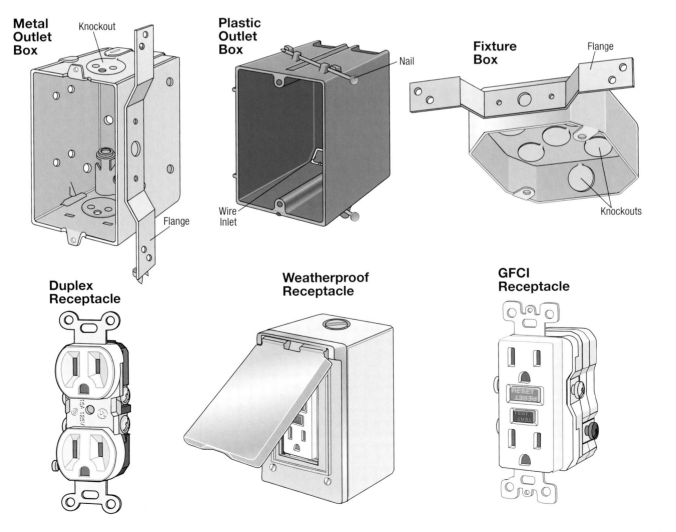

Metal Outlet Box — Knockout, Flange

Plastic Outlet Box — Nail, Wire Inlet

Fixture Box — Flange, Knockouts

Duplex Receptacle

Weatherproof Receptacle

GFCI Receptacle

Setting up Service

If you are wiring your barn for new electric service, you will surely have a service panel, the gray metal box that holds the circuit breakers. The service panel for a sizable structure takes the utility power coming into the barn, typically a 120/240-volt, 100-amp service delivered through three wires. The two hot service wires (usually black) each deliver 120 volts, and they attach to two corresponding terminals of the main disconnect. The 120-volt circuits deliver power to the individual barn circuits through a "hot bus," which is typically the chassis into which the breakers plug. Most common appliances run on 120 volts, but heavier machinery often requires a 240 supply.

Before working on or even checking an existing service, turn off the power with the main breaker switch mounted at the top of the service panel. With the power off, remove the cover plate and note the breaker arrangement. Each breaker in use is connected to a cable; a label on the cover should identify each. Check whether there are any breakers not in use or spare slots for additional breakers. If there are no spares but there are empty slots, generally there is room to add a new circuit. If all of the slots are in use, you may be able to add a double (twin) breaker, which puts two breakers in the space of one.

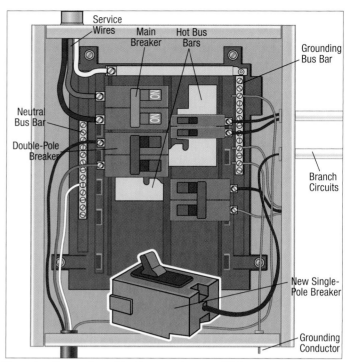

New circuits can be added to a service panel if there are spare breakers or empty slots along the bus bars. If there are no empty slots, new circuits should be added by a licensed electrician.

Adding a Circuit

To add a new circuit to your house's main service panel, first be sure the main breaker is turned off. Remove the panel's cover plate, and then use a screwdriver to pry out a perforated knockout from the side or top of the panel box. Attach a cable clamp and thread 12 inches of the cable through the connector, the hole in the box, and the locknut. Tighten the two screws against the cable, and tighten the locknut. Remove about 8 inches of the outer sleeve of the end of the cable, and strip the wire ends. Insert the ends of the white (neutral) wire and the bare ground wire into holes along

the bus bars intended for these wires at the side or bottom of the panel (note how the other circuits are connected), and tighten the setscrews.

If a spare breaker is not already in place, snap one into its slot on the panel board. Loosen the screw of the breaker, and insert the black wire of the cable into the hole below. Then retighten the screw to secure the wire end. Screw the cover back on the panel and record the new circuit on the panel door. To prevent a power surge, turn off all the individual breakers and then turn on the main breaker. Turn the individual breakers back on one by one.

The main breaker, mounted at the top of the panel, controls power entering the hot buses. Turn off the power by moving the double handle to the off position.

A new breaker can be added to a spare slot in the panel. If there are no spare slots, you'll need to have a licensed electrician add a subpanel.

A circuit's hot wire is secured beneath a circuit-breaker screw. You insert the bare wire end in the terminal hole and tighten down the screw.

Basic Wiring Plans

The diagram on this page indicates the elements of a basic wiring plan for a typical barn (top) and shows how those basic individual elements are wired into the cables (bottom). In this plan, three separate circuits are run from the main service panel: a series of GFCI-protected power receptacles (illustrated in green); two overhead lights that are controlled by two switches (in red); and an exterior weatherproof receptacle with a switch-controlled floodlight (in blue).

Local building codes will dictate how many receptacles or fixtures can be put on each 20-amp circuit, as well as what variety and gauge of wire you must run. The illustration below shows how each item is wired in these three circuits. The black and white lines represent the black (hot) and white (neutral) wires in the cable; the green lines represent the grounding wires, which are usually bare copper but sometimes have a green covering.

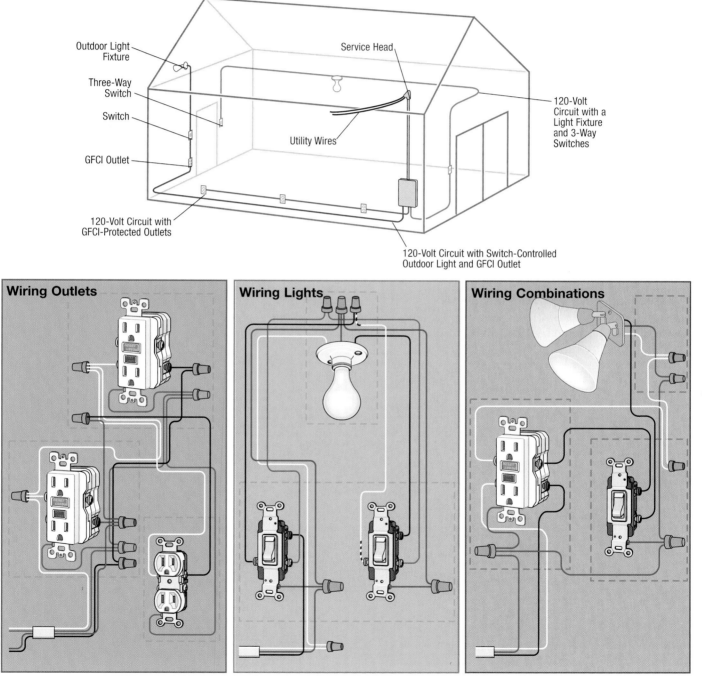

Wiring Outlets

Wiring Lights

Wiring Combinations

For a circuit that needs more than one receptacle protected by GFCIs, wire as shown. This requires two- and three-wire cables.

These two switches can be installed at opposite ends of a room so that whichever way you enter, you can turn on a light.

A switch need only be wired to the positive or "hot" wire of a circuit to be effective. Cutting the power loop here turns off the light.

Roughing-In Cable

If you're running cable from your house's service panel to an outbuilding, you can do it either aboveground or underground. Aboveground is less work, but it's unsightly, and there's always the danger that wires will be blown down by the wind, pulled down by ice, or knocked down by a big delivery truck. Running cable underground means digging a trench, generally 18 to 24 inches deep, from your house to the outbuilding.

Wiring in unfinished outbuildings should be considered outdoor wiring, which must be installed with special weatherproof switches, outlets, and light fixtures. Generally, local codes require that wiring inside an unfinished building be NM cable protected by rigid nonmetallic conduit or special NMC (corrosion-resistant) cable whenever it is installed aboveground. If you'll be finishing the interior of your outbuilding, you should run the cable through the framing without conduit. Most codes allow buried cable to be Type UF (underground feeder); some require that Type TW (thermoplastic—wet) wire and conduit be used. Always check and observe your local codes when planning an outdoor wiring project.

Preparing the Framing

If local codes permit, consider running the new wiring in the framing yourself and letting a professional electrician make the hookups at the power source. Also, pay the pro to check your work so that you will be assured that it is safe and up to code.

You'll need a power drill or hand brace and a ⅝- or ¾-inch bit to make holes through studs. The edge of the hole should be no less than 1¼ inches from the facing edge of the stud. If you can't leave 1¼ inches of space between the hole and the edge of the framing member, put a steel plate on the framing member for the necessary protection.

Electricians don't measure and mark each cable hole but create an unobstructed path through framing. Holes are centered to stay clear of nails driven through drywall or paneling.

Steel plates are used to protect wires that run through holes drilled through studs. They prevent you from drilling, nailing, or screwing into the wire, causing damage to the wire and potential electrical shock.

Nailing plates, which are available at electrical supply stores, work as a shield to prevent punctures from surface nails driven through drywall and paneling.

Installing the Cable

Once new framing is ready to be wired and electrical boxes have been put in place, carefully begin pulling the cable through the framing. When you insert a cable end into an electrical box, leave about 8 inches of extra cable. Using a wire staple, secure the cable at a maximum of 8 inches above the box. After all of the cables have been run through the framing and into their respective electrical boxes, rip back and remove the sheathing from the cable ends in each box, and then strip the ends of the wires. Before a typical rough-in inspection is made, you must also splice together the grounding wires, using either green wire connectors or wire crimping ferrules. Be sure to include a bare copper wire pigtail that will be connected to the green grounding screw of a device, and neatly push all the wires back into the box for protection.

Installing Switches & Receptacles

After a rough-in inspection is performed, the receptacles and switches may be installed. However, it is best to wait until the wallboard is in place before doing this work. When the walls are completed and all of the boxes wired, install cover plates and turn on the power. Be certain to check each receptacle using a plug-in receptacle analyzer to verify that all of the wiring has been properly done. Install the light fixtures, and then confirm that they are all in working order. Once you have completed this work, the job will be ready for final inspection.

Running Cable in New Construction

TOOLS & MATERIALS

- Basic carpentry tools
- Chalk-line box
- Circular saw
- Handsaw or reciprocating saw

- Sheathing material
- 6d or 8d common nails

1 Use a measuring tape and a pencil to measure and mark the height where utility boxes will be situated; generally this is 12 in. off the floor for receptacles and 44 in. for switches.

2 Nail utility boxes in place on the stud. Set the box out from the stud to account for the thickness of the drywall. Be sure that the boxes will be flush with the finished wall surface.

3 Using a power drill with a spade bit, drill holes through wall studs at the same height to run the electrical cable through. Drill in the center of the stud to avoid compromising its strength.

4 For vertical runs, attach the cable to the side of the stud using staples designed for use with the cable. These staples are attached by hammering them into the stud, over the cable.

5 Where the cable passes into a device box, use a clamp connector. This not only protects the cable from chafing, it clamps it in place so that it can't be easily pulled out.

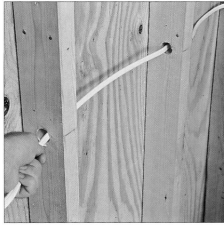

6 To run the cable horizontally, fish it through the studs, one at a time, using the holes you have drilled with a spade bit. Avoid kinking the cable or tearing the insulation.

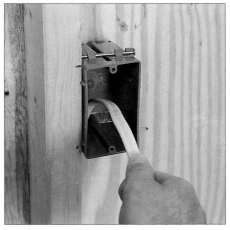

7 Pull the cable up into the device boxes you have mounted. Be sure to pull an ample amount through, as the cable access ports on device boxes act as traps, making it hard to retract.

8 After connecting the proper wires to the proper terminals, mount switches or receptacles securely to the device box. A tight physical connection is essential for safety.

Installing Outdoor Cable

Underground feeder and branch-circuit cable, known as UF cable, is designated for outdoor wiring because it is weatherproof and suitable for direct burial. UF cable looks somewhat like ordinary NM cable, so be sure that the UF designation is clearly written on the sheathing. The wires are molded into plastic rather than wrapped in paper and then sheathed in plastic as NM cable wires are. Aboveground UF cable must be protected with conduit where subject to injury.

Direct-burial cable must be buried deeply enough to be protected from routine digging. The NEC specifies minimum depth requirements for underground cable: 24 inches for direct-burial cable; 18 inches for rigid nonmetallic conduit; and 6 inches for rigid and intermediate metal conduit.

If your cable is protected by a GFCI, you may be permitted to trench less deeply, but this is not recommended—you might someday plant a tree or shrub over the cable and risk cutting it while digging. Though the ground-fault circuit interupter will prevent shocks, it's not going to save you the time needed to dig up and replace the line.

Any special characteristics of newer types of cable insulation will be identified on the sheathing, such as sunlight and corrosion resistance. Note that the plastic sheathing on UF cable encases the insulated conductors inside it, making the individual wires somewhat difficult to strip.

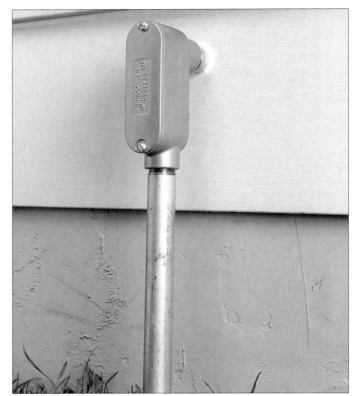

Outdoor cable run underground must be protected in rigid conduit where it enters or emerges from the trench.

Outdoor Electrical Boxes

There are two main types of outdoor boxes, raintight and watertight. Raintight boxes typically have spring-loaded, self-closing covers, but they are not waterproof. This type of box has a gasket seal and is rated for wet locations as long as the cover is kept closed. It is best to mount a raintight box where it is not subject to water accumulation or flooding. Watertight boxes, on the other hand, are sealed with a waterproof gasket and can withstand a soaking rain or saturation. These boxes are rated for wet locations.

Conduit, Connectors & Fittings

Outdoor wiring is typically protected by rigid conduit—both aboveground and wherever it enters or emerges from underground trenching. Rigid and intermediate metallic conduit (IMC) are most commonly used, but many local codes permit the use of rigid nonmetallic conduit, which is made of polyvinyl chloride (PVC). Regardless of which type of rigid conduit you are permitted to use, you will have to make a variety of connections. These are available for metal and nonmetallic conduit, including bushings for straight pieces and elbow connections, locknuts, offsets, and various couplings. Be sure that the connectors you select match the material and category of conduit you are using.

At the point where cable runs through the exterior wall of your home, you will need a special L-shaped connector called an LB conduit body. An LB encloses the joint between your indoor cable and the outdoor UF cable (UF cable is also permitted for indoor use) that runs down the side of your house

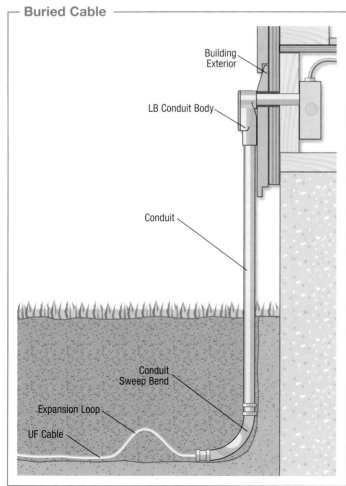

Buried Cable

Building Exterior

LB Conduit Body

Conduit

Conduit Sweep Bend

Expansion Loop

UF Cable

Running Cable Underground

TOOLS & MATERIALS

- Insulated screwdrivers • Measuring tape
- Needle-nose pliers • Caulking gun
- Sledgehammer • Electrician's hammer
- Power drill-driver with spade or masonry bit
- Star drill • Knockout punch

- 12-3 or 12-2 with ground NM cable
- Mounting bracket
- Rigid conduit • Masonry anchors
- Cable clamps • Cable staples
- Junction box • LB fitting
- Conduit sweep bend • Conduit nipple
- Pipe straps

1 Make a mark for the access hole at least 3 in. from any structural framing. Using a spade or masonry bit, drill an access hole through the exterior wall or header joist.

2 Mount the junction box over the access opening with screws, and run the branch-circuit cable from the breaker box through the hole on the side of the box.

3 Use a short length of conduit, called a conduit nipple, and make a connection between the LB fitting and junction box. Turn the long end of the LB fitting down toward the ground.

4 Begin a trench through which the cable can travel. Connect a length of conduit from the LB fitting into the cable trench. Fasten it to the wall just above the point that makes contact with the ground.

5 A conduit sweep bend is attached below the first length of conduit. It safeguards the cable as it goes underground. A bushing at the end prevents the cable from chafing.

6 Stake out a trench, running from the LB fitting to wherever your outdoor box or fixture will be located. Carefully set aside the sod as you dig the trench so that you can replace it when you're done.

7 Feed exterior UF cable up the sweep bend, through the conduit and LB fitting, to the junction box inside. If you need to run conduit through the entire trench, you can do it now.

8 Splice the NM cable and exterior UF cable inside the interior junction box, or you can continue the run of cable because UF cable can be used indoors as well.

and into an underground trench. LB conduit bodies are fitted with a gasket that seals the cable connection against the weather.

Another type of fitting that you may find useful is a box extension which is used to increase the volume of an existing outdoor receptacle or junction box when you need to tap into it to bring power where it is required. This is often done to avoid extensive rewiring and renovation work.

Outdoor Receptacles

Weatherproof receptacle boxes must be used when installing outdoor receptacles. They are made of a variety of materials, both metal and plastic. Check your local code for any variations in these basic rules.

An outdoor receptacle box must be completely weatherproof, regardless of whether it will be mounted on a wall, post, or length of rigid metal conduit. Attach special brackets, called mounting ears, to the back of the receptacle box if it will be attached to a wooden post; then screw the box securely in place. For a conduit mounting, first anchor a conduit sweep bend and a vertical section of rigid conduit at the end of your underground cable trench. Next, using a compression fitting, mount the receptacle box on top of the vertical section of conduit. Be sure the box is between 12 and 18 inches above the ground.

Attach a plastic bushing to the end of the conduit sweep; then fish the UF cable from the trench up through the pipe to the receptacle box. Pull the cable into the box; then secure it in place. Split and pull back about 10 inches of the cable sheathing to expose the inside wires. Cut away the peeled-back sheathing; then strip the wires using a multipurpose tool. Wire the GFCI-protected receptacle as you would anywhere else, connecting the wires to their proper terminals. Place the foam gasket over the box, and screw the waterproof box cover over the gasket to complete the installation.

Installing an Outdoor Receptacle

TOOLS & MATERIALS

- Measuring tape
- Power drill-driver
- Fish tape
- Combination tool
- Screwdriver
- Neon tester

- Weatherproof box
- Galvanized screws
- Cable
- Staples

1 Use a fish tape to run the cable from inside the house to the spot where you plan your outdoor receptacle to be. This usually means drilling a hole through the stringer joist, sheathing, and siding.

2 Knock out the metal or plastic blocking the hole in the back of the box so that you can run the cable through it. Secure the cable, and screw the box to the outside of the building.

3 Screw the white wire to the silver screw and the black wire to the brass screw on either side of the receptacle. Standard receptacles should be connected to a GFCI-protected circuit.

4 A typical cover plate will only protect a receptacle from dust and nuisance contact. To seal the receptacle against weather, use a UL-listed weatherproof box.

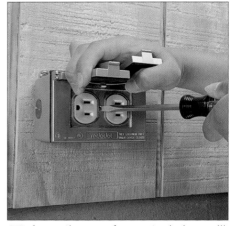

5 A weatherproof receptacle box will need a gasket between the box and the cover plate. The spring-loaded cover will close tightly enough to keep out the weather.

Outside Lights

For outdoor lighting, either type R (reflector) or type PAR (parabolic aluminized reflector) lamps are suitable. These long-lasting lamps have a reflective interior surface that maintains a bright light and resists weathering. Although PAR lamps are not affected by inclement weather, not all type R lamps are acceptable for outdoor use; check the package labeling. To mount lamps of this kind, you must install weatherproof lamp sockets. Outdoor sockets for single-, double-, and triple-lamp installations are available. Some mounts can also accommodate a motion-sensor control switch.

You can also install 120-volt or low-voltage (12-volt) exterior accent lighting. Mount a light fixture on a post to provide general lighting or on a ground spike pointing upward to show off a beautiful part of your landscape. If you choose low-voltage lighting, then you will also need to install a voltage transformer on the exterior wall.

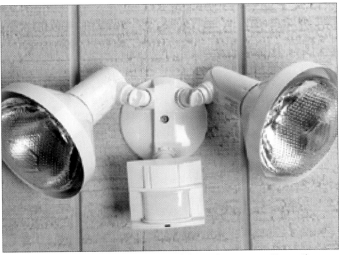

Exterior lights can be fitted with 24-hour timers or with motion sensors that turn on the lights automatically whenever someone comes within the range of the sensor.

Installing a Floodlight

TOOLS & MATERIALS

- Screwdriver
- Power drill-driver with screwdriver bit
- Caulking gun

- Floodlight
- Weatherproof fixture box
- Wire connectors
- Cable
- Staples
- Screws
- Caulk

1 To bring power to your new floodlight, break one of the knockout tabs out of an opening in an existing ceiling electrical box. Be sure the power to the circuit has been turned off.

2 Extend power from this box to the switch box that will house the switch you will be using to control the floodlight. Then run cable from the switch box to the fixture.

3 Most fixtures have two lamp holders that swivel to cover a large area. Many also have motion sensors and timer switches that provide security and make it easier to find your keys at night.

4 Connect wire leads from the lamps to the power leads (and ground) in the box with wire connectors. Caulk the top of the box to keep water from collecting and rotting the siding.

5 Mount the box cover, and adjust the lights to suit. The beams can be pointed in almost any direction. Use bulbs rated for outdoor use, even under a roof overhang.

7 WIRING & PLUMBING

Installing Outdoor Cable **141**

Basic Utility Plumbing Plan

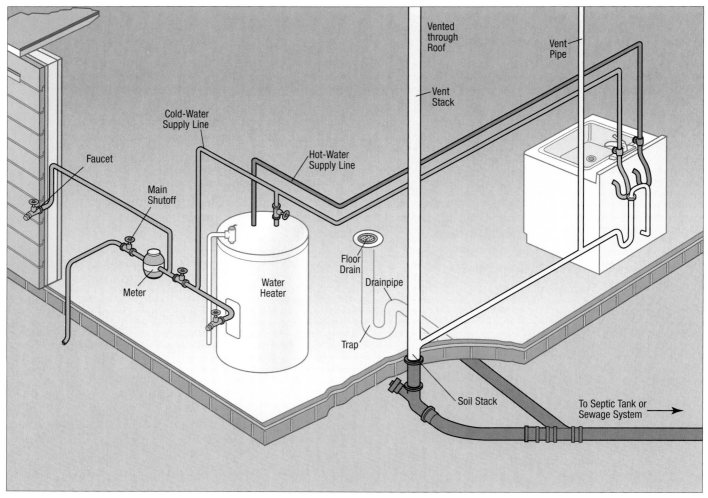

Vented through Roof

Vent Pipe

Vent Stack

Cold-Water Supply Line

Hot-Water Supply Line

Faucet

Main Shutoff

Floor Drain

Drainpipe

Meter

Water Heater

Trap

Soil Stack

To Septic Tank or Sewage System →

The supply and drainage system for any structure is a system that works together to supply fresh water and get rid of waste. Vent Pipes allow air in at the appropriate junctures to allow for proper drainage.

Plumbing Basics

A modern plumbing system has two basic parts: water pipes that supply water, and a system that carries wastewater out (the DWV, or drain-waste-vent, system). Country houses draw water from underground wells, but most houses today are supplied by municipal water pipes. A water meter keeps track of how much is used.

Inside the structure, the main supply line splits, with one branch feeding all the cold-water pipes and the other supplying water to the water heater. The hot-water line coming out of the water heater branches, paralleling cold-water lines throughout the structure. Many barns need only a utility sink, a few outdoor hose-bibcock faucets, and perhaps a floor drain.

Drains & Vents

One part of the DWV system channels water to the main drain. The other part consists of pipes (called vents) that rise up out of the drainpipes to the roof. Vents allow in outside air to replace the air displaced by flowing water. Without them, the negative pressure would suck the water out of the traps. The trap's main purpose is to prevent noxious and poten-

tially lethal sewer gases from rising up through the drains. Because of their shape, traps always have water in them, which provides an airtight seal. The traps are always near a drain opening, although some may be hidden below the floor (such as those on floor drains) or out of sight in the basement.

Each drain must be vented. Vent pipes are usually located near the drain opening after the trap; sometimes multiple drains are served by one vent, a system called wet venting. Vents connect to a drainpipe and run either directly to the roof or horizontally to another vent. Without them, wastewater flowing down the drain would empty the trap due to siphoning action. Instead, vents allow outside air to flow into the pipe, breaking the siphon action.

Plumbing an Outbuilding

The most basic plumbing setup consists of cold-water supply pipes (from your house's municipal or well system) providing water at faucets and utility sinks, and drainpipes bringing waste to the sewer system or septic tank. Pipes from your house will need to be buried underground below the local frost line so that they don't freeze and burst—it may be 4 or even 5 feet in some Northern locations. Because

Typical Septic System Plan

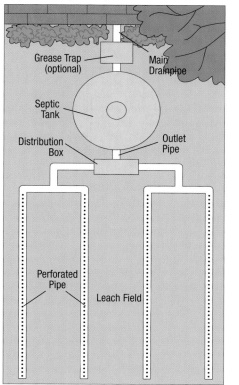

Grease Trap (optional)

Main Drainpipe

Septic Tank

Distribution Box

Outlet Pipe

Perforated Pipe

Leach Field

Typical Gray Water System

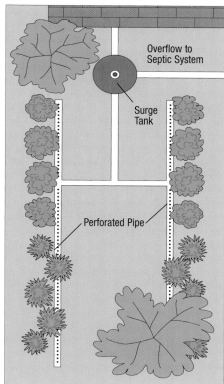

Overflow to Septic System

Surge Tank

Perforated Pipe

of this digging, you should have a plumbing plan drawn up before you start construction on the foundation.

If you want to have hot water, you'll need to install a separate water heater in the barn—preferably, close to its main point of use.

Septic Systems

Water that leaves your house must be separated from solid wastes and treated before it can be returned to the environment. Buildings that don't have septic tanks feed into enormous waste-treatment plants, some of which handle millions of gallons of sewage a day. The plumbing in most barns, however, will be connected to septic systems.

A septic system has three main sections: the septic tank, the distribution box, and the leach field (also called the drainfield). As sewage enters the tank, it is poured into a mix of waste and anaerobic bacteria. Most of the solids are quickly broken down, and the liquid effluent leaves the tank and enters the distribution box, from which it flows into the leach field's perforated pipes and drains into the ground. What remains behind in the tank are solids, which sink to the bottom, and grease, which rises to the top. If not cleaned out, eventually new solids in the tank won't have enough room to settle properly and can infiltrate the leach field, clogging its pipes. The grease layer, if left to accumulate, can flow past the tank's outlet baffle and out into the leach field, where it limits absorption. If the sludge or grease gets this far, the entire leach field may have to be replaced.

To keep this from happening, you should have a septic tank professionally pumped out periodically. How often depends on the tank capacity and how many people use the system.

Typically two people using a 1,000-gallon tank only need to pump it out every six years or so, but six people using a 2,000-gallon tank should have it pumped out every three years.

In some regions, you can install a graywater system. This allows you to channel water from dishwashers, clothes washers, and other non-septic systems into the yard.

Making a Plan

The most compelling reason to bring water to a barn is livestock. After all, you're not going to want to haul dozens of gallons of water from a spigot on your house to your barn or trip over a hundred feet of hose all summer (and have it freeze solid in the winter).

Some livestock operations, such as dairying, have very specific plumbing code requirements (particularly for manure removal in confinement buildings), and will need hot water to clean equipment. For other buildings, such as a workshop or potting shed, you need to weigh the convenience of water versus the expense. Your plumbing layout should be as efficient as possible, with the shortest possible pipe runs and a minimum of fixtures. Of course, one of the main expenses will probably be the digging of the trench for the supply lines and the cost of having a professional make the hookups to your supply and waste systems.

With this expense in mind, note that ripping apart your foundation and walls in order to retrofit a barn with a toilet and shower to convert it to living space isn't going to be cheap, either. If you suspect you may want to convert part of your barn into living space at a later date, you can rough-in the plumbing into the foundation and beneath the finished floor and walls and leave the installation for another time.

In any case, once the basic plan has been prepared (along with a list of parts and materials), get a copy of your local plumbing code from the office of the municipal plumbing inspector. You will find important information regarding such things as the required size and type of supply and DWV pipes, the slope required for horizontally positioned soil and waste pipes, allowable venting methods, and the placement of soil- and waste-pipe cleanout plugs.

After deciding where new fixtures and appliances are to go, make a drawing to show how you're going to get new water distribution and soil/waste pipes from here to there. Sketch in obstacles that are in the path. Do the roughing-in procedure to pinpoint the exact spots where water and soil/waste pipes will come into the room to align with the new fixture or appliance. The drawing should be a precise layout, or you'll pay a price later in lost time and money.

Working with Pipe

Water supply lines usually range from ½- or ¾-in. diameter (common in houses) up to 1-in. piping for main supply lines. The pipe walls have to be reasonably thick because the water these pipes carry is under pressure. Structures built before the 1960s may have galvanized steel water pipes, while newer buildings have copper or plastic pipes. Local codes regulate what kinds of supply lines you can use.

Waste pipes, usually at least 1½ inches in diameter, carry wastewater from sinks, showers, and appliances. Soil pipes, which handle solid wastes from toilets and serve as the main drain, are 3 or 4 inches in diameter. Most drain lines lead to the building's main drain, called the soil stack. Soil pipes and their vents are made from cast iron or plastic. Waste drain lines and vents are usually iron or plastic. Vent pipes tend to be slightly smaller than the drains to which they connect.

Plastic Pipe

Lightweight plastic pipe ranges in diameter from 1½ to 6 inches. Plastic waste pipes are made of ABS (black) or PVC (white) plastic. Check with the local plumbing inspector to find out which type is acceptable for your project. Most plastic DWV lines are installed with just a few simple tools. You join them with solvent cement. Be sure to match the solvent cement to the type of plastic used in the pipe. You can even join a new section of plastic pipe to an existing cast-iron waste line with compression clamp fittings consisting of flexible gaskets and metal band clamps.

Measure the lengths required, allowing for the fittings. Unless you are cutting pipe already in place, put the lengths you're planning to cut in a miter box. Cut the pipe with a backsaw or hacksaw. Use a utility knife or emery cloth to remove burrs so that it will slide smoothly into the fitting. After cutting the pipes, test-fit the parts. Use PVC

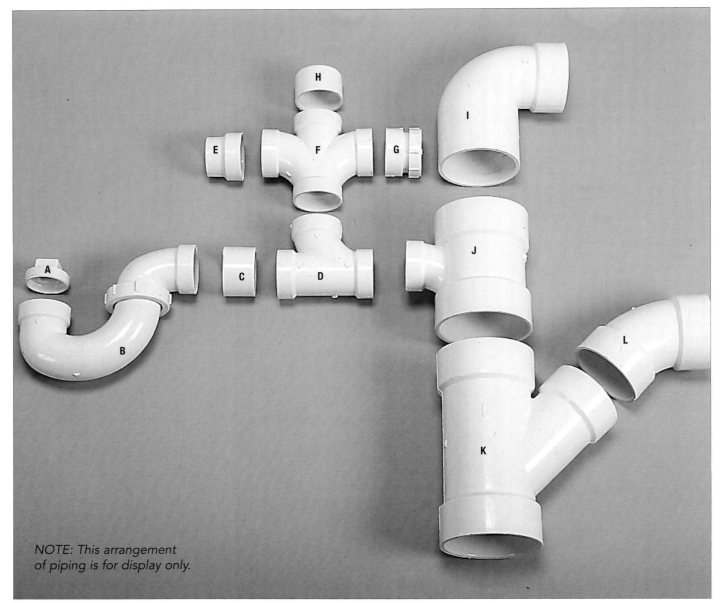

NOTE: This arrangement of piping is for display only.

PVC DWV fittings include: (A) cleanout plug, (B) P-trap, (C) coupling, (D) vent T-fitting, (E) reducer, (F) cross, (G) ground-joint adapter, (H) cap, (I) 90-deg. elbow, (J) sanitary reducing T-fitting, (K) sanitary Y-fitting, (L) 45-deg. elbow

primer to clean the ends of PVC pipe and fittings. Coat the ends of each pipe and the inside of the fittings with the solvent cement. Then insert the pipe into the fitting, and twist the two parts against each other about one-quarter turn. Hold the pieces together for about ten seconds. If you fit the joint properly, the solvent cement will form a continuous bead around the joint. Wipe off any excess cement around the pipe and fitting with a cloth.

Copper Pipe

Copper tubing is often available in 20-foot-long lengths of rigid tubing or coils of flexible tubing. The advantage of flexible tubing is that you can bend it to snake through curves in existing walls and floors without making joints. The downside is that curves have to be gentle and without kinks. Making the bends requires a little practice. By contrast, each turn in rigid tubing requires a joint with a

soldered or threaded coupling, which can be hard to make in tight spots.

Copper tubing is available in several different grades. Rigid tubing is sold in three grades: K (the thickest-walled), L, and M (the thinnest). Type K is most often found in underground lines. Type L is required by code for most commercial systems; type M, somewhat easier to work with, is usually acceptable for homes.

Flexible tubing comes in two grades: K and L. Another grade, DWV, generally has been replaced by plastic pipe, for the most part. Always consult with the local building inspector to find out which types they accept before planning any additions to your plumbing system.

In any system you may also want to include special fittings, such as an anti-hammer device to prevent pipe noise, and a freeze-proof exterior spigot. These have an exterior handle but turn off the water supply inside.

Connecting Plastic Pipe

TOOLS & MATERIALS

- Fine-toothed saw or tubing cutter
- Utility knife
- Felt pen (for marking)

- Rigid plastic pipe & fittings
- Solvent glue
- Pipe primer

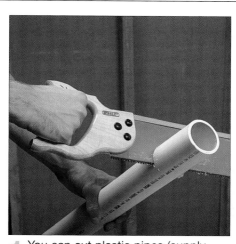

1 You can cut plastic pipes (supply lines, drains, and vents) with almost any saw, but a fine-toothed blade makes a cleaner cut. For cuts close to a wall you can use a flexible wire saw.

2 When you cut through plastic, even a fine-toothed saw can leave burrs and small shavings. Trim them off with a utility knife inside and out. A medium grit sandpaper also works well.

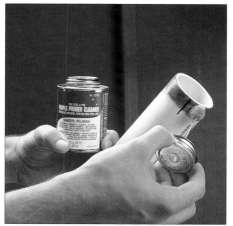

3 You can use one coat of adhesive in many cases, but it's best to start with a primer that cleans the surface for better adhesion. Use the primer and adhesive in a well ventilated area.

4 Apply liquid cement for plastic pipe to mating surfaces. Be sure to read and follow all label cautions. Avoid contact between your hands and the cement. It can cause serious skin irritation.

5 Plastic pipe cement softens mating surfaces. They become one when the surfaces harden. You need to work quickly. Always make a one-quarter turn when you mate pipe fittings.

Cutting Copper Pipe

Use a wheel-type cutter to cut copper pipe. It is possible to make cuts with a hacksaw, but it can be difficult on existing pipes where there isn't much room. Fit the cutter around the pipe, and tighten the handle. After you rotate the cutter around the pipe once or twice, you'll feel less resistance as the wheel deepens its cutting groove. Tighten the handle again to make the wheel bite in. Continue rotating and tightening until the wheel cuts all the way through. With some practice, you'll get the knack of tightening the handle gradually while you're rotating the cutter. If the wheel is biting in too deeply, you should back off on the handle a bit.

Sometimes even a relatively clean cut needs smoothing around the inner edges. This additional step will improve water flow and prevent buildup of mineral deposits on the pipe's inner wall. There are reaming tools for cleaning up burrs; many wheel cutters have fold-out reamers. You can also use a small piece of carbide sandpaper or a round metal file.

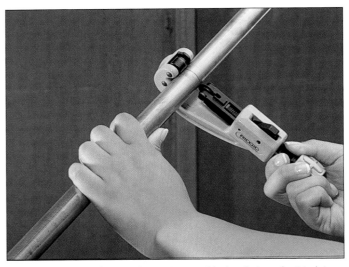

A pipe cutter can be used to cut many kinds of pipe. Just twist the tool around the pipe, tightening the blade.

Connecting Copper Pipe

TOOLS & MATERIALS

- Hacksaw or tubing cutter
- Propane torch
- Spark lighter
- Wire brush or sandpaper
- Flux brush
- Work gloves
- Safety goggles or glasses
- Rags

- Copper pipe and fittings
- Solder
- Flux

1 Plumbers use a small tool with metal wires inside to brighten copper for the best solder bond. Use sandpaper or a regular wire brush in a pinch. The surface of the copper should appear bright.

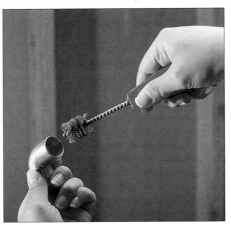

2 To brighten the interior surfaces of a connection, use a wire brush that looks similar to a bootle brush. Rotate it several times inside the fitting to remove any tarnish.

3 To draw solder completely into the joint (even uphill against gravity), coat mating surfaces with soldering paste, called flux. Use a brush to apply flux to the mating surfaces.

4 Assemble the connection, and apply heat evenly to the entire fitting. Wear gloves and use clamps to handle heated pipes. Test the heat by touching the solder to the pipe opposite from the flame.

5 When the copper is hot enough to melt solder, remove the flame and move the solder around the joint until it's filled. Also be careful of molten solder drips.

Roughing-In Plumbing

To extend the existing copper-pipe water system to a new plumbing fixture, turn off the water supply and drain the system. If you are tapping into the existing pipe at an elbow, rather than cutting the pipe, use a propane torch to heat the elbow until solder melts. Then free the pipe from the elbow. Discard the elbow. (Wear thick gloves and use adjustable pliers to avoid burning your hands. Also be sure to protect building materials from the torch frame.) After the pipe cools, use an abrasive, such as sandpaper or steel wool, to clean residue from the ends of the pipe.

Solder a copper T-fitting between the two ends of the original copper pipe, and use the open end of the T-fitting as the supply source for your line. You can add adapters to copper and other types of pipe to continue the run in plastic where codes allow.

Supporting Pipes

To prevent sagging, water pipes should be supported with hangers at the time they are installed, generally against floor joists, at minimum 32-inch intervals. If copper pipe is used to bring water to a new plumbing fixture or plumbing appliance, be sure the hangers are of the same metal to avoid a galvanic reaction.

DWV pipes also need to be supported. You can use riser clamps to support vertical runs of DWV pipe. Supported horizontal runs of DWV pipe are at intervals of at least 3 feet. Don't forget to provide support at the fittings as well. This can be done by bracing the pipe with cinder block, brick, or strap hangers nailed to the foundation wall. If a DWV pipe runs overhead, parallel with the joists, it can be braced with wooden supports nailed between the joists. Provide some free play to allow for expansion so that the pipes will not bind as they expand, causing them to make noise.

To give water pipes maximum support, bore holes in joists and studs. Holes in joists should stay at least 2 inches from the edges of the joist. Never cut a hole larger than one-third or a notch deeper than one-sixth the depth of the joist. Any notches on the edge of a joist should be no longer than one-third of the depth of the joist and should never be put in the middle one-third of a joist. This is where the force is greatest on the joist. Similar considerations should be taken when cutting through studs in bearing walls.

Typical Rough Plumbing Layout

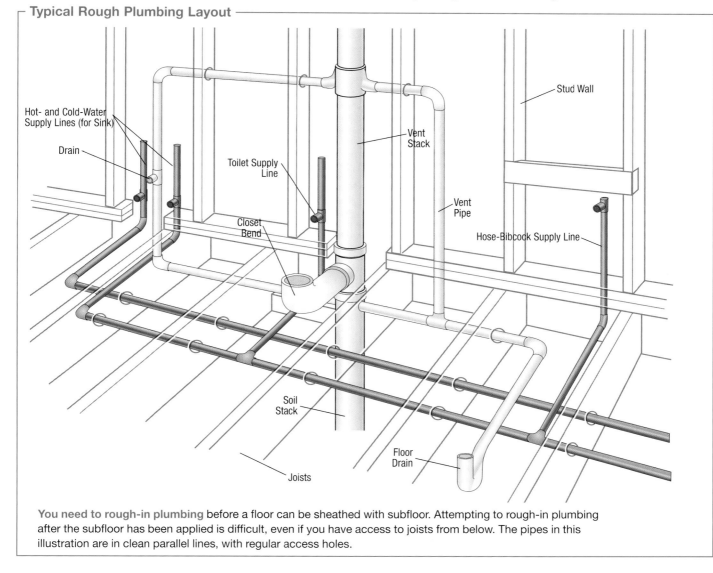

- Hot- and Cold-Water Supply Lines (for Sink)
- Drain
- Toilet Supply Line
- Closet Bend
- Vent Stack
- Vent Pipe
- Stud Wall
- Hose-Bibcock Supply Line
- Soil Stack
- Floor Drain
- Joists

You need to rough-in plumbing before a floor can be sheathed with subfloor. Attempting to rough-in plumbing after the subfloor has been applied is difficult, even if you have access to joists from below. The pipes in this illustration are in clean parallel lines, with regular access holes.

Sinks & Toilets

According to most regional codes, sinks and lavatories must have a device to retain water in the basin and to trap matter floating in the water so that it can't flow into the waste pipe and cause a clog. Most lavatories have pop-up stoppers that are controlled by liftrods. Older lavatories and utility sinks use plain rubber or metal stoppers that you insert into and remove from drain inlets by hand. The drain inlets of these lavatories and sinks are outfitted with cross bars that will trap much of the debris floating in the water so that it can't run into the waste pipe.

Drain Inlets

The drain inlets of a kitchen sink and that of a sink in a utility room must be at least 1½ inches in diameter. The drain inlets of bath sinks are at least 1¼ inches in diameter. Although not required by most regional codes, bath sinks may also have one or more openings called an overflow. The overflow is located approximately three-quarters of the way up on one wall of the basin. It allows water to drain so that it doesn't overflow, flooding the countertop or floor.

Supply & Drain Lines to Sinks

Running supply and drain lines from your roughed-in plumbing to sinks is relatively easy, because these parts often come in a kit that you assemble. Someone else has engineered the pipe assembly for you and made sure that all the pipes and fittings are the same size and that all the bolts, nuts, and washers are in place.

The drains are typically PVC, arranged to form a water-filled P-trap that keeps foul gases from reaching the living area. The trap is attached to the sink drain, often by screwing a collar-type fixture onto the drain of the sink. Below the sink drain, the trap joins the pipes that take the wastewater to the septic system.

Installing a Sink

TOOLS & MATERIALS

- Adjustable wrench
- Groove-joint pliers

- Sink
- Faucet kit
- Drain kit
- Plumber's putty

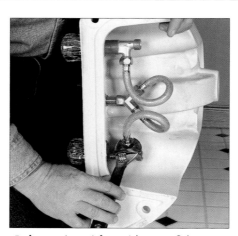

1 A counterset faucet has an 8-in. spread between valves. Join the control valves to the spout with flexible tubing. Some faucets mount differently. This one is probably the most difficult.

2 Coat the drain flange with plumber's putty. Tighten the nut on the drain tube from below, and attach the pop-up lever to the lift rod. This controls the drain mechanism.

3 The trap for a pedestal lavatory is hard to reach later, so attach it to the basin drain before setting the basin. You probably won't use a chrome trap in your barn. A PVC one is more appropriate.

4 Set the basin on the pedestal, and join the faucet to the valves with supply tubes. Tighten the compression nuts to make a solid connection between the water supply and the faucet.

5 To connect the trap, slide a compression washer and nut onto the trap arm. Insert the arm into the drain, and tighten. Open the supply valves under the sink, and try the faucet.

The supply line is usually not plastic (CPVC), but copper or flexible stainless-steel-mesh tubing. Here too, the fittings and tubing lengths will be part of an integral kit that links to your faucet. The only real challenge here is linking the kit fittings to your hot- and cold-water rough-ins.

Supply & Drain Lines to Toilets

Running supply lines to toilets is as easy as running supply lines to sinks. Drain lines to toilets are not, as with sinks, sold as kits. Indeed, they take some real skill and know-how to install. Call in a plumber on this one (or consult a more detailed specialty textbook) if you are doing this for the first time. Here a mistake can be a terrible mess to clean up.

The toilet drain is nothing more than a pipe with a flange on top. The pipe optimally drops straight down from the toilet. This flange is called a closet flange. The lip of the flange screws in place to the subfloor of the bathroom. Be sure to make elevation accommodations for tile or other finished flooring. If you screw a closet flange to the subfloor and then improperly finish the floor with tile or wood, the finished flooring may lift the toilet away from the flange and prevent a proper seal.

Once the closet flange and drain line are in place, they dictate the placement of the toilet because the two bolts that hold the toilet in place are attached to the closet flange. The distance to the wall from the back of the toilet is crucial (the tank must fit snugly), so it is imperative that you situate the closet flange properly. Too far from the wall, and you have a gap between the tank and the wall; too close to the wall, and your tank won't fit. Position your flange carefully in accordance with your toilet's requirements.

Once the closet flange is in place and you are ready to set the toilet, a wax seal is typically placed between the closet flange and the toilet. When cinched tight, the bolts that hold the toilet in place will pull the toilet up snug against this seal to keep leaks from forming at the toilet's base.

Installing a Toilet

TOOLS & MATERIALS

- Adjustable wrench
- Groove-joint pliers

- Toilet
- Water supply tube
- Wax gasket
- Closet bolts
- Pipe joint compound

1 Insert the heads of closet bolts into the grooves in the flange so that the threads of the bolts stick up out of it. If the bolts have plastic washers, use them to hold the bolts in place.

2 Install the new gasket on the flange, and stick it in place between the bolts. If you prefer, you can insert the gasket into the drain hole on the underside of the bowl.

3 Using the closet bolts as guides, set the bowl onto the flange gasket. Site through the China bolt holes. Tighten the nuts onto the threaded ends of the closet bolts.

4 Prepare the tank by inserting the tank bolts through the tank and securing them with nuts and washers, if provided. Do not overtighten the nuts. The porcelain may break.

5 Carefully set the tank into position on the back of the bowl, and tighten the tank bolts. Level the tank by loosening and tightening the nuts, but don't overtighten them.

CHAPTER 8

Finishing

Finishing your barn can be as easy as nailing up rough pine boards around doorjambs and windows or as difficult as mitering trim around openings and installing precisely cut corner boards. If you plan to use the barn space as living space—as when you build a studio or loft over a barn main floor—you'll want to spend a few extra dollars and put in the additional time to trim out the space so that it looks more finished and attractive. If you are going to use the barn for a work space or to quarter animals, a stop down to the local saw mill or lumberyard for one-by rough-cut spruce, pine, or fir will suffice. On the outside, most barns have basic trim with butt joints that cover the end grain on the siding.

Rough Storage

Because a barn or outbuilding is generally not a finished space, you don't want to put huge amounts of time or money into building storage systems. Finished one-by pine boards are expensive, and it can cost as much as $200 to put up 150 running feet of shelving.

But shelf space is nice to have, especially if you've finally built a storage shed to house all those boxes and who-knows-what-else you've been storing in the basement, attic, and back hallway all these years.

Basic shelf systems are easily adaptable to nearly any structure or area. These shelves and table systems are framed using principles similar to those used to frame partition walls. It might be tempting to screw steel L-brackets into the studs and place inexpensive ½-inch CDX plywood on top of them to create shelves. But these types of shelves don't hold much weight. An inexpensive alternative is to create a 2×4 frame that you can deck with plywood. Run 2×4s floor to ceiling, tied into the floor and the joists above, and hang the framed shelves between them. This makes a sturdy, strong alternative to either lightweight steel L-brackets or shelf kits.

You can build a basic benchtop from a frame of 2×4s screwed together on edge and a piece of ¾-inch plywood screwed on top of the frame. (Using liberal amounts of construction adhesive also helps.) Use 2×4s or 4×4s for legs. You can use regular wood screws to attach the legs to the benchtop, or for extra durability, use hex-head lag screws. After the legs are attached, screw some cross bracing between the legs. You can add a shelf below the tabletop by securing plywood to the cross bracing.

This shelf and work surface is angle-braced to the wall below a series of sunny windows, providing a perfect place for growing and caring for potted plants.

Shallow storage shelves can be made of 2x4s (or 2x6s depending on the width of your studs) set on blocks that are screwed to the inside of the stud bay.

A sturdy workbench can be made from common dimensional lumber and one or two sheets of ¾-in. plywood. The height, width, and depth can be manipulated to suit your needs.

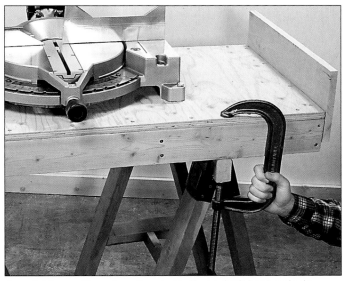

A portable workbench makes sense if you don't have a single workspace for many operations. This chop-saw table is made of plywood screwed to a 2x4 frame. The end panel supports long boards.

Stalls & Partitions

If you want a multipurpose barn where you can handle car and truck repair, keep a few animals, and have a large workshop and storeroom, you may need some walls, partitions, and stalls.

In most barns, the outside walls are the load-bearing, although there are often interior posts. But most walls that divide space within a barn are nonload-bearing walls, better known as partition walls. You might build them by screwing a two-by top plate to the underside of the bottom webs of the trusses or the underside of the joists, and then shooting a two-by into the slab with power-actuated fasteners or screwing a two-by plate to the wood floor for a sill plate. With these two plates in place, you can simply frame walls as you would when building any structure.

Half-walls for stalls are framed the same way, but because each stud doesn't run all the way to the top plate, it's good to have a post or double stud at each end.

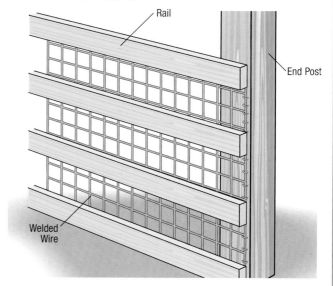

Half-Wall Partitions

Rail

End Post

Welded Wire

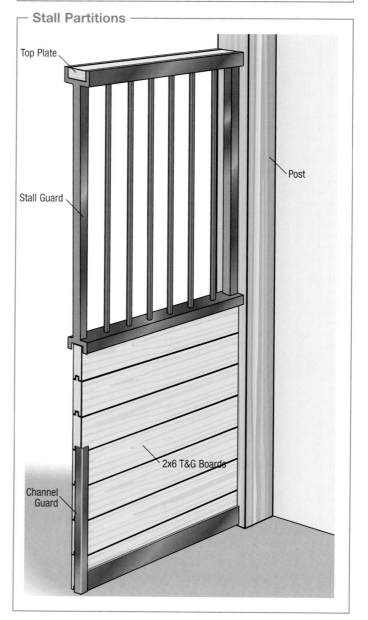

Stall Partitions

Top Plate

Post

Stall Guard

2x6 T&G Boards

Channel Guard

Raising horses requires a large barn with individual stalls designed for each animal. Unique gable-end framing can contain combinations of windows to let in light and air.

Planning Animal Stalls

The best information on what type of area and square footage is required for animals is available from your state or university agricultural extension service or from a local 4H group. You will find that large animals need a lot of room, and stalls that run 10×10, or 12×12 feet can eat up an enormous amount of space in a 24×50 barn. Even smaller stalls can gobble up space. For instance, a cow under 1,400 pounds generally requires a stall at least 4 feet wide by 5½ feet long. For heavier cows, the recommended stall size grows to 5 feet wide and 6 feet long. A horse that's 14 hands needs a 10×10-foot stall, and a 16-hand horse needs a stall 12×12 feet. Stalls for two 16-hand horses can take up the entire width of a 24-foot-wide barn.

You can build stalls with wide rough-cut boards such as 2×6s or 2×8s. Many suppliers offer treated 2×6s that add strength to partitions with single and sometimes double tongue-and-groove joints. You need to check care-fully about the wood treatments that will be safe for animals in stalls. For example, you should not paint parti-tions because many animals will chew on the materials. Some livestock barns also need to be fitted with watering systems. There are basic containers you fill by hand and automatic systems connected to supply piping.

Feeders

The kind of hay feeder or grain feeder you have in your barn will depend on the type of animals you keep. The hay feeder shown below can provide food for many different kinds of animals.

Feeders need not be made of wood. Depending on the type of animals you are feeding, there are a number of metal feeders in round, oblong, and rectangular shapes that you can buy from feed and grain supply centers. Some of these feeders are on wheels and can be brought in and out of a barn, depending on access and weather.

Building a Feeder

TOOLS & MATERIALS

- Power drill-driver
- Circular saw

- 2×4s
- ¾" plywood
- 2×8s
- 2×2s
- Galvanized deck screws

1 Cut 2x4 legs, and build the two end sections by adding two supports. Then connect the two sides with longer 2x4 supports, notch the plywood cor-ners, and fasten the sheet with screws.

2 Screw down a 2x6 cleat on top of the plywood. This will hold one end of the spokes. Use screws short enough so that they will not stick out of the other side, where the animals could injure themselves.

3 Screw angled blocks at the tops of the front legs. The blocks should be angled with the lower part pitching toward the back of the feeder. Screw a wide board, such as a 2x8 to the blocks.

4 Screw 2x2 spokes to the inside of the front plate. Space them equally with about 3 to 4 in. between each spoke. The bottom end of each spoke is placed behind the cleat on the plywood deck.

5 After all of the spokes have been screwed in place, screw a section of plywood to the rear of the back legs to act as a back for the feed bin. This type of feeder is meant to back up to a wall.

Creating Living Space

If you plan to use part of a barn for living space, you'll need to insulate part of the structure and make a plan for heating, plumbing, wiring, and other residential features.

One possible scenario is to have a living loft with a work area below. This will take a substantial amount of planning, as you will have to furnish the loft with hot water, heat, and a stairway.

You will also have to install some kind of bathroom and accommodate sewer lines to a new or existing septic system. Drain and supply lines will have to be run not only for a bathroom but possibly to a kitchen area as well, escalating the cost and complexity of the design. Even modest mechanical systems for basic conveniences can double construction costs.

You also have to consider that motorized vehicles or fume-producing paints or solvents used in a work area below will seep into a loft living area above unless you create an entirely separate space in the barn for those activities and provide substantial ventilation. You may need extra sheets of plastic or foil to completely isolate living spaces.

A more likely scenario is that the entire barn is used for living area or that the barn has some of its space for living and the remaining space for low-impact activities in a pottery or painting studio, workshop, carpenter's shop or gardening space.

One drawback to turning a barn into a living space is that barns tend to be either squares or rectangles. Structures designed and built for living often have sections of walls that are offset to admit light and air and to add some variety to the interior traffic patterns. You are dividing up a box when you partition a barn for living.

Sealing up Living Space

To cut heat loss while gaining moisture and preventing damage, it is necessary to reduce the passage of air and moisture through walls and ceilings. Selecting and applying the appropriate caulks, gaskets, or sheet materials is an important part of the process.

Air Barrier House Wrap. This lightweight house-wrap sheeting stops the bulk of air movement through walls. Apply it over the outer walls beneath the siding. Materials used for house wraps allow water vapor to escape to the outside but at the same time keep out wind.

Some materials, such as spun polyester, are able to do this because of their porosity. Other nearly impermeable materials, such as polyethylene, are perforated with many tiny holes to make them moisture permeable. Air-barrier house wrap is available in rolls 9 feet wide for large wall surfaces and in shorter widths for wrapping sill and head plates.

Vapor Barriers. Vapor-barrier sheeting blocks both air and water vapor. To do this, it must be impermeable to moisture. To be acceptable as a vapor barrier, the permeance rating should be less than 1. Unpainted drywall has a permeance rating of 50 and is not considered a vapor barrier. The asphalt-backed kraft paper used to face some blanket and batt insulation has a permeance rating of 1; it is a marginal vapor barrier. Two excellent vapor barriers are polyethylene sheeting, which has a permeance rating of 00.08 to 0.04, and aluminum foil which has a rating of 0.

Weatherstripping. Weatherstripping is made with many different materials and comes in many shapes. Its purpose is to create an effective barrier at openings between the inside of a structure and the outdoors. You can choose packaged kits that contain rigid strips intended for average-sized doors or windows, or rolls of flexible mate-

---

Insulation Options

Spraying loose fill is one of the easiest ways to add insulation in an attic. Typically, this work is done by contractors with special equipment that delivers loose fill from a supply truck.

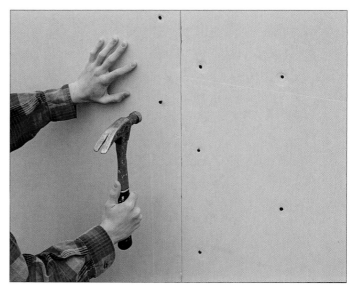

Rigid foam insulation adds significant R-value to the exterior walls of your barn or other structure but adds only a 1- to 2-in. layer of material.

rial you cut yourself. You apply some types simply by sticking them to the window or door while others have to be tacked to the frame.

Venting Options. While typical barn venting consists only of louvers and a natural draft through construction that is not intended to be airtight, living spaces require more complex systems. Aside from interior vents near moisture sources, such as kitchens and baths, you'll also need to ventilate the space between the finished ceiling and the roof. Typically, you can do this with a balanced combination of soffit vents along the eaves and ridge vents, attic gable-end vents, or through-roof vents.

Insulation Options. Two main factors affect your choice of insulation: the configuration (for instance, loose fill or rigid foam board) and the R-value. But you should also consider ease of application, how the material is packaged, and potential drawbacks such as possible skin irritation. But many lumberyards and home centers stock only fiberglass and a few types of foam boards.

Insulation is commonly available in four forms: batts to fit between 16- or 24-inch-wide framing, either paper- or foil-faced; loose fill to blow or pour into structural cavities; and foam boards, used mainly on roofs and on the outside of walls and foundations. The other type, sprayed-in-place foam, is more expensive and not as widely used.

To create a thermal envelope around your living space, particularly in the framing compartments of an existing building, you may want to use more than one type of insulator. Smaller spaces, such as where pipes enter walls, can be more easily filled with foamed-in-place urethanes; partially closed walls can be filled with loose cellulose; open walls can get batts of fiberglass; and walls and ceilings with exposed framing are easier to insulate with rigid foam.

Fiberglass insulation is made to fit between studs. Its thin strands of glass can irritate skin, so be sure to wear gloves, a long-sleeve shirt, and a dust mask when handling it.

Materials

Fiberglass is the most common wall and ceiling insulation material. It has an R-value that ranges (depending on thickness) from R-11 to R-38, and is available in many sizes with different types of backing.

Fiberglass

Extruded polystyrene board is a dense board that offers R-5 per inch for more insulating value. Expanded polystyrene is made of a material similar to that used to make foam coffee cups. It has an R-value of about 3.5 per inch.

Extruded polystyrene

Cellulose fiber is a paper-based product and has roughly the same R-value as fiberglass, about R-3.5 per inch. Typically, it is made from shredded recycled paper combined with a fire retardant. Loose fill can be blown in using a pressurized air hose. Several newer insulating materials use a mix of about 75% recycled cotton fiber (even scraps of old blue jeans) with 25% polyester to bind the fibers together. The material comes in batts and as loose fill. Its R-value is about the same as that of cellulose.

Cellulose loose fill

Polyurethane foam can be sprayed by contractors into open framing cavities where it provides a thorough seal against air leaks and a thermal rating of about R-6.0 per inch. It also comes in pint-sized quantities—in a spray can with a nozzle so that you can use foam for small jobs, like filling openings in the building envelope.

Polyurethane foam

Polyisocyanurate board is a rigid foam board rated at about R-6.3 per inch. In 1 inch of space you get almost double the thermal resistance provided by an inch of fiberglass.

Polyisocyanurate

Drywall

Also known as plasterboard, wallboard, and often by the registered trade name Sheetrock, drywall provides a solid foundation for interior finishes such as wallpaper, paneling, or tile. But because its paper-covered face can easily be painted, drywall often serves as the finished surface.

Drywall sheets are quickly cut and installed using a hammer and nails, or screws and a power drill-driver with a Phillips head screwdriver bit. Pros generally use a special drill with a torque limiter and other features that allow them to load a screw and just pull the trigger. The drill stops when the screw is set just into the panel surface with a neat and easily spackled dimple.

On wall studs spaced 16 inches on center, fasteners should be spaced every 8 inches for nails and 12 inches for screws. Use screws if possible to prevent nail pops.

The standard drywall panel for new construction and remodeling is ½-inch thick. Drywall is generally available in 4-foot widths and 8-, 10-, 12-, and 14-foot lengths. It may seem easiest to hang 4×8 sheets vertically, running the long dimension from floor to ceiling. And it's true that a 4×8 sheet, which weighs about 54 pounds, is easier to maneuver and install than longer sheets—especially on ceilings. But whenever possible, you should install sheets horizontally on walls. Choose the longest practical length to minimize the number of joints. You'll probably need a helper, but horizontal installation saves work during the time-consuming process of taping and finishing.

When you handle drywall during installation, remember to treat it gently because it breaks easily if dropped or hit. You can quickly crush a corner and ruin an entire panel if you put the full weight of a sheet on it. Stack drywall flat to prevent warping if you don't plan on using it right away.

Installing Drywall

TOOLS & MATERIALS

- Measuring tape • T-square
- Utility knife • Pencil
- Drywall hammer or power drill-driver
- Caulking gun • Panel lifter
- Eye protection
- 3-, 6-, and 12-in. drywall taping knives
- Sanding pole • Mud tray or hawk
- Tape dispenser (optional)
- Stepladder or scaffolding (as required)

- Drywall panels
- Construction adhesive
- Drywall nails or screws
- Joint compound
- Drywall tape
- Sandpaper

1 To cut drywall, score the surface with a utility knife against a straightedge such as a drywall T-square. Snap-break the panel along the cut, and slice through the paper backing.

2 Install the top wall panel first, butting it against the ceiling. If you're working alone, a few nails under the panel can support it. If you have a partner to help, things will go faster.

3 Butt the bottom panel against the top by pushing down on a panel lifter with your foot. If there is a small gap near the floor, it will be covered by the baseboard trim.

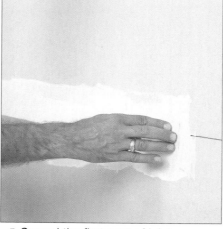

4 Spread the first coat of joint compound over the seam. Embed a length of paper drywall tape in the first coat of compound by smoothing it against the wall with a drywall knife.

5 Once the coat dries, apply second and third coats of compound with a wider taping knife. Smooth compound carefully to reduce sanding time. Sand lightly between coats as needed.

Trimwork

Most of the trimwork you'll do in your barn will be with rough-cut 1×4 or 1×6 pine. The same material works quite well inside and out. For doors and windows, you can either miter the joint, butt the joint, or use corner blocks.

For exterior trim you can usually use No. 2 lumber. This type of spruce, pine, or fir is a medium-grade stock. You'll find a lot of minor defects, such as knots. Treat them and exposed end grain with a stain-killing, shellac-based primer. This will keep the pitch in the knots from bleeding through after you paint the trim. Omit this step if you plan to use a stain or clear sealer instead of paint, but be sure to seal these weak points adequately to keep moisture and insects from penetrating the wood. Finishing exterior trim is important because this kind of lumber is very susceptible to damage caused by insects and weather.

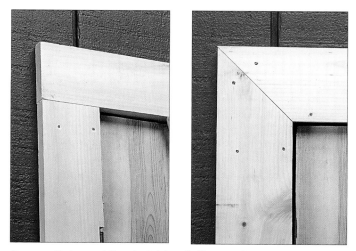

Over rustic barn siding, butt joints (left) generally look fine, although you can dress up the the trim by mitering (right).

1 You can rely on a ruler, but DIYers are wise to rough-cut boards and set them in position to mark the miter cuts. Be sure to mark the direction of any miter cuts so that there is no confusion.

2 For accurate miter cuts (45-deg. cuts on mating boards), use a power miter saw that swivels or a miter box with fixed stops at 45-deg. in either direction. These will give you consistent accuracy.

3 Begin installation by driving 8d finishing nails almost, but not quite, flush with the wood surface to avoid marring the wood with hammer blows. Accuracy is important here.

4 Use a nail set to focus the power of the hammer, and drive the nails home. If you plan to carpet the floor, it's wise to apply a finish to the baseboard before you install it, or at least before you carpet.

5 Work around the room, one board to the next. Leave the leading edge of each board rough-cut until the joint fits perfectly, and then measure the run to determine the piece's final length.

8 FINISHING

Installing Rake Boards

A rake board is basically a trim board, often used with one or more strips of smaller trim, that covers the outermost gable-end rafters. Its main functions are to conceal the rough lumber of the end rafter, which generally is construction-grade material, and to cover the top edges of siding on the gable-end walls. But you can also mount a rake board on blocking, and use trim along the top and bottom edges to increase its overall thickness and add detail to the roof line.

■ **Rake board lumber** is typically 1×6 or 1×8 pine. But you may need a different size depending on the depth of the rafters. Generally, the rake follows the lines of the rafters. For example, it will have the same plumb cut at the ridge where one rake board joins another. But to trim the roof neatly, the rake board should extend a bit below the rafter. This can allow sheathing and siding, in some cases, to tuck underneath the lower edge. You also need to plan the cuts on the downhill side where the gable-end rake often joins a one-by fascia made of the same material. The fascia covers the rafter tails. On more finished barn designs, fascias and rakes form a continuous belt of trim around the edges of the roof.

■ **Boxed-out rake boards** can create a soffit along the gable ends. But this requires extra labor, such as nailing up and venting a soffit in an area that is difficult to work in comfortably and safely without a fairly elaborate setup of ladders or scaffolding. Don't attempt this work from the roof, even if it has a shallow slope.

■ **Rake board thickness** can be several inches in a design where the board is blocked out and away from the rafters. But even when the rake board is attached directly to the outer rafter, overall roof width is increased by at least 1½ inches due to rakes on both gable ends. So it's important to plan and install the rakes and the rake flashing before you shingle the roof. If you jump the gun and shingle first, you're likely to discover that the shingles are too short.

Finishing a Building with Trim

TOOLS & MATERIALS

- Hammer
- Circular saw
- Caulking gun

- Finishing nails
- Paintable exterior caulk
- One-by stock casing trim

1 Corner boards give siding something to butt into. The two boards can be mitered, but it is easier and just as attractive to set one flush with the wall and set the other so that it caps its edge.

2 Nail boards to cover the undersides of rafters. This will keep flying insects and birds from making their home in your building. If you plan to finish the interior, these boards should be vented.

3 Case moldings around windows and doors also give the siding something to butt into. These can be made of one-by stock or any molding you prefer. Many windows are made with trim attached.

4 Install rake board on the last rafter at both ends of the building. This trim will give a more finished appearance to your building. Simple one-by lumber should be fine here.

5 Run a bead of caulk along any seam that might let air or insects through to the inside. A good time to do this is after you have primed your siding and trim. This way all the wood gets primed.

Gutter System Assembly

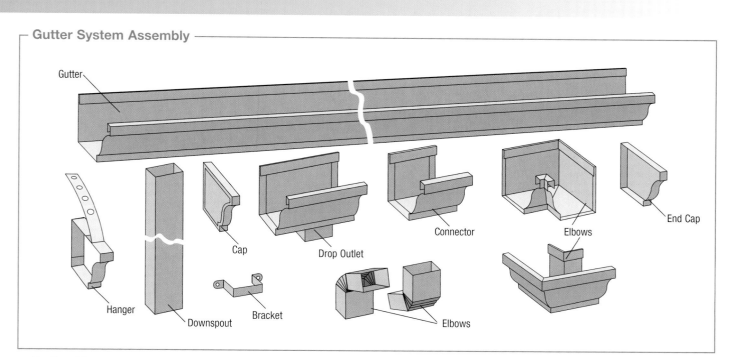

Gutter

Hanger

Downspout

Cap

Bracket

Drop Outlet

Elbows

Connector

Elbows

End Cap

Gutter Cleaners

A wire basket that rests in the gutter, over the downspout opening, will keep debris out of the pipe.

Screens that cover the entire gutter are designed to trap wet debris where it can dry and blow away.

Some systems replace standard gutters with louvers that disperse the flow onto the ground.

Gutter Hangers

Spikes and ferrules are the standard hanging system. The ferrule (a tube around the spike) prevents crimping.

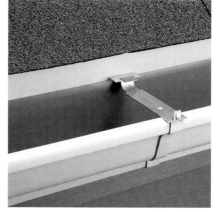

Brackets nail into the fascia board and clip into the gutter edge. Space brackets about 3 ft. apart.

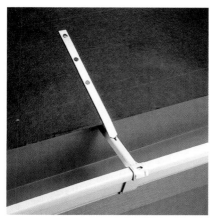

Straps wrap around the gutter and are nailed to the roof deck under the first course of shingles.

Paint & Stain

Painting or staining your barn or outbuilding will not only protect and preserve the new siding, but it will add color and accent. How well your paint or stain stands up over time depends on a number of factors, including which finish you use and what quality you buy. It also depends on how well you prepare the wood and apply the finish.

Paint Types

Paint is a mixture of solids, pigments, solvents, and binders that sit on the surface of the wood when dry. It protects the wood as long as there are no cracks to admit water, sun, or insects. For paint, your choice is either latex (water-based) or alkyd (oil-based) products. Most recent research shows that a top-quality latex paint will outlast a top-quality alkyd paint. That's because the latex paint is flexibile and permeable, so it doesn't crack as often when stressed with the movement of the siding or continuous assaults by water. Oil-based paints, though stiffer and more brittle when dry, are still the best when you want the paint to really penetrate, as is the case when painting bare wood.

Also, water-based paints are much easier to clean up (use water), and they have a lower volatile organic compound (VOC) content, making them marginally safer for the environment and safer too for the painters applying them.

High-gloss paints (enamels) are shiny and reflective. They produce a strong water-resistant coating, but surface flaws show up readily. Semigloss paints (eggshell, or satin) leave a somewhat shiny surface that doesn't resist moisture as well as high-gloss paint. Flat, or matte-finish, paints leave no gloss or shine. This paint is great for siding with imperfections, such as No. 2 spruce. A flat siding paint with semigloss trim is a good traditional combination.

Finishing Options

The same boards can look dramatically different depending on the type of protection you apply. The most practical are clear sealers and semitransparent stains. They do not crack or chip like paint and some heavy-bodied stains. And as they fade over time the surfaces will look slightly weathered but retain some of their color. Best of all, these coatings are easy to renew. Clear sealers in particular require no preparation work. These pictures show a series of different applications made on the same kind of Douglas fir. Before you select a finish, it's wise to test it on some of your scrap lumber.

Semitransparent stains allow some grain to show but add an overall tone to the boards. The stains come in many colors, in water-based or oil-based solutions.

Solid-body stains cover the wood grain completely the way paint does. They can also unify cheaper grades of lumber that have surface blemishes as well as different hues.

Paint provides the most opaque finish but lies on the surface instead of penetrating the wood. When a paint film cracks and begins to peel, it is more difficult to touch up than stain.

Oil-based clear sealers are the easiest to apply because they are so thin and easy to spread. You will need more than one coat on raw wood, and particularly on rough-grained barn siding.

Latex-based clear sealers feature easy cleanup, but the sometimes milky-looking finish may not be as durable as a comparable oil-based finish. Be sure to test finishes on scrap lumber.

Different Tools for Painting

Wall brushes are usually 4, 5, or 6 in. wide. Use smaller brushes for trim—angled bristles are good for cutting in.

Rollers apply coats of paint quickly and easily. They leave a stippled surface that is more pronounced with longer naps.

Paint sprayers apply a fine mist. Using one requires some practice, but it can greatly speed up application.

Finishing New Siding

TOOLS & MATERIALS

- 4-in. exterior wall brush
- 1½-in. sash brush
- Caulking gun
- Drip rags, dropcloths
- Ladders
- Putty knife
- Sanding block
- Scaffolding (optional)

- Primer, exterior paint (or stain)
- Caulk
- Sandpaper
- Wood putty

1 Fill holes with exterior-grade putty. Deep holes will need two or more coats. Allow the putty to dry, and then sand it. Prime the dry patch so that it doesn't show under paint or stain.

2 Apply a weather-resistant caulk around window and door openings and where siding butts against corner trim. This will help keep out drafts, water, and insects.

3 There is no set application rule for paint or stain. But it works well to cover seams before brushing out the surface. Don't miss the underside of clapboards, or other hidden edges.

4 On the finish coat of paint or stain, work on small sections between trimmed borders. Start by cutting in the edges. A sash brush is the best tool for this job, even if you're using a sprayer.

5 Work from the top of the wall down to the bottom so that you can pick up any drips before they dry, or scrape them away with a paint scraper or joint compound knife.

Part 2 Designs

10 Practical Outbuilding Designs

The barns and outbuildings described in this section have been built and continue to serve the needs of their owners. They are grouped in four categories, according to the complexity of their construction: simple framing, standard framing, pole framing, and advanced framing. The photos, drawings, and descriptions can serve as case studies to inform your own projects. Depending on your needs, however, you will want to vary the dimensions, floor layouts, rooflines, or window and door placements. For all buildings except perhaps a simple shed, you should probably hire a professional to draw up plans for you. A pro will be able to create the floor plan and elevations required by most building inspectors, as well as framing plans that specify key structural elements, such as diagonal bracing, headers, and beams. If you hire a licensed architect or engineer, complying with local codes should be no problem. In any case (and if you use stock plans), be sure to check the complete design and plans with the local building department.

Simple Framing Projects

1 Garden Tool Shed (page 166)
2 Backyard Storage Shed (page 169)
3 Gambrel Shed (page 172)

These easy-to-build projects can be completed in several days. All are constructed with simple 2×4 wall, floor, and roof frames. Although these sheds are relatively small structures, all the projects resemble the larger structures described later in their basic outlines. If you can build one of these, you are well on your way toward building any of the other projects.

Simple Foundations Each shed project described here has been built on a different foundation. The Garden Tool Shed rests on a small pier-and-beam foundation. The piers are formed in 6-inch-diameter form tubes filled with concrete, leveled off, and tied together with a doubled 2×6 pressure-treated grade beam.

The Backyard Storage Shed uses a simple post foundation made by sinking 4×4 pressure-treated posts in concrete. The tops of these posts are tied together with pressure-treated 2×6s that lap the outside of the posts. In both cases, the floor is framed with pressure-treated 2×6 joists nailed into the grade beams. The third project—the Gambrel Shed—is built on a small structural slab.

Rough-Sawn Lumber The first two sheds, like several of the larger barns and outbuildings described later, have been built with rough-sawn lumber, which is often available from local sawmills. This lumber comes full-dimension, meaning a 2×4 measures close to 2 inches by 4 inches (although the actual dimensions of each piece might be a ¼ inch or so wider or narrower).

Rough-sawn lumber is cheaper than finished lumber, but it may require additional time to season (or dry out), and it requires careful handling to avoid splinters. Plan some extra time to evaluate the moisture content of your material. If it is slightly green, consider buying it in advance and stacking it on-site with small boards, called stickers, between each layer. This allows air to circulate through the lumber pile.

Several months of drying time may be needed before green lumber is fully cured. However, all of the projects described here that use rough-sawn

Livestock Barn

lumber can be built with slightly green material. Although the wood will shrink as it dries, these rough-sawn-lumber projects do not include finished interiors that will be affected. The projects that do include interior finishing have been built with seasoned framing material.

Basic Framing These sheds are small, not subject to extreme loading conditions, so studs can be spaced 24 inches on center. Install horizontal 2×4s as blocking, placed at approximately the mid-height of studs. This blocking stiffens the structure and provides useful, if shallow, shelves in the open wall cavities of an unfinished shed.

Once you have raised the four walls and nailed the bottom plates to the top edge of the grade beams or sill plates, add diagonal let-in bracing. As long as the wall area does not exceed that of the Garden Tool Shed, these diagonal struts will be sufficient to prevent the walls from racking. The larger gambrel shed requires plywood sheathing—in this case, T1-11 plywood that can double as finished siding where allowed by code.

Standard Framing Projects

The three projects described in this section qualify as full-scale buildings, with large wall and roof areas that exert wind and snow loads equal to those of a full-sized house.

Foundation Choices Two of these projects are built over monolithic slab-on-grade foundations. This foundation type was chosen for these outbuildings because it provides a ready-made, durable floor to support vehicles and equipment without any additional floor framing. Structural slabs are also a good choice where rocky soil makes it difficult to excavate for piers and foundation walls.

The third project—a livestock barn—was built on a pier-and-beam foundation similar to the one used for the garden shed project. But it does not have a floor framed over most of the area, and provides a dirt floor for the livestock. A plank floor has been added

only at the back of the barn, where a flat, level surface was needed for storing farm equipment.

Basic Framing These projects all exemplify the standard framing procedures described in Chapter 4 (pages 56 to 67). In many cases, this is the method of framing you will find in modern wood-framed houses.

However, one important difference between these first two projects and standard-framed housing is the bracing. The large garage and the livestock barn described here are braced with let-in metal strapping. Siding is attached to horizontal purlins—rough-sawn 1×4s at the top, middle, and bottom of the outside walls. This creates open wall cavities that are not suitable for insulated spaces. Only the artist's studio, which has insulated 2×6 walls finished on the interior with drywall, uses plywood sheathing as the wall bracing.

Agricultural Metal Roofing The agricultural metal roofing panels—commonly known as ag-panels—used on all these structures is a common roofing option for a variety of buildings, including even some residential housing. Metal roof panels can be installed quickly and last a long time. However, because the roof areas on these structures are relatively large, the panels are subject to cumulative expansion and contraction due to changes in temperature. Make sure you carefully follow the detailing described on pages 106 to 108.

Pole Framing Projects

7 Pole Barn (page 185)
8 Three-Bay Garage (page 188)

Pole construction often proves to be an economical alternative for large agricultural structures. The building projects described in this section all use 6×6 or 6×8 pressure-treated timber posts—a type commonly available at a lumberyard or building-supply center. These pressure-treated posts, encased in concrete pilings and extending all the way to the top of the

walls, serve as both the foundation and the skeleton of the structure.

Pole Choices For any of these projects, you can substitute round pressure-treated poles for dimensioned timbers. Round treated poles can be less expensive, but they can also complicate the building process. It's usually much easier to build with square-edged timbers than it is to join round poles and dimensional lumber.

Beam Connections The structural integrity of a pole building depends on the strength of its connections. These connections are best made with 8-inch bolts, threaded rods, and lag screws. Always predrill to the exact diameter of the bolt shank to reduce the possibility for slipping, and use large steel washers to distribute the loads over a wide surface area. Spikes should be used only when a beam is supported from below or notched into a post. To reduce the chance of the bolts splitting the timbers, offset bolt holes so they don't line up along the grain.

Lumber-Braced Walls The poles create an open skeleton, typically with diagonal bracing crossing between each pole but with little else to support the siding. This support is provided by horizontal 2×4 girts, running from grade beam to cross beam on 2-foot centers. These help to brace the skeleton and provide a nailing base for siding.

Advanced Framing Projects

9 Gambrel Barn (page 191)
10 Timber-Frame Garage (page 194)

The two projects described in this section represent the largest and most ambitious projects in this book. The first project—a large gambrel barn—combines many of the standard framing practices discussed in the text with traditional gambrel roof framing. The second project uses traditional timber joinery to create an elegant timber-framed garage. Timber framing calls for expert carpentry skills, and a sound knowledge of construction.

Garden Tool Shed

1 Garden Tool Shed

Located near an orchard and a large garden plot, this shed provides much-needed storage for a range of yard and garden tools, hoses, and apple storage bins. The large double doors provide easy access for a riding lawn mower. This is the simplest project in the book, and, once the materials have been delivered, you will probably be able to build it over the course of a few days.

Foundation Six concrete piers, poured into form tubes, support the shed. Make sure the piers extend below the frost line to prevent frost heaving, and bring the tops of the tubes several inches above grade so that they can be cut level with each other. Although concrete piers by themselves are fine, you can add a few inches of gravel in the base of the hole to improve drainage before filling the form with 2,000-psi concrete.

The tops of the piers are tied together with a double 2×6 grade beam made from pressure-treated lumber. After filling each form tube with concrete, run strings to mark the centerlines of the grade beams 1½ inches in from the outside of the building wall.

At each corner where two string lines intersect, embed an anchor bolt in the fresh concrete so that it extends at

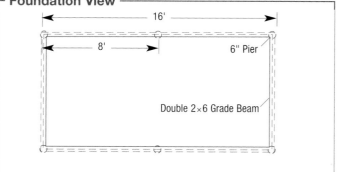

Foundation View

16'

8'

6" Pier

Double 2×6 Grade Beam

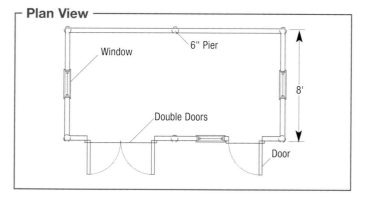

Plan View

6" Pier

Window

8'

Double Doors

Door

Side Elevation

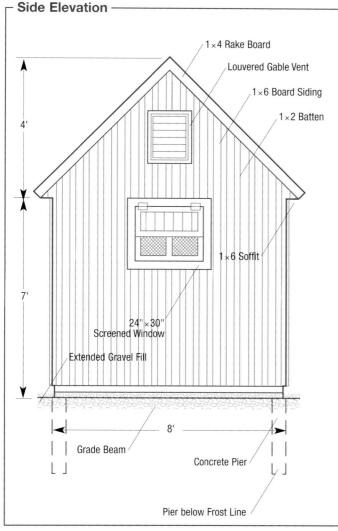

- 1×4 Rake Board
- Louvered Gable Vent
- 1×6 Board Siding
- 1×2 Batten
- 1×6 Soffit
- 24"×30" Screened Window
- Extended Gravel Fill
- 4'
- 7'
- 8'
- Grade Beam
- Concrete Pier
- Pier below Frost Line

least 4 inches above the concrete between the two 2×6s of the grade beams. You can add a washer and nut at each location to lock each beam in place on the piers.

Framing Once the grade beam has been built, frame conventional 2×4 walls with studs 24 inches on center. You may not need residential-quality construction, but it's wise to build walls with a single sill plate and two top plates that overlap at corners. (One option is to build the long walls as two 8-foot walls to avoid using 16-foot-long lumber that may be hard to handle or transport.) The doubled top plate will provide sufficient support above the door and window openings along the front elevation, but the local building department may require headers.

Install at least one horizontal row of blocking to support the siding, stand up the walls, check them for plumb, and brace the corners with diagonal 2×4s.

The shed has a steep 12-in-12-slope gable roof. (Refer to the gable framing section of Chapter 5, pages 85 to 90.) Once you have cut the rafters and positioned them along the top plates in line with the studs, install 2×4 collar ties and sheathe the top of the roof with 1×8 rough-sawn boards spaced approximately 12 inches apart.

Roofing & Siding You can let the sheathing boards run a few inches past the gable-end walls, add supporting blocking, and nail a rough-sawn 1×8 along the rake to create an overhang and cover the tops of the siding boards. Finish the roof with agricultural metal roofing panels. (See Chapter 6, pages 106 to 108.)

This shed has been sided with vertical rough-sawn 1×6 boards and 1×2 battens. Space the boards about 1/2 inch apart to allow for seasonal swelling and shrinking.

Back Elevation

- Metal Roofing Panels
- Awning Window
- Board & Batten Siding
- 16'

Front Elevation

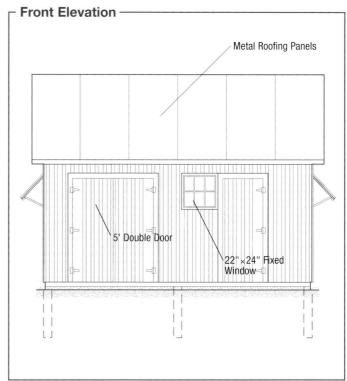

- Metal Roofing Panels
- 5' Double Door
- 22"×24" Fixed Window

Windows & Doors You can add windows and vents anywhere, as long as they fit between the framing. A louver vent under the ridge will help air out the shed during summer months.

The gable-end windows are actually top-hinged shutters backed with screening. Box in the opening with 2×4s and a beveled 2×6 sill, as shown in the detail drawing below. No headers are required in the gable end, where roof loads are distributed to the side-wall top plates.

The double doors are constructed with 1×6 siding laid edge to edge. Use a 1×8 on the hinge side to provide anchorage for strap hinges, as shown in the front elevation drawing on page 167. The boards are held together by a 1×6 Z-frame on the interior. Screw the door together using 1½-inch galvanized screws. Finish it off by nailing battens over the edge joints to mimic board-and-batten siding.

Window Detail

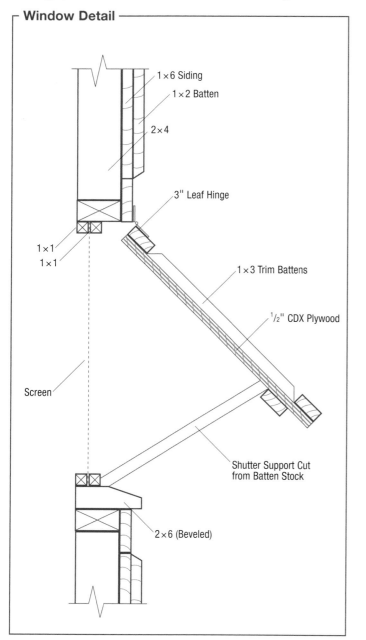

- 1×6 Siding
- 1×2 Batten
- 2×4
- 3" Leaf Hinge
- 1×1
- 1×1
- 1×3 Trim Battens
- ½" CDX Plywood
- Screen
- Shutter Support Cut from Batten Stock
- 2×6 (Beveled)

Framing Section

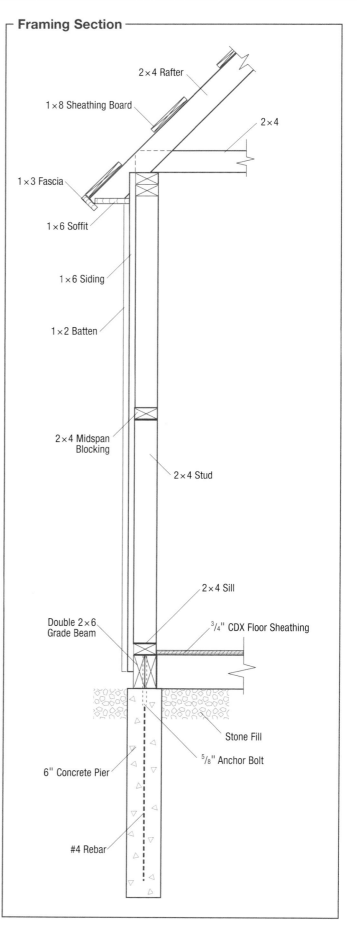

- 2×4 Rafter
- 1×8 Sheathing Board
- 2×4
- 1×3 Fascia
- 1×6 Soffit
- 1×6 Siding
- 1×2 Batten
- 2×4 Midspan Blocking
- 2×4 Stud
- 2×4 Sill
- Double 2×6 Grade Beam
- ¾" CDX Floor Sheathing
- Stone Fill
- ⅝" Anchor Bolt
- 6" Concrete Pier
- #4 Rebar

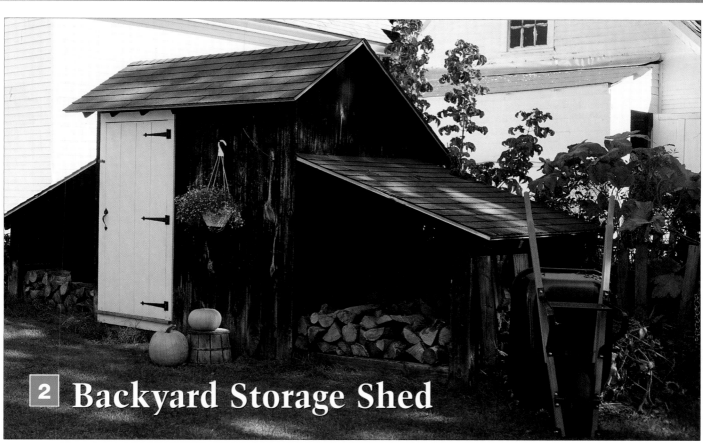

2 Backyard Storage Shed

This small shed is used for storing yard and garden tools. It is essentially a smaller version of the larger Garden Tool Shed but with two open storage wings that the owner uses for keeping his firewood dry. But it would also make a good place for keeping bikes, play equipment, or a garden tractor out of the weather.

Foundation This shed is supported on a post foundation. Four 4×4 pressure-treated posts are placed at the corners of

the main shed, and four more are placed 5 feet off the corners of the main shed to support the ends of the storage wings. (See Plan View, below.) The four posts for the main shed structure are tied together with pressure-treated 2×6s that box in the tops of the posts, as shown in the foundation perspective drawing (page 171). Because the 2×6s lap over the face of the posts, the posts must be aligned 1½ inches inside the outside walls. A single 2×6 spans the distance between the two piers for the storage wings on each side. It's

Plan View

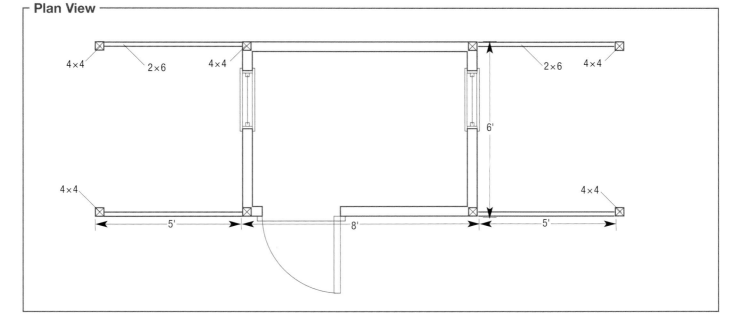

important that all the posts extend below the frost line for your area so that heaving ground will not displace the main shed from the storage wings.

Framing When using a simple post-and-beam foundation, the easiest way to install floor framing is by nailing 2×6 joists running the short dimension of the building to the grade beams. The grade beams essentially function as the rim joists and headers. Before framing the floor, lay down plastic to prevent weeds from growing below your shed and to keep moisture from rising. A layer of gravel will help drainage. Frame the walls with 2×4s spaced 24 inches on center, and install horizontal blocking as a nailer for the siding. Stand the walls with the outsides flush with the 2×6 ties on the post foundation. Sheathe the floor with ¾-inch plywood and the roof with ½-inch CDX plywood.

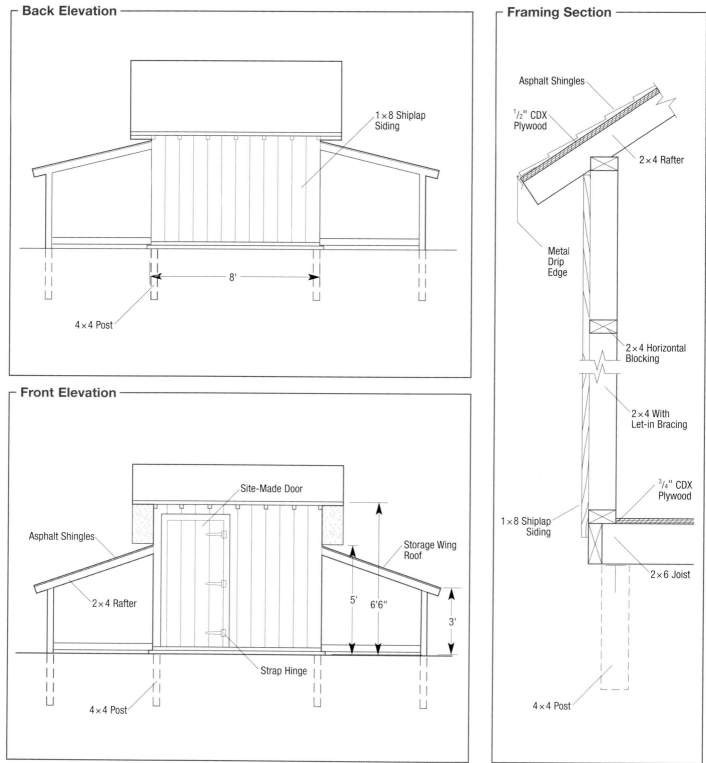

Back Elevation

1×8 Shiplap Siding

8'

4×4 Post

Front Elevation

Site-Made Door

Asphalt Shingles

2×4 Rafter

Strap Hinge

Storage Wing Roof

5'   6'6"

3'

4×4 Post

Framing Section

Asphalt Shingles

½" CDX Plywood

2×4 Rafter

Metal Drip Edge

2×4 Horizontal Blocking

2×4 With Let-in Bracing

¾" CDX Plywood

1×8 Shiplap Siding

2×6 Joist

4×4 Post

Roofing and Siding This shed was sided with 1×8 vertical shiplap siding. The eaves were left open. Run metal drip edge on all sides of the roof, tack down roofing felt, and cover it with asphalt roofing shingles.

Window and Door It's useful to have a little natural light in any small shed to make it easy to find things during the day. This shed was built with one fixed-pane window placed in the gable end above the roof line of one storage wing. You can frame out the opening and mount a fixed-frame window on hinges to provide extra ventilation.

The door has two layers—a sheet of ¼-inch exterior-grade plywood faced with siding boards—and is framed with 1×2s. (See page 170.) Bond the two layers with panel adhesive and ¾-inch-long galvanized screws, placed 6 inches on center along the door edges and 12 inches in the field.

Left Side Elevation

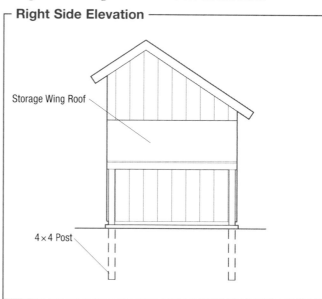

Fixed Window

Storage Wing Roof

4×4 Post

8'

6'

Right Side Elevation

Storage Wing Roof

4×4 Post

Foundation/Floor Perspective

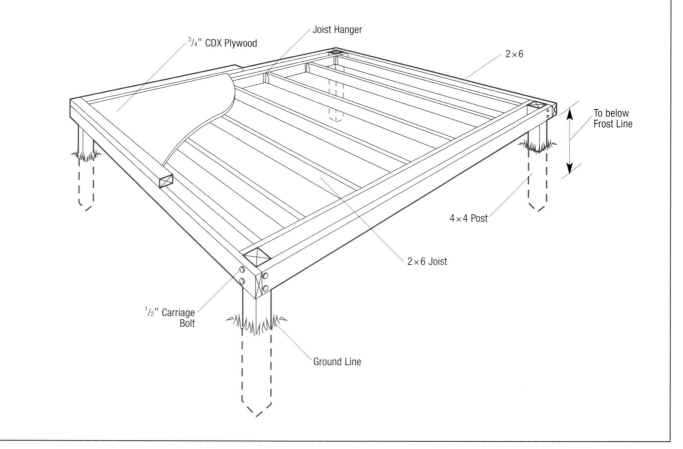

¾" CDX Plywood

Joist Hanger

2×6

To below Frost Line

4×4 Post

2×6 Joist

½" Carriage Bolt

Ground Line

3 Gambrel Shed

This rugged storage shed serves as a garage for a small tractor and provides ample storage for supplies in the upper loft. The gambrel design offers greater storage area below the roof than a conventional gable roof does. The roof structure can be built with standard rafters or made with either site-built or factory-ordered trusses.

Slab Foundation This particular shed was built on a structural slab. For a small shed of this size, the thickened edge, which serves as the footing of the slab, needs to be only 8 inches thick. However, the center area of the slab between the thickened edges still needs to be a full 4 inches thick to resist cracking under load.

After excavating for the footings, spread gravel below the slab area, and cover with 6-mil polyethylene before laying down 6 × 6-inch 10/10 welded-wire mesh. Make sure this mesh is supported on chairs so that it rests in the lower third of the slab. Place two lengths of #4 rebar, supported on chairs, at the bottom of the footing trench. Use 2×10 form boards, staked into the ground, to define the perimeter of the slab. Check to be sure that the form boards are square by measuring equal diagonals before pouring concrete. Pour the slab with 3,000-psi concrete specified for monolithic pours. Set anchor bolts in the midspan of the walls (and about 10 inches from each corner and to either side of the door opening) along the perimeter to receive a 2×4 pressure-treated sill plate.

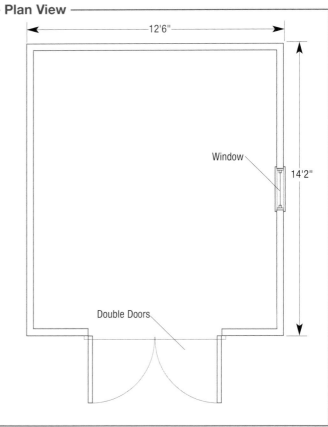

Plan View

12'6"

14'2"

Window

Double Doors

Typical Gambrel Truss Design

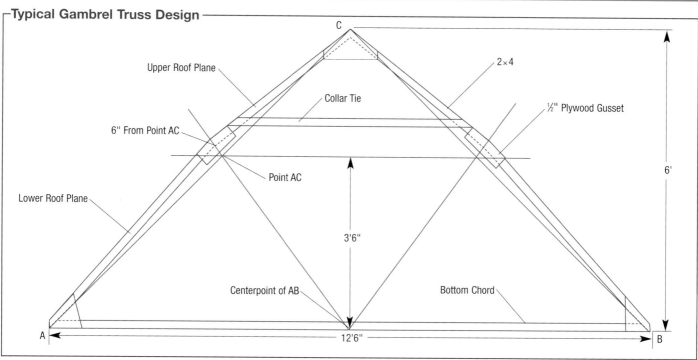

- Upper Roof Plane
- Collar Tie
- 2×4
- ½" Plywood Gusset
- 6" From Point AC
- Point AC
- Lower Roof Plane
- 6'
- 3'6"
- Centerpoint of AB
- Bottom Chord
- A
- 12'6"
- B
- C

Front Elevation

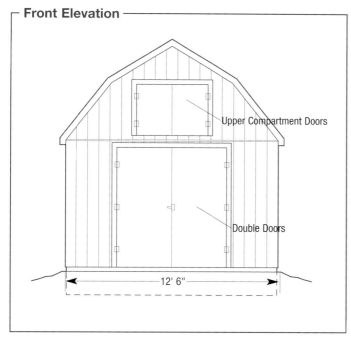

- Upper Compartment Doors
- Double Doors
- 12' 6"

Side Elevation

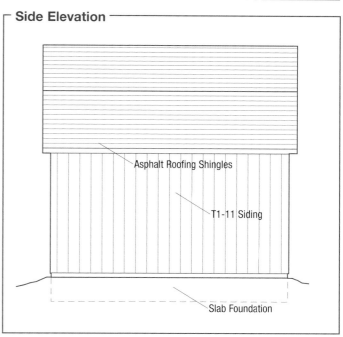

- Asphalt Roofing Shingles
- T1-11 Siding
- Slab Foundation

Trusses Build (or order) your trusses before framing the walls. The easiest way to lay out these trusses is to sweep the slab clean, and snap out a full-scale drawing of the truss on the slab using a chalk-line box with nonpermanent blue chalk. Start by snapping a base line (12 feet, 6 inches) across the long dimension of the slab, about 18 inches in from one end so that you won't run into the anchor bolts that are sticking out of the concrete.

Find the center of your baseline (6 feet, 3 inches from each end in this case), and snap a line perpendicular to the baseline. Measure and mark a point 6 feet above the baseline to define the peak. Then snap diagonals running from the peak to each end of the baseline, as if you were defining the

bottom edge of two gable rafters. Next, snap a line that runs about 3½ feet above and parallel with the baseline, and snap two lines running from the midpoint of the baseline through the intersections with the diagonals (gable lines).

There are no hard-and-fast rules governing the offset of the two gambrel roof planes. This roof has a 6-inch offset, as shown on the detail drawing on this page. This provides enough room for the loft doors. Once the offset points are established, snap the bottom edges of the gambrel lines, running the chalk line from the peak to the offset point and from the offset point to the end of the baseline on both sides. Lay down 2×4s along these gambrel lines, and mark the top edges to complete the full-scale plan of the truss.

Use this full-scale plan as a pattern to cut the 2×4 pieces of the trusses. Lay 2×4s on your full-scale drawing to mark the cut angles at the peak and at each offset point. Keep in mind that this full-scale plan does not define the overhang of the lower roof plane.

Once you have the pieces for the upper and lower roof planes, you need a bottom chord, cut from one long, straight 2×4. Mark and cut the angle on each end of this 2×4 to match the angle of the lower roof plane members. You'll also need to cut a collar tie.

Cut enough pieces to build 11 trusses—one at each end and nine trusses in between, spaced 16 inches apart. (One bay will be less than 16 inches.) Join the five intersections at the peak, at the two offset angles, and at each end of the bottom chord with gussets cut from 12 × 12-inch squares of ½-inch exterior-grade plywood. Nail off the gussets with 12 4d nails (six evenly spaced over the end of each 2×4 truss piece). If building trusses seems too challenging or time consuming, it's easy to order them, and often cost-effective, as well.

Framing & Siding Now you can lay out, cut, and bolt down the pressure-treated sill plates. Lay out the walls with 2×4 studs 16 inches on center, sheathe the walls with T1-11 siding, and attach them to the sill plate. Frame two narrow walls (31 inches wide) to stand on each side of the large door opening. The sill plates below these narrow walls will extend an additional 1½ inches to support jack studs in the door opening. The jack studs fall 2 inches below the upper edge of the top plates and support a 2×6 header nailed at the

bottom chord on the first truss. The step between the lower edges of the 2×4 truss chord and the 2×6 header create a stop for the top of the large double door.

After you have erected the walls and trusses, frame an opening for the loft door, using a double 2×4 header. Cut one of these 2×4s to fit between the upper truss chords of the first truss, and the second to lap over the inside face of the chords. Fill in the studs above and on each side of the opening with 2×4 studs on 16-inch centers. Before applying the T1-11 siding above the top plates on each end, run a length of Z-flashing (available at building-supply centers) along the top edge of the plywood on the walls.

Exterior Trim & Roofing Install a 1×4 fascia along the truss ends, and nail an L-bracket to the siding to hold aluminum soffit. Over the sheathed end trusses, nail 2×4 blocking in line with the upper and lower chords of the end trusses. Over this blocking, install 1×6 rake boards. Install aluminum vented soffit material below the truss ends. You can also use plywood sheeting cut for plug vents or strip vents.

Sheathe the roof, and install metal drip edge on all sides. You are now ready to tack down your roofing felt, and complete with asphalt shingles.

Doors All the doors on this gambrel shed have been built from T1-11 siding laminated to ½-inch exterior-grade plywood and trimmed with prepainted 1×2 pine.

┌ Framing Section ─────────

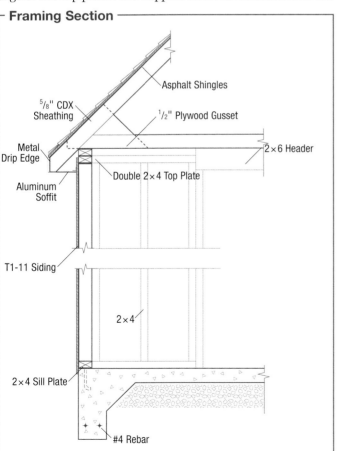

- Asphalt Shingles
- ⅝" CDX Sheathing
- ½" Plywood Gusset
- Metal Drip Edge
- 2×6 Header
- Aluminum Soffit
- Double 2×4 Top Plate
- T1-11 Siding
- 2×4
- 2×4 Sill Plate
- #4 Rebar

┌ Door Frame Detail ─────────

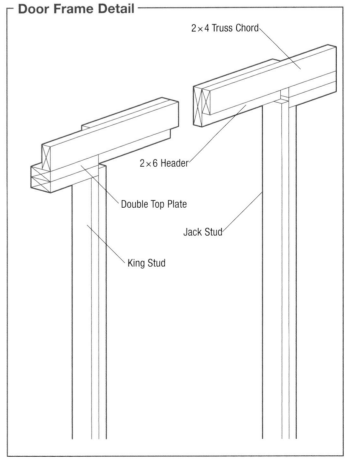

- 2×4 Truss Chord
- 2×6 Header
- Double Top Plate
- Jack Stud
- King Stud

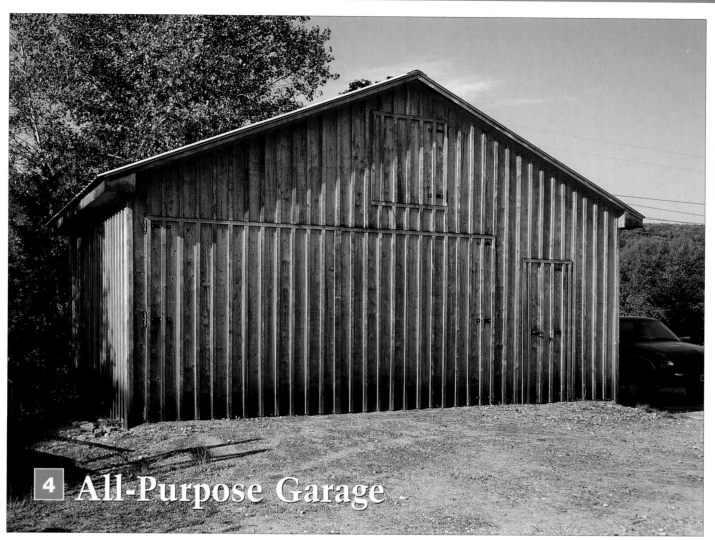

4 All-Purpose Garage

This large garage offers ample work area for a small mechanic's shop, for storing tools, or parking a small tractor. Its structural integrity depends on metal cross-bracing in the walls, a large built-up beam for the garage-door header, and standard W-trusses for the roof.

Slab Foundation This building needs a full-size structural slab with a minimum 12-inch-wide footing around its perimeter, as described in Chapter 3 (pages 44 to 46). After excavating for the footings, spread gravel below the slab area, and cover it with 6-mil polyethylene before laying down 6 ×6-inch 10/10 welded-wire mesh. Make sure this mesh is supported on chairs so that it will sit in the middle of the 4-inch slab section. Place two lengths of #4 rebar, supported on chairs, at the bottom of the footing trench. Use 2×10 form boards, staked into the ground, to define the perimeter of the slab. Measure diagonals to check that the form boards are square before pouring concrete. Pour the slab using fortified 3,000-psi concrete specified for monolithic pours. Set anchor bolts every 6 feet (and about 10 inches from each corner, and to either side of the door openings) around the perimeter to receive a 2×4 pressure-treated sill plate.

Plan View

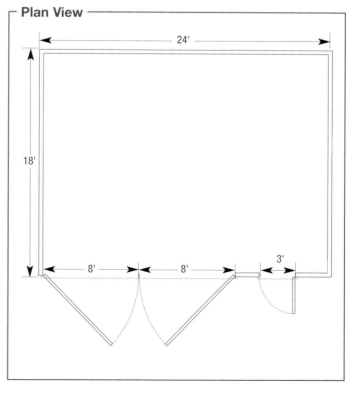

Framing Section

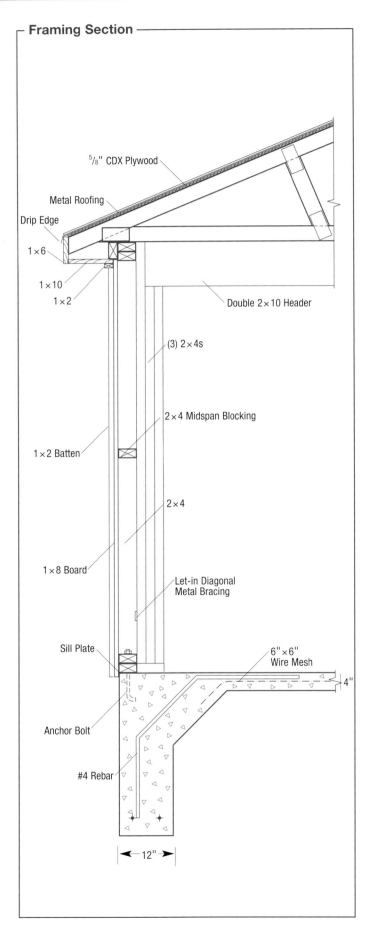

5/8" CDX Plywood

Metal Roofing

Drip Edge

1×6

1×10

1×2

Double 2×10 Header

(3) 2×4s

2×4 Midspan Blocking

1×2 Batten

2×4

1×8 Board

Let-in Diagonal
Metal Bracing

Sill Plate

6"×6"
Wire Mesh

4"

Anchor Bolt

#4 Rebar

12"

Wall Framing This shed was framed using full-dimension rough-sawn 2×4s spaced 16 inches on center, but common dimensional 2×4s will work just as well. Install midspan blocking and let-in diagonal bracing. Run the metal bracing from near the top plate at each corner at about a 45-degree angle down to the sill plate of the walls.

Garage Door Framing Build a garage door header using two 16-foot-long 2×10s, nailed every 12 to 16 inches with a row of four 16d common nails. This heavy beam should be supported by double jack studs on each end, as shown in the Framing Section at left. Because of the large opening, the front wall can't be braced with metal strapping. But this wall still requires bracing to prevent racking, especially around the two garage doors. Do this by sheathing the inside face of the wall with ½-inch CDX plywood. The strength of the plywood bracing will come from its nailing. Nail it off every 4 inches along the edges with 8d common nails.

Roof Trusses Trusses were used on this project to create a clear span over the floor without interruption from supporting walls or posts. Trusses should be ordered before you begin construction, to allow time for them to be made and delivered to the site. The trusses on this garage were ordered with a 24-foot-long bottom chord and 10-inch plumb cut overhang. In this case, the open webs of the truss were going to be used to store lumber (with access through the loft door), and the truss manufacturer had to be aware of these loading conditions. Follow the guidelines for erecting trusses found in Chapter 5 (pages 94 to 96). Another option is to pay for delivery and installation, which often is cost-effective if you have the building prepared for trusses.

Fill in the gable-end studs above the back wall plates and front headers. Box in a loft opening with 2×4s. The end truss will distribute roof loads to the side walls, so this loft opening does not need a header. Sheathe the roof with ⅝-inch CDX plywood. Hang the sheathing about 6 inches over the gable-end rakes, and support this overhang with short 2×4 blocks nailed to the end truss.

Siding & Roofing Install vertical 1×8 rough-sawn board siding covered by 1×2 battens. Space the boards about ½ inch apart to allow for seasonal movement. Battens should overlap the seams to avoid any gaps when the large boards lose moisture and shrink. Because this is an unheated garage with open-wall framing, a vented roof is not necessary. You can box the eaves with rough-sawn one-by material, and run this same material up the rakes, nailed to the support blocks. Run metal drip edge around the entire perimeter of the roof, and install metal roofing panels.

Doors These large, swinging garage doors have been framed like small wall sections, using dimensional 1×3 studs and metal bracing. Be sure to run the bracing from the top hinge-side corners on a diagonal down to the corners where one door meets the other. The exteriors of all the doors have been sheathed with board-and-batten material, and box-trimmed with batten stock. You will need to notch the batten trim to allow long strap hinges to pass underneath. For large doors, you will need at least three and probably four very large strap hinges per side. As an alternative you may prefer to buy and install an over-head style garage door. It may take some looking and possibly special ordering to get a 16-foot-wide overhead door, but it may still prove to be easier than building and hanging these large barn doors yourself.

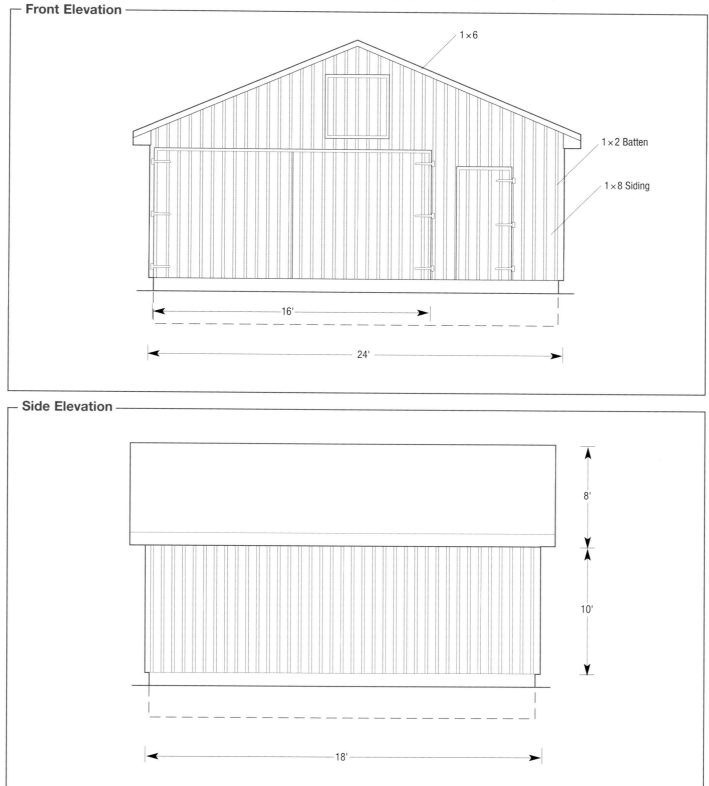

Front Elevation

1×6

1×2 Batten

1×8 Siding

16'

24'

Side Elevation

8'

10'

18'

5 # Livestock Barn

Plan View

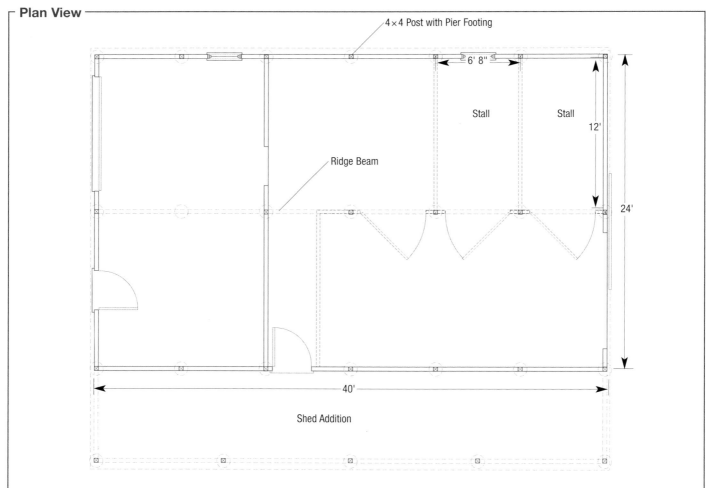

4 × 4 Post with Pier Footing

6' 8"

Stall   Stall

Ridge Beam

12'

24'

40'

Shed Addition

Built for a commercial sheep farmer, this Livestock Barn provides space for animals as well as storage for farm implements. While most of the walls were framed using standard 2×6 studs, many of the post-and-beam connections introduce some of the construction techniques used in the next group of projects—pole structures.

Foundation The pier-and-beam foundation for this large shed consists of a series of piers spaced approximately 6 feet apart. A row of piers has been added down the center of the main gabled structure to support 4×4 posts that in turn support the collar ties and ridge beam for the roof.

A row of piers spaced 10 feet apart support the shed addition along the length of one side. You can most easily form these piers by digging straight-sided holes with a posthole digger or power auger, and inserting 8-inch-diameter or larger form tubes. Make sure the piers extend below the frost line to prevent frost heaving, and bring the tops of the form tubes several inches above grade so that they can be cut level with each other. In most cases you simply pour concrete into the tubes once they are braced or backfilled in a plumb position. You can add a few inches of gravel in the bottom of the hole for drainage, and strengthen the pier with rebar. But there are two main keys to preventing heaving and settling: dig the hole below the frost line, and pour over well-compacted or undisturbed soil.

The tops of the piers that define the perimeter of the main gabled structure are tied together with a double 2×6 grade beam made from pressure-treated lumber. Run string lines to mark the centerlines of the grade beams and to position the anchor bolts, as described in the Garden Shed project (pages 166 to 167).

Framing Frame the walls with 2×6 studs spaced 24 inches on center. You can build your walls in 12-foot sections, stand them on the grade beam, and tie the sections together with a second top plate. You will probably need a helper (or mechanical raising jacks) to set them as one unit. The large (42×30-inch) window openings along the sides and the large door openings on each gable end require doubled 2×6 headers. As always, you should check these sizes with your local building department and increase them if need be.

A center beam runs down the length of this barn. It is built with double 2×6s spanning the distance between the 4×4 posts. The boards are secured to the posts with lag bolts. Knee braces, cut from 4×4s with a 45-degree angle on each end, stabilize each post. The center beam supports 2×8 rafter ties that span the distance between the side walls above the top wall plates. Break the rafter ties over the center beam, overlapping the two pieces at least 16 inches. The porch beam for the shed addition is built in the same manner as the center beam.

Frame a conventional roof with a 5-in-12 slope, using a 2×8 ridge beam and 2×6 rafters spaced 24 inches on center, as described in Chapter 5 (pages 86 to 90). You can install a second set of posts (bearing directly over the first

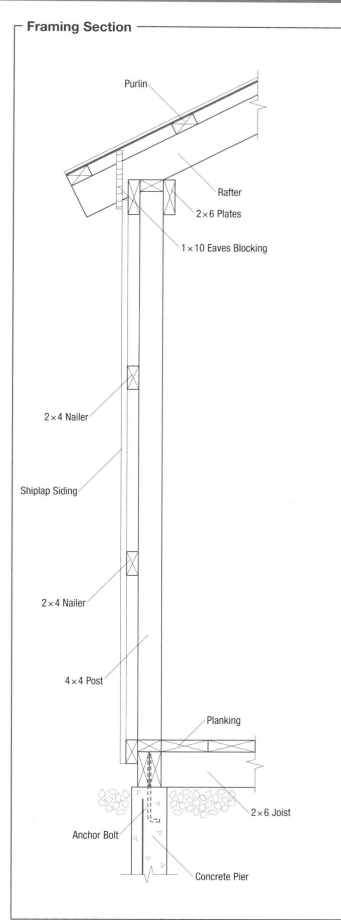

Framing Section

Purlin

Rafter

2×6 Plates

1×10 Eaves Blocking

2×4 Nailer

Shiplap Siding

2×4 Nailer

4×4 Post

Planking

2×6 Joist

Anchor Bolt

Concrete Pier

set) to support the ridge beam. An option is to install longer poles that reach through the center beam to the ridge.

Reinforce the roof with rough-sawn 2×4 purlins. Align the first purlin at the edge of the square-cut rafter tails, and space the boards about 12 inches apart. It's wise to check these specs with the ag-panel manufacturer.

The back third of this barn has been sectioned off with a wall framed with 2×4 studs spaced 24 inches on center

and supported on another 2×6 grade beam secured to the side beams and the center posts. Pressure-treated 2×6 joists, spaced 12 inches on center, support a 2×6 plank floor, making a solid deck for farm equipment.

Siding & Roofing Nail horizontal 2×6s at the top and 2×4s at the midspan and bottom of the exterior walls as a nailing base for 1×8 vertical shiplap siding. Install this siding mate-

Front Elevation

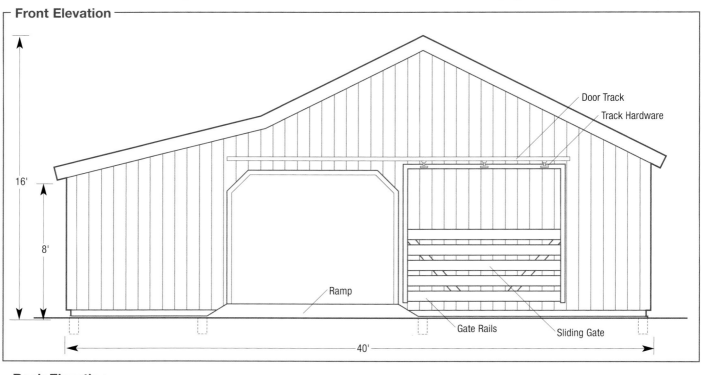

Back Elevation

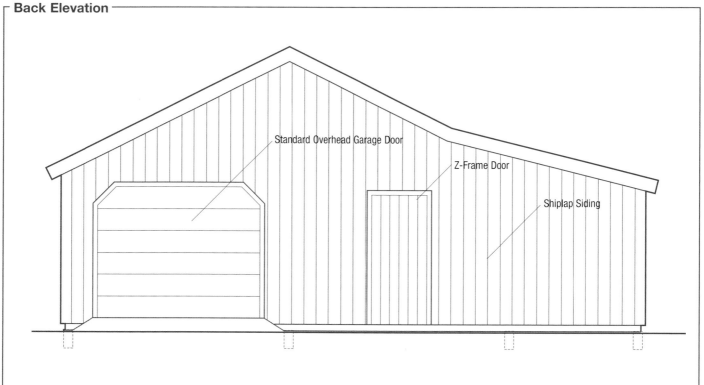

rial with 1½-inch galvanized spiral or ring-shank nails.

Because this is an unheated structure with open walls and roof framing, a vented roof is not necessary. The square-cut rafter ends are left open, and 1×10 eaves blocking fits in between each rafter. In warm climates you might substitute heavy screening or even louvers in these areas. Run metal drip edge around the perimeter of the roof, and install metal roofing panels, as described in Chapter 6 (pages 106 to 108).

Windows & Doors The window openings hold single plastic-glazing panels held in place with 2×2 stops. The entry doors (on the back and shed addition) are shiplap siding material supported by a Z-frame, as described in Chapter 6 (page 117). The large opening on the back elevation has a standard overhead garage door to keep equipment secure, while the large front opening has a sliding gate, which uses heavy-duty sliding hardware available from agricultural supply centers.

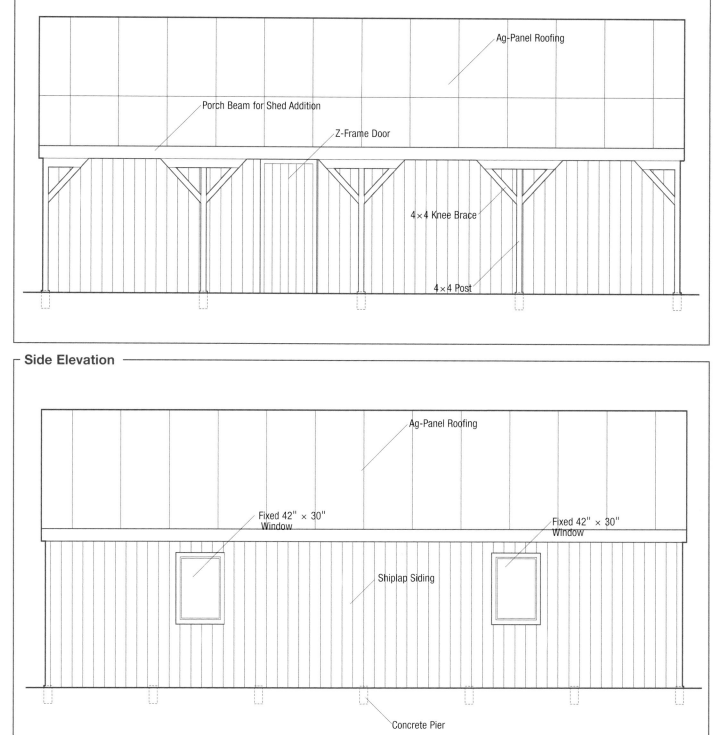

Side Elevation

Ag-Panel Roofing
Porch Beam for Shed Addition
Z-Frame Door
4×4 Knee Brace
4×4 Post

Side Elevation

Ag-Panel Roofing
Fixed 42" × 30" Window
Fixed 42" × 30" Window
Shiplap Siding
Concrete Pier

6 Artist's Studio

Plan View

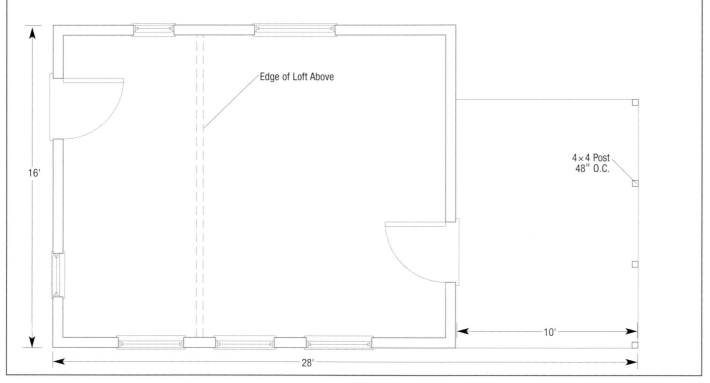

Edge of Loft Above

4 × 4 Post
48" O.C.

16'

10'

28'

This simple but elegant ceramics studio offers good light and ample loft storage for a working artist. It is built much the same as a small house would be and, in fact, could make a charming guesthouse. Insulated walls and a drywall interior make it suitable for use year-round with the addition of a heat source. A rear porch extends both work and storage areas in the summer months.

Slab Foundation This building needs a full-size structural slab with a minimum 12-inch-wide footing around its perimeter, as described in Chapter 3 (pages 44 to 46). After excavating for the footings, spread gravel below the slab area, and cover it with 6-mil polyethylene sheeting before laying down 6 × 6-inch 10/10 welded-wire mesh.

Make sure this mesh is supported on chairs so that it will sit in the lower third of the 4-inch slab. Place two lengths of #4 rebar, supported on chairs, at the bottom of the footing trench. Use 2×10 form boards, staked into the ground, to define the perimeter of the slab. Measure diagonals to check that the form boards are square before pouring concrete. Pour the slab with a fortified 3,000-psi concrete specified for monolithic pours. Set anchor bolts every 6 feet and about 10 inches from each corner and to either side of the door opening around the perimeter to receive a 2×6 pressure-treated sill plate.

Framing Lay out, cut, and bolt down the sill plates. Frame the walls with 2×6 studs spaced 24 inches on center, and sheathe them with ½-inch CDX plywood. Stand the walls, and add a second top plate to tie them together.

Frame a conventional roof with an 8-in-12 slope, using a 2×8 ridge beam and 2×6 rafters spaced 24 inches on center, as described in Chapter 5 (pages 86 to 90). Sheathe the roof with ⅝-inch CDX plywood.

Half of this one-room structure is open all the way up to the rafters. The other half is covered by a loft storage area. Run 2×8 rafter ties over the top wall plates, and sheathe the top edges with ¾-inch CDX or PT plywood as a loft floor.

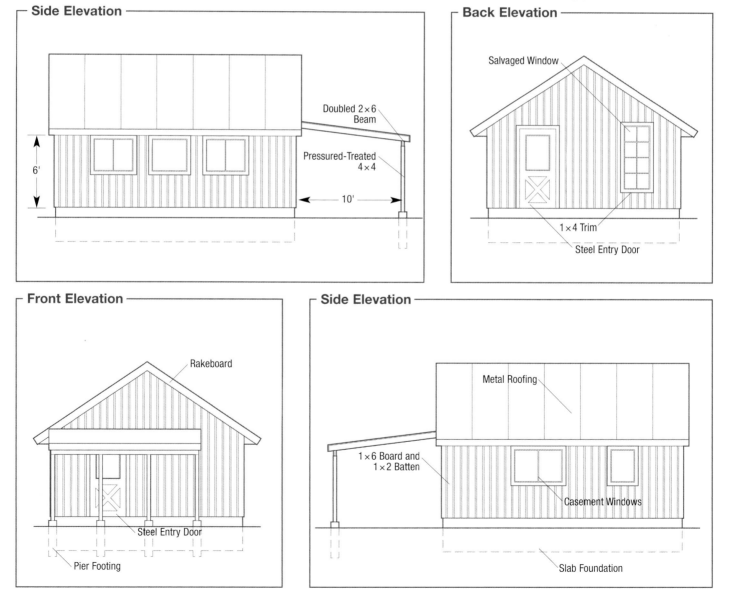

Side Elevation
- 6'
- Doubled 2×6 Beam
- Pressured-Treated 4×4
- 10'

Back Elevation
- Salvaged Window
- 1×4 Trim
- Steel Entry Door

Front Elevation
- Rakeboard
- Steel Entry Door
- Pier Footing

Side Elevation
- Metal Roofing
- 1×6 Board and 1×2 Batten
- Casement Windows
- Slab Foundation

Porch Four concrete piers, poured into fiber tubes and spaced 4 feet apart, support a shed porch along the back wall of the studio. Make sure the piers extend below the frost line to prevent frost heaving, and bring the tops of the fiber tubes several inches above grade so that they can be cut level with each other.

Erect 4×4 posts, and install a doubled 2×6 beam to support the lower end of the shed rafters. The upper end of the rafters are notched into a 2×6 ledger nailed over the exterior sheathing on the back wall of the studio, as shown in the detail drawing below. Nail down rough-sawn 1×4 purlins, spaced about 12 inches apart for metal roofing panels. Remember to check the support requirements with the ag-panel manufacturers. You will find that the size of the strapping can be altered, depending on the spacing of the rafters among other variables.

Siding & Roofing This shed has been sided with vertical rough-sawn 1×6 boards and 1×2 battens. Before installing the siding, cover the exterior walls with housewrap or felt paper. Space the siding boards about 1 inch apart so that the battens have ample support and provide coverage should the main boards shrink.

Because this is an insulated, heated space, the roof must be ventilated. This means building a ventilated soffit. Before installing the siding, run short lengths of 2×4 from the lower edges of each rafter, and toenail them into the walls, as shown in Framing Section, below. Next install vent channel (available from building-supply centers), and piece in ½-inch exterior-grade plywood as a soffit. Install a 1×8 fascia to the rafter ends, allowing it to hang down slightly below the soffit, and then nail up a 1×2 drip fascia. Run metal drip edge around the entire perimeter of the roof, and install metal roofing panels as described in Chapter 5.

Windows & Doors The windows in this studio were purchased from a salvage yard. Each one is different, which lends a unique charm to the building. When using salvaged windows, purchase them before you begin framing the walls so that you can be sure to frame the correct rough openings. Bear in mind that some regions have strict energy codes and may not allow old, single-pane glazing. The door is a standard prehung insulated steel entry unit.

Insulation & Drywall Once you have closed in the studio, you are ready for insulation and drywall. This building was insulated with R-19 fiberglass batts, though other insulation choices are available. The rafter cavities should also be insulated, but first you must install vent channels. These plastic channels staple to the underside of the roof sheathing to prevent the insulation from blocking air flow. Finish the interior with ½-inch drywall.

Porch Roof Connection Detail

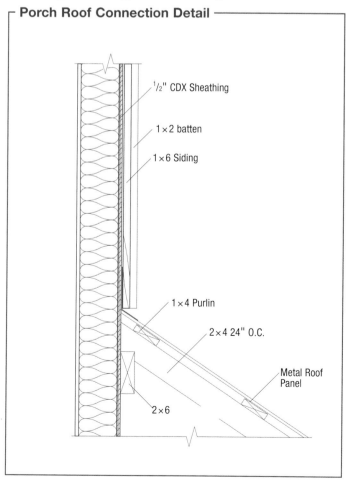

Framing Section

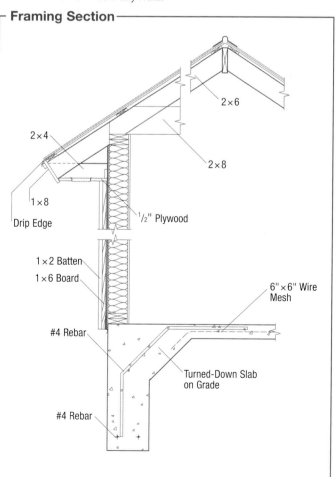

7 Pole Barn

Plan View

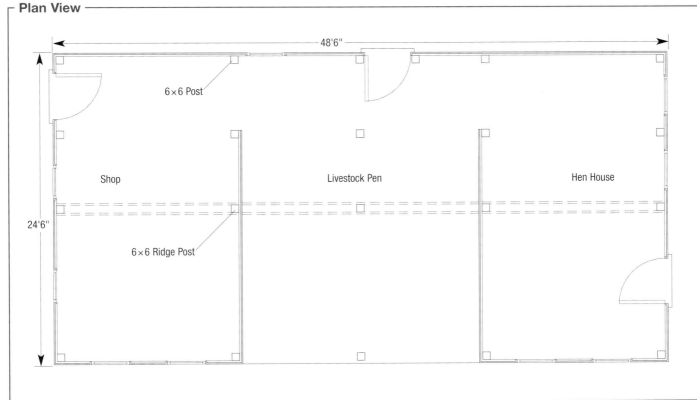

48'6"

6 × 6 Post

Shop

Livestock Pen

Hen House

24'6"

6 × 6 Ridge Post

This large-scale barn includes a livestock pen, poultry house, and small workshop. A large second-story hay loft provides ample dry storage. Although the design is a pole barn, this structure has square-edged timbers.

Framing The structure for this barn consists of a grid of 6×6 pressure-treated timbers embedded in 2,000-psi concrete to below frost depth. Through the center of the barn, a row of ridge posts rise all the way to the peak at 16 feet. The posts that define the exterior walls rise 9 feet above grade to the top wall plates, and the interior row of posts that support the loft rise to approximately 13 feet.

Girts Set the skeleton posts, brace them in plumb position, and allow the concrete to harden. (You can tie the posts together with temporary girts.) When the layout is complete and the concrete has set, you can tie the tops of the long exterior walls together with two 2×8 girts. These 2×8s are stacked on edge. The lower one is bolted with a pair of 8-inch threaded rods secured with large washers and nuts, and the upper one is spiked. You can also use a single larger board to serve the same purpose.

Next, install the center beam—a pair of 2×10s on either side of the tall ridge posts. The top of this beam will be 9 inches lower than the side-wall girts. Secure a single 2×10 along the row of interior posts that define the loft. This 2×10 functions as the loft-floor header joist. Run 2×10 joists, framed 16 inches on center from this header, across the center beam, and into joist hangers on the wall girt on the far side. Deck this floor area with ¾-inch plywood. Then run 2×6 cross ties from the back wall girt to the interior row of posts, and brace with 2×4 knee braces.

Finally, set the ridge girt, a pair of 2×8s on each side of the ridge posts, approximately 16 feet above grade. The 2×8 rafters have an upper bird's-mouth that sits on this ridge beam, as well as a lower bird's-mouth that sits on the top

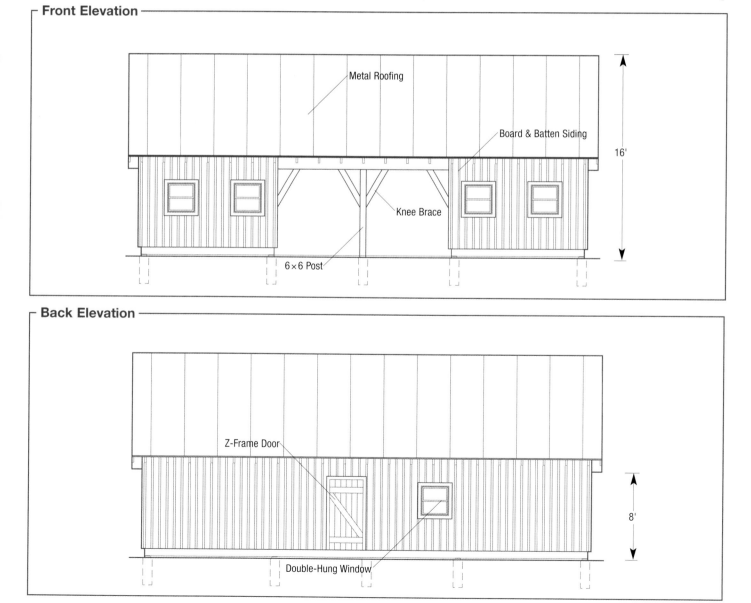

Front Elevation

Metal Roofing

Board & Batten Siding

16'

Knee Brace

6×6 Post

Back Elevation

Z-Frame Door

8'

Double-Hung Window

wall plates. Reinforce the roof with rough-sawn one-by material spaced about 12 inches apart. Brace the skeleton with diagonal 2×4s, and run the horizontal 2×4s every 2 feet on center on the outside of the exterior walls.

The center area of this barn is used as a livestock pen. The area on the right has been sectioned off with a 2×4-framed wall for use as a hen house. The area on the left is used as a wood shop and has a framed floor. Secure pressure-treated 2×6s to the base of the skeleton posts as rim header joists for the floor framing, and in-fill with pressure-treated 2×6 joists. You'll probably have to use joist hangers, which are typically required by code.

Deck the joists with ¾-inch plywood. Use exterior-grade in these rough-service spaces. Before framing the floor, lay down 6-mil polyethylene sheeting, weighted down with gravel to prevent ground moisture from rising. (You will probably want to install the roofing and siding before decking the shop and loft floors to protect them from weather.)

Siding & Roofing This structure was sided with vertical rough-sawn 1×6 boards and 1×2 battens. Space the siding boards about ½-inch apart to allow for seasonal movement, and attach the battens.

Because this is an unheated barn with open wall and roof framing and open-web trusses, a vented roof is not necessary. The rafter ends have been cut square and left open. Run metal drip edge around the entire perimeter of the roof, and install metal roofing panels as described in Chapter 5.

Windows & Doors Frame the window and door openings in the walls with 2×4s nailed into the horizontal 2×4 nailers. This barn has only one door, built from 1×8 siding material secured by a Z-frame, as described in Chapter 6. The windows in this barn have been purchased from a salvage yard. When using old windows (if allowed by energy codes), purchase them before you begin framing so you know exactly what the rough-opening sizes will be.

Framing Elevation

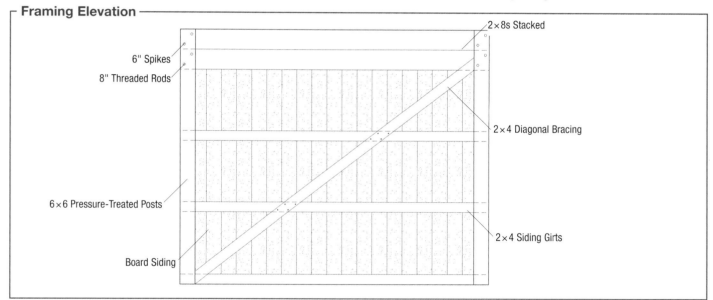

- 6" Spikes
- 8" Threaded Rods
- 6×6 Pressure-Treated Posts
- Board Siding
- 2×8s Stacked
- 2×4 Diagonal Bracing
- 2×4 Siding Girts

Side Elevation

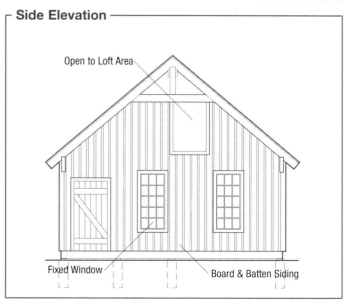

- Open to Loft Area
- Fixed Window
- Board & Batten Siding

Side Elevation

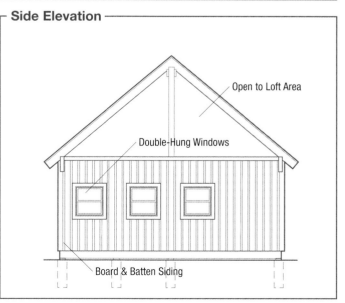

- Open to Loft Area
- Double-Hung Windows
- Board & Batten Siding

8 Three-Bay Garage

This large three-bay garage provides ample storage for a variety of vehicles, from automobiles to farm equipment such as tractors and trucks. The structure also includes an insulated room that can serve as a carpenter's or machinist's shop. The saltbox-style roof can be framed with trusses or dimensional timbers.

Framing The framed structure that supports this garage consists of a grid of 6×6 pressure-treated timbers embedded in 2,000-psi concrete to below the local-area frost depth. There are 15 posts in all. The posts that define the back exterior walls rise 8 feet above grade to the top wall plates. The posts that define the front wall and the posts that support the center beam rise to a height of 10 feet above grade.

Girts Set the skeleton posts, and tie the tops of the front and back exterior walls together using two 2×10 girts bolted to each side at the top of the posts. Bolt the girts to the posts with 8-inch threaded rod. Nail a 2×8 top plate over the tops of the posts, aligned with the outside of the exterior 2×10 girt. Cut 2×6 knee braces with a 45-

Plan View

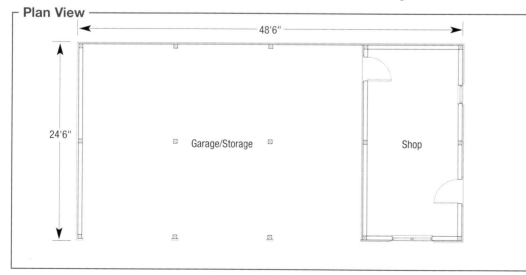

48'6"

24'6"

Garage/Storage

Shop

degree angle to stabilize each post. Nail these knee braces near the top of each post to the underside of the 2×8 top plate. Run vertical 2×6s along the length of the front posts that section off each bay of the garage, and box in the remaining two sides of each post with vertical 1×10s.

Next, install the center beam, which is made of a pair of 2×10s bolted to either side of the center posts with 8-inch threaded rods. Brace the skeleton posts with diagonal 2×4s, and run horizontal 2×4s every 2 feet on center on the outside of the exterior walls.

Roof Structure There are two ways to frame the roof of this building. You can certainly do the work using traditional framing techniques and dimensional lumber. The easiest approach is to carefully measure the span, calculate the roof angles, allow for the overhangs, and order trusses. Notice that the front and back walls rise to different heights, so the peak of the roof actually rises forward of the center beam. Such a detail does not present any difficulty for most truss fabricators, although the offset design may cost a bit more to execute.

If you do order trusses, it's wise to do it before construc-

Side Elevation

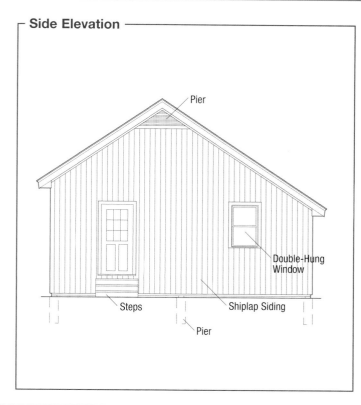

Front & Back Elevations

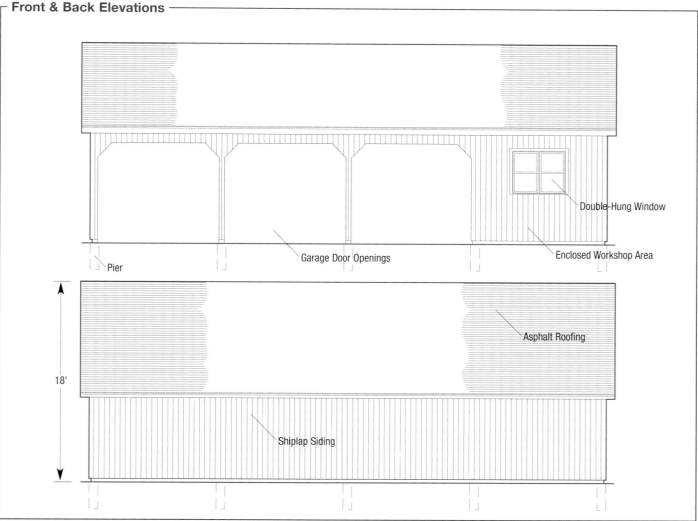

If you do order trusses, it's wise to do it before construction on your garage begins to allow time for them to be made and delivered to the site.

The illustration below shows a custom-framed roof. You can frame this roofline using 2×6 rafters. The high end of each rafter is connected to a 2×8 ridge beam. The lower end of each rafter intersects the top plate of the wall in a bird's-mouth cut. Sheath the roof with ⅝-inch CDX plywood.

Insulated Shop Area The right-hand quarter of the garage has been enclosed to create an insulated shop area. Begin by framing an elevated floor, as shown in the Framing Section below. Secure 2×10s to the base of the skeleton posts about 22 inches above grade as a rim joist for the floor framing. Fill in with 2×10 joists and deck the joists with ¾-inch plywood. Use joist anchors at the connections. Insulate the floor with at least R-22 fiberglass batts, and sheathe the underside of the joists with ¼-inch luan plywood. Lay down 6-mil polyethylene sheeting, and weight it down with gravel to prevent the dampness from rising.

Frame the wall sections with 2×6 studs spaced 24 inches on center. Nail these walls to the skeleton posts so that the bottom plate lines up with the bottom edge of the 2×10 rim joist. Insulate these walls with R-19 fiberglass batts, and install ½-inch drywall on the interior faces.

Siding & Roofing This structure was sided with vertical 1×6 shiplap material. Nail this siding to the horizontal 2×4s of the lumber-braced walls. (Note that walls of the shop area have 2×4 in-fill walls covered by lumber-braced exterior walls for a consistent exterior.)

Because part of this structure is an insulated, heated space, this section of the roof must be ventilated. This means installing gable vents and building a ventilated soffit. Before installing the siding, run short lengths of 2×4 from the lower edges of each rafter to a nailer on the siding. Then install vent channel, and piece in ½-inch AC plywood as a soffit. Install 1×8 fascia to the ends of the rafters, allowing it to hang down slightly below the soffit, and then nail up a 1×2 drip fascia. Run metal drip edge around the entire perimeter of the roof, tack down building felt, and complete with asphalt shingles, as described in Chapter 6 (pages 112 to 114).

Windows & Doors The door into the shop area is a standard prehung insulated steel entry unit. (You can order it with a lockset already installed.) The windows are double-hung units. The window openings do not require headers because the roof loads are supported by the pole skeleton.

Framing Section

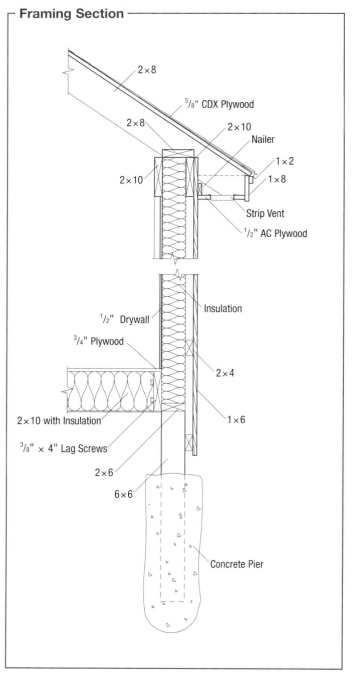

Framing Section

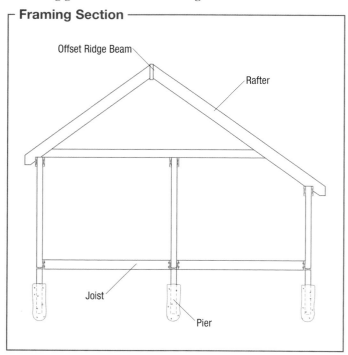

9 Gambrel Barn

Gambrel roof framing on this barn affords two floors of usable space with a minimum of framing. Originally built as a horse barn, this traditional gambrel now provides first-floor storage for farm implements with an insulated second-story artist's studio.

Slab Foundation This building needs a full-size structural slab with a minimum 12-inch-wide footing around its perimeter, as described in Chapter 3 (pages 44 to 46). After excavating for the footings, spread gravel below the slab area, and cover it with 6-mil polyethylene before laying down 6 × 6-inch 10/10 welded-wire mesh.

Make sure this mesh is supported on chairs so that it will sit in the lower third of the 4-inch slab section. Place two lengths of #4 rebar, supported on chairs, at the bottom of the footing trench. At the locations of the interior support posts, excavate for a 2-foot-square pad to the same depth as the thickened edge. Place short pieces of #4 rebar to make a square, supported on chairs at the bottom of these pads. Use

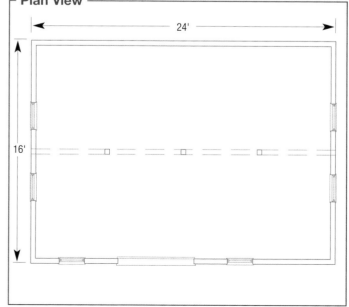

Plan View

24'

16'

2×10 form boards, staked into the ground, to define the perimeter of the slab. Measure diagonals to check that the form boards are square before pouring concrete. Pour the slab with a fortified 3,000-psi concrete specified for monolithic pours. Set anchor bolts every 6 feet (and about 10 inches from each corner and to either side of the door openings) around the perimeter to receive 2×6 pressure-treated sill plates. Set a metal post anchor in the center of each pad to receive the 4×4 center posts.

Wall & Floor Framing Lay out, cut, and bolt down the pressure-treated 2×6 sill plates. Frame the walls with 2×6 studs spaced 16 inches on center, and sheathe them with ½-inch CDX plywood. Frame window openings with a doubled 2×6 header, and the large door opening with a doubled 2×12 header. Stand the walls, and add a second, overlapping top plate to tie them together.

Set 4×4 center posts in the metal post anchors. Brace the posts with temporary 2×4s. Build the center beam from three 2×8s, and set it on the posts. Set 2×8 rim and header joists on the top wall plates, and run 2×8 joists spaced 16 inches on center. These joists butt into the center beam and are supported by metal joist hangers.

Next, frame the second-story walls with 2×4 studs spaced 16 inches on center. Measure in 4 feet from the outside of the rim joist, and snap a line across the tops of the floor joists. Stand the second-story walls along the inside of this chalk line, and tie the walls together with a second top plate. You can sheathe the outside with ½-inch plywood, but it's not necessary. Nail 2×4 ceiling joists to the sides of the studs below the top plates, as shown in the Framing Section, page 193. Between the second-story walls, deck over the 2×8 floor joists with ¾-inch plywood.

Gambrel Roof Framing Once the walls are up you are ready to frame the gambrel roof. Start by running the 2×6 rafters for the lower roof plane, spaced 16 inches on center. These are cut like conventional rafters at a steep 27-in-12 slope. They have a plumb cut at the top that butts the top of the second-story walls, and a bird's-mouth that sits on

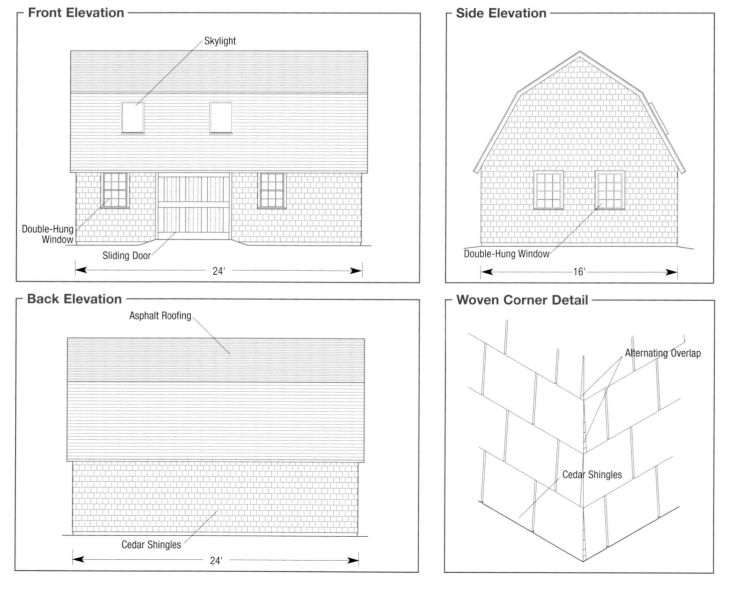

Front Elevation

Skylight

Double-Hung Window

Sliding Door

24'

Side Elevation

Double-Hung Window

16'

Back Elevation

Asphalt Roofing

Cedar Shingles

24'

Woven Corner Detail

Alternating Overlap

Cedar Shingles

the header joist of the second floor. Square cut the ends of the rafters, and run 2×6 fascia across the ends. Frame the rafters for the upper roof plane by first installing a 2×8 ridge beam. Support the ridge beam about 4 feet above the second-floor ceiling joists using temporary 2×4 posts and bracing. The rafters run at a 7-in-12 slope from this ridge beam down to the top plate of the second-story walls, intersecting in a special bird's-mouth. Sheathe the roof with ⅝-inch CDX plywood.

Shingle Siding This barn has been sided with durable cedar shingle siding. Start by applying a layer of felt paper over the exterior wall sheathing. The shingle exposure depends on the length of the shingles you'll use.

The barn as shown has 16 × 8-inch No. 1-grade cedar shingles installed with a 7½-inch exposure. To install the shingles, snap a level chalk line on the building felt 15 inches above the bottom edge of the wall sheathing, so that the first course of shingles hangs an inch below.

Nail each shingle with a pair of 4d galvanized siding nails

about 8 inches above the bottom edge. Apply a second layer over these to create the starter course. Subsequent courses will have just one layer of shingles. Leave a ⅛-inch gap between adjacent shingles. Corners are overlapped in alternate courses to create a woven corner, as shown in the detail drawing on page 192.

Roofing Cover the sheathing with building felt, and install metal drip edge along the perimeter. The intersection between the upper and lower roof planes must be flashed with 16-inch aluminum coil stock. Complete the roof by installing asphalt shingles.

Windows & Doors The windows in this barn—large double-hungs with divided lights—add an elegant traditional flair. The large sliding door is built of 1×6 tongue-and-groove vertical siding boards secured by an overlapping grid of 1×6, 1×8, and 1×10 boards. It hangs from a 2×6 ledger nailed to the inside of the wall, using heavy-duty sliding-door hardware, available from agricultural supply centers.

Siding and Foundation Section

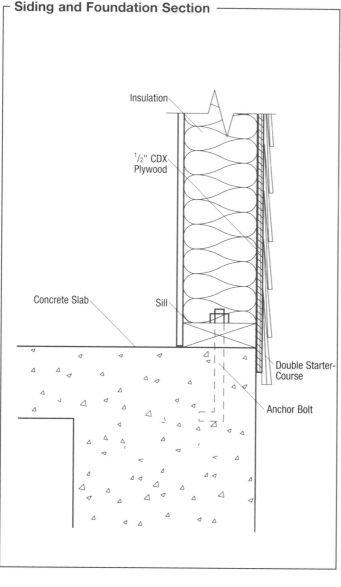

Insulation
½" CDX Plywood
Concrete Slab
Sill
Double Starter-Course
Anchor Bolt

Framing Section

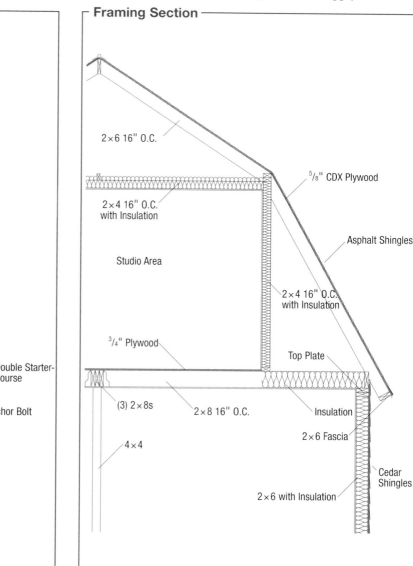

2×6 16" O.C.
2×4 16" O.C. with Insulation
Studio Area
¾" Plywood
(3) 2×8s
4×4
2×8 16" O.C.
2×6 with Insulation
⅝" CDX Plywood
Asphalt Shingles
2×4 16" O.C. with Insulation
Top Plate
Insulation
2×6 Fascia
Cedar Shingles

10 Timber-Frame Garage

This elegant open-bay garage with an enclosed garden shed relies on traditional timber-framing techniques combined with modern framing. The skeleton structure consists of four saltbox-style timber bents that stand parallel with each other, forming three bays. The bay on the left is enclosed with walls on all four sides to create a shed, shop area, or studio.

The other two bays are open in the front, and serve as the garage. The four bents are tied together by crossbeams joining the tops of the three upright posts in each bent and by a sill beam running along the back. Between the bents of this skeleton structure, conventional rafters complete the roof structure, while a conventionally framed floor structure supports a loft storage area.

Bear in mind that timber framing techniques are among the most challenging in the building trades. This project description will give you a sense of the steps involved. However, it's best not to attempt such as ambitious building without the assistance of an experienced timber framer. This project assumes that you have ordered precut bents or

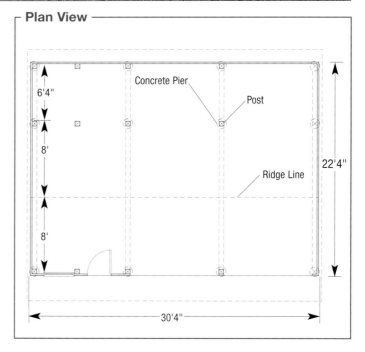

Plan View

6'4"

8'

8'

Concrete Pier

Post

Ridge Line

22'4"

30'4"

will cut the timber joints with an experienced joiner who can be sure that the structure is sound and that the framing will pass local code inspection.

Foundation The timber bents will be supported on concrete piers located below each post in the timber bent. These piers should be excavated for 8-inch fiber form tubes. (You may need larger-diameter forms to support the weight of some timber-frame materials.) Make sure the piers extend below frost line to prevent frost heaving, and bring the tops of the form tubes several inches above grade so that they can be cut level with each other.

Timber Bents The Building Perspective shows the locations of the timber bents. Begin by laying out and mortising the sill beams. Assemble the bents, and brace across the face of each joint with temporary 2×4s to stabilize it as the bents are lifted into place. Lift the bents with a crane, and brace them with temporary two-by material. Lift the cross-tie running between the bents near the tops of each vertical post, and place the sill beams along the back as you go.

Once the skeleton structure is up, you will begin framing in the roof. Nail blocks to the face of each bent at the peak to support a 2×8 ridgeboard. Cut rafters for a 12-in-12-slope roof, as described in Chapter 5 (pages 86 to 90), and install

Building Perspective

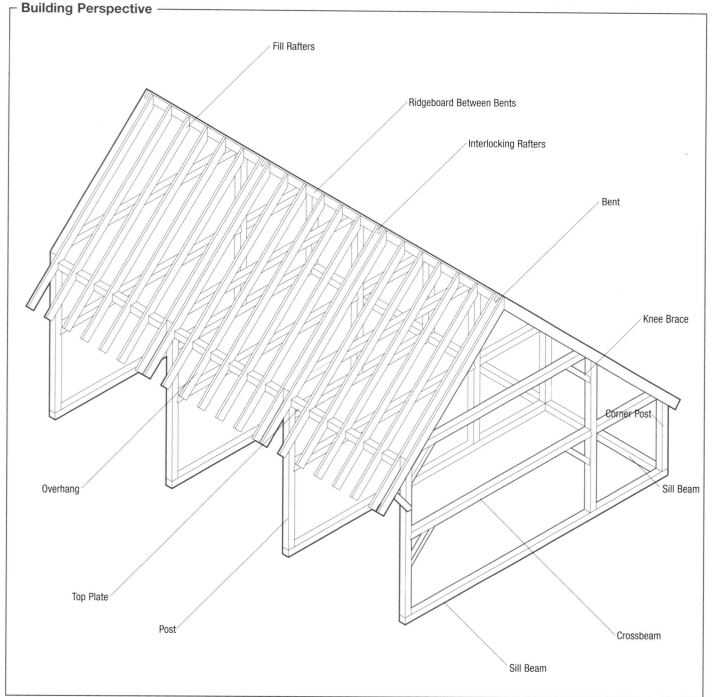

Fill Rafters

Ridgeboard Between Bents

Interlocking Rafters

Bent

Knee Brace

Corner Post

Sill Beam

Overhang

Top Plate

Post

Crossbeam

Sill Beam

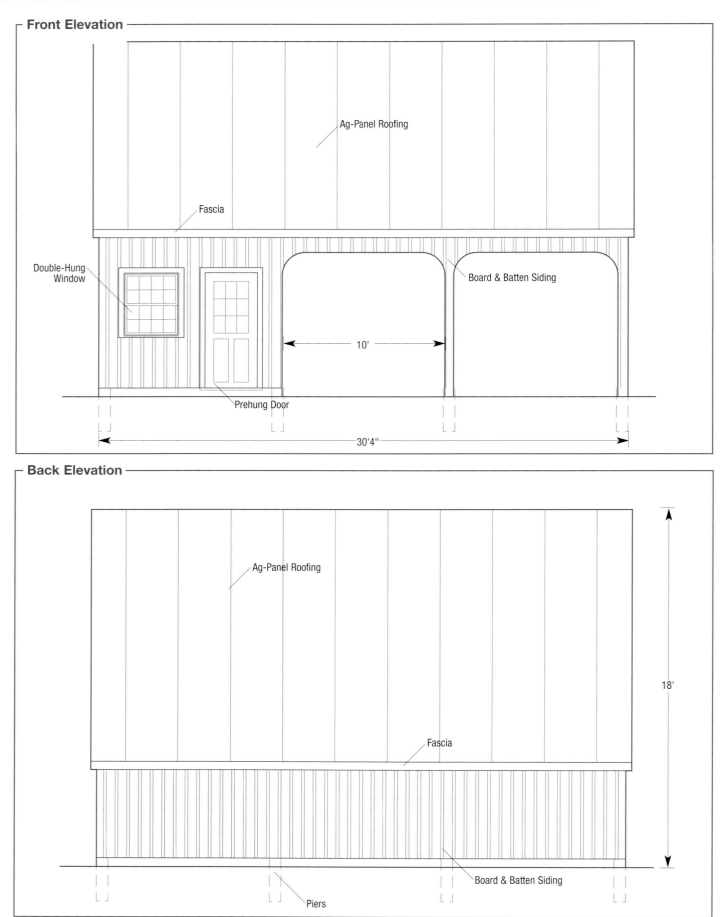

Front Elevation

Ag-Panel Roofing

Fascia

Double-Hung Window

Board & Batten Siding

10'

Prehung Door

30'4"

Back Elevation

Ag-Panel Roofing

18'

Fascia

Board & Batten Siding

Piers

these with the bird's-mouth sitting on the front crossbeam. Square-cut the ends of the rafters so that the ends extend 32 inches horizontally from the outside wall line.

Frame the loft by running a 2×6 rim joist around the perimeter and in-filling with 2×6 joists over the tops of the center girts of each bent.

Enclosed Shed The left-hand third of the garage has been enclosed for use as a garden shed. Begin the enclosure by framing an elevated floor. Before framing the floor, however, lay down 6-mil polyethylene sheeting, weighted down with gravel to prevent ground moisture from rising. Cut a 2×6 header joist to sit on top of the timber sill, flush with the outside on each side. In-fill the floor with 2×6 joists, and deck them with ¾-inch CDX plywood.

Frame wall sections to fit between the bents on all four sides of the shop area using 2×6 studs spaced 24 inches on center. Note that the walls fitting inside the bents will sit between the knee braces. Stand these walls on the framed floor.

Siding & Roofing Nail a horizontal 1×6 every 2 feet on center to the exterior as a nailing base for the siding. On the tall gable-end walls, run 2×4 horizontal nailers above the 8-foot line instead of the one-by nailers. This allows you to break the siding in an even line. Make the upper siding boards overlap the lower boards by at least ½ inch to create a more weather-resistant joint between boards.

This garage has been sided with vertical rough-sawn 1×6 boards and 1×2 battens. Space the siding boards about ½ inch apart to allow for seasonal movement.

Because this is an unheated garage with open wall and roof framing, a vented roof is not necessary. The rafter ends have been cut square and left open. Nail blocks over the siding along the roofline, and install a 1×8 fascia down the rake and over the ends of the rafter tails.

Note the attractive curve where the siding on the end walls meets the wide front overhang. (See Side Elevation, below.) These pieces of siding are supported by a 2×6 diagonal brace that extends from the rafter end to the front post of the bents at each end of the building. (See Building Perspective, page 195.) Nail the siding pieces so that they hang well below the brace, and cut the gentle arc using a saber saw.

Run metal drip edge around the entire perimeter of the roof, and install asphalt shingles as described in Chapter 6 (pages 112 to 114).

Windows & Doors The door into the shed area is a standard prehung entry unit. The windows are prebuilt double-hung units. Frame the window rough openings in the loft area of the gable-end walls with 2×4s nailed into the horizontal 2×4 nailers. The window and door rough openings in the shed area can be box-framed with 2×4s. These do not need structural headers because the timber bents support the loads.

Side Elevation

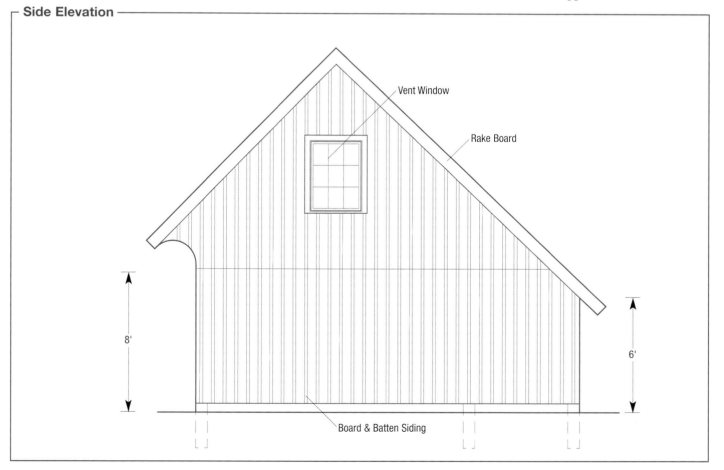

Vent Window

Rake Board

8'

6'

Board & Batten Siding

American Lighting Association

2050 Stemnons Freeway, Suite 10046
Dallas, TX 75207
(800) 605-4448
Web site: www.americanlightingassoc.com

The American Lighting Association is devoted to the lighting of any area or space of the home or yard. With valuable insights and tips, its Web site is packed with extensive safety and planning information, as well as a guide to manufacturers.

APA—The Engineered Wood Association

P.O. Box 11700
Tacoma, WA 98411
Web site: www.apawood.org

APA is a nonprofit trade association, the U.S. and Canadian members of which produce a variety of engineered wood products. Primary functions include quality inspection and product promotion. Write for free brochures.

Barn Journal

Web site: museum.cl.msu.edu/barn/
Web master: barn@museum.cl.msu.edu

A web site dedicated solely to barns and traditional farm architecture. A reader-supported site, the Barn Journal is dedicated to both the appreciation and the preservation of your farm structure.

Better Barns

12 Main Street South,
Bethlehem, CT 06751
(203) 266-7989
Web site: betterbarns.com

Specializing in the construction of the outdoor structure. Better Barns offers a wide range of styles and designs for cabins, sheds, and barns, and will even install your structure for you.

Calgary Cupola & Weathervane

96 Havenhurst Crescent SW
Calgary, Alberta, Canada T2V 3C5
(403) 630-0968
Web site: www.cupola4me.com

Cupola & Weathervane manufactures and sells handcrafted wooden cupolas directly to you. Design your own cupola or pick from its numerous designs. Visit the Web to order or inquire about a specific project or design.

The Flood Company

(800) 321-3444
Web site: www.floodco.com

Flood is a 150-year-old family-owned corporation that makes a variety of paint-related products, including penetrating stains, sealers, wood renewers, and cleaners. The company Web site offers a full rundown of products, information on application tools, and a store locator.

Handy Home Products

6400 East 11 Mile Road
Warren, MI 48091-4101
(800) 221-1849
Web site: www.handyhome.com

Handy Home Products is a leader in ready-to-assemble wooden storage buildings, gazebos, timber buildings, and children's playhouses. Call or write with inquiries.

Hearthstone Homes

1630 East Highway, 25/70
Dandridge, Tennessee 37725
(800) 247-4442
Web site: www.hearthstonehomes.com

Hearthstone Homes produces quality logs, timber, projects, and plans to custom-design your home, and offers on-site assistance or technical advice upon building.

Hyde Manufacturing Company

54 Eastford Road
Southbridge, MA 01550
1-800-USA-HYDE

Web site: www.hydetools.com
Hyde makes a variety of hand tools, including those for masonry, drywall, and setting and finishing tile.

Louisiana-Pacific Corporation

805 SW Broadway
Portland, Oregon 97205
(800) 648-6893
Web site: www.lpcorp.com

LP is a premier supplier of commodity and specialty building products serving the retail, wholesale, homebuilding, and industrial markets. Visit the Web for questions or information.

Metal Roofing Alliance

Phone: (888) METALROOF
Web site: www.metalroof.org

A coalition of metal-roofing manufacturers and related companies in the metal-roofing industry, whose primary focus is to educate homeowners on the many benefits of metal roofing for residential applications. Call or visit its Web site for a free video on metal roofing.

Southern Pine Council

P.O. Box 641700, Kenner, LA 70064
Web site: www.southernpine.com

A nonprofit trade promotion group supported by manufacturers of Southern Pine lumber. For construction details and building tips, complete project plans, and other helpful information write for a free catalog.

North American Insulation Manufacturers Association (NAIMA)

44 Canal Center Plaza #310
Alexandria, VA 22312
(703) 684-0084
Web site: www.naima.org

NAIMA is a trade association of N. American manufacturers of fiberglass, rock wool, and slag wool insulation products. Visit its Web site for publicaitons on these products.

The Stanley Works

1000 Stanley Drive, New Britain, CT 06053
Phone: (800) STANLEY
Web site: www.stanleyworks.com

The Stanley Works provides a line of hand and power tools for contractors and homeowners. Its speciality products include a series of ergonomically designed products and a line of extra-durable contractor tools for the job site.

Porter-Cable Corporation

4825 Hwy. 45 North, P.O. Box 2468, Jackson, TN 38302-2468
Phone: (800) 4US-TOOL
Web site: www.porter-cable.com

Porter-Cable is a leading manufacturer of portable electric and cordless power tools, nailers, compressors, and related accessories for commercial and residential construction, plumbing, and electrical markets.

Summerwood Products

733 Progress Ave., Toronto, Ontario M1H 2W7
Phone: (800) 663-5042
Web site: www.summerwood.com

Summerwood Products offers dozens of shed and gazebo designs, each with many configuration options and extras. The company also sells its products in precut kits that can easily be assembled in a weekend.

Ryobi North America

1424 Pearman Dairy Rd., Anderson, SC 29625
Phone: (800) 525-2579
Web site: www.ryobi.com

Ryobi produces portable and bench-top power tools for contractors and DIYers. It also manufactures a line of lawn and garden tools. Call its toll-free customer service line for free literature, or go on-line.

Timber Frames by R. A. Krouse

46 Titcomb Lane, Arundel, Maine 04046
(207) 967-2747
Web site: mainetimberframes.com

Richard A. Krouse is one of a handful of builders in New England specializing in timber-frame construction. Visit its Web site for more information on building and designing your timber home or project.

Simpson Strong-Tie Company

4637 Chabot Dr., Suite 200, Pleasanton, CA 94588
Phone: (800) 999-5099
Web site: www.strongtie.com

One of the most widely used brands of framing hardware, with hundreds of different fasteners. Call for a free catalog or for plans for deck construction and other home projects.

Western Wood Products Association

522 SW 5th Ave., Suite 500, Portland, OR 97204-2122
(503) 224-3930
Web site: www.wwpa.org

WWPA establishes standards and levels of quality for Western lumber and related products in Western softwood species. Technical information is available on its Web site.

Actual dimensions The exact measurements of a piece of lumber, pipe, or masonry. See "Nominal dimensions."

Ampere (amp) A unit of measurement describing the rate of electrical flow.

Anchor bolt A bolt set in concrete that is used to fasten lumber, brackets, or hangers to concrete or masonry walls.

Apron Architectural trim beneath a window stool or sill.

Backfill Soil or gravel used to fill in between a foundation or retaining wall and the ground excavated around it.

Barge rafters The last outside rafters of a structure. They are usually nailed to outriggers and form the gable-end overhangs. Sometimes called fly rafters.

Battens Narrow wood strips that cover vertical joints between siding boards.

Batter board A level board attached to stakes and used to position strings outlining foundations and footings.

Beam A steel or wood framing member installed horizontally to support part of a structure's load.

Bearing post A post that provides support to a structure's framing.

Bearing wall A wall that provides structural support to the framing above.

Bent A complete cross-section frame assembly (typically including wall, ceiling, and roof components) in a timber-frame building.

Bird's mouth The notch made of a level and plumb cut near the tail end of a rafter where the rafter edge rests on a top plate or horizontal framing member.

Blocking Lumber added between studs, joists, rafters, or other framing members to provide a nailing surface, additional strength, spacing between boards, or firestopping within a framing cavity.

Board-and-batten siding A siding style that uses long siding boards installed vertically, with the gaps between them covered by one-by or two-by battens.

Cable Two or more insulated electrical wires inside a sheathing of plastic or metal.

Carriage bolt A bolt with a slotless round head and a square shoulder below the head that embeds itself into the wood as the nut is tightened.

Center pole In pole framing, the center ascending poles or posts that provide structural support for the roof and internal framing.

Chord The wood members of a truss that form the two sides of the roof and the base, or ceiling joist. (See also "Web.")

Circuit breaker A protective device that opens a circuit automatically when a current overload occurs. It can be reset manually.

Cleat A small board fastened to a surface to provide support for another board, or any board nailed onto another board to strengthen or support it.

Collar tie A horizontal board installed rafter-to-rafter for extra support.

Concrete necklace The concrete that is poured around a post in the ground to provide additional support.

Conduit Metal or plastic tubing designed to enclose electrical wires.

Corner boards Boards nailed vertically to the corners of a building that serve as a stopping point for siding and as an architectural feature.

Cornice Generally called a roof overhang, the part of the roof that overhangs the wall.

Cupola Small ventilating stuctures built on top of the roof with louvered slides to allow for airflow.

Cripple studs Short studs that stand vertically between a header and top plate or between a bottom plate and the underside of a rough sill.

Curing The hardening process of concrete during which moisture is added or trapped under plastic or other sealer. Proper curing reduces cracking and shrinkage and develops strength.

Dead load The weight of a building's components, including lumber, roofing, and permanent fixtures.

Double top plate The double tier of two-by lumber running horizontally on top of and nailed to wall studs.

Drip cap Molding at the top of a window or door.

Drip edge A metal piece bent to fit over the edge of roof sheathing, designed to shed rain.

Dry well A hole in the ground filled with rocks or gravel, designed to catch water and help it filter into the soil. The outline of a dry well often is formed with concrete block or a perforated steel drum.

D-W-V Drain-waste-vent; the system of pipes and fittings used to carry away wastewater.

Easement The legal right for one person to cross or use another person's land. The most common easements are narrow tracts for utility lines.

Eaves The lower part of a roof that projects beyond the supporting walls to create an overhang.

Expansion bolt A bolt used to anchor lumber to masonry walls. The jacket of an expansion bolt expands to grip the side walls of a pilot hole due to wedge pressure at its base.

Face-nailing Nailing perpendicularly through the surface of lumber.

Fascia One-by or two-by trim pieces nailed onto the end grain or tail end of a rafter to form part of a cornice or overhang.

Flashing Thin sheets of aluminum, copper, rubber asphalt, or other material used to bridge or cover a joint between materials that is exposed to the weather—for example, between the roof and a chimney.

Floor joists The long wooden beams generally set horizontally 16 inches on center between foundation walls or girders.

Footing The part of a foundation that

transmits loads to the soil; also, the base on which a stone wall is built. Typical footings are twice as wide as the wall they support and at least as deep as the wall is wide.

Foundation The whole masonry substructure of a building upon which the rest of the structure stands.

Frost heave Shifting or upheaval of the ground resulting from alternate freezing and thawing of the moisture in soil.

Frost line The maximum depth to which soil freezes in the winter.

Full stud Vertical two-by lumber that extends from the bottom plate to the top plate of a wall.

Gable roof A roof in the shape of an inverted V with two triangular ends.

Gable end The triangular wall section under each end of a gable roof.

Gambrel roof A roof design common on barns and utility buildings that combines two gable roofs of differing slopes. The lower slope on each side is steep, which provides more usable space in lofts.

Girder A horizontal wood or steel member used to support part of a framed structure. Also called a beam.

Girder pocket The recessed seat created in a foundation wall in which the end of a girder sits.

Girt Horizontal perimeter timbers used in timber framing that funciton as nailers for vertical sheathing or siding.

Grade The identification class of lumber quality. Also shorthand for ground level—the finished level of the ground on a building site.

Ground The connection between electrical circuits or equipment and the earth. Designed to reduce shock hazards.

Ground-fault circuit interrupter (GFCI) A device that detects a ground fault or electrical line leakage and immediately shuts down power to that circuit.

Gusset plates Metal or plywood plates used to hold together the chords and webs of a truss.

Header The thick horizontal member that runs above rough openings, such as doors and windows, in a building's frame.

Header joist A horizontal board, installed on edge, that is secured to the ends of the floor joists.

Heartwood The inner, nonliving part of the tree that is typically the more durable portion due to denser wood grain.

Hip roof A roof that has a central ridge and slopes in four directions creating an overhang on every side of the building.

Jack rafters Short rafters, typcially in a hip roof, that run at an angle between a rafter and a top plate.

Jack stud A stud that runs from the bottom plate to the underside of a header. Also called a trimmer.

Jamb The upright surface forming the side in an opening, as for a door or window.

Joist Horizontal framing lumber placed on edge to support subfloors or hold up ceilings.

Joist hanger Bracket used to strengthen the connection between a joist and a piece of lumber into which it butts.

Junction box Metal or plastic box inside which all standard wire splices and wiring connections are made.

Kerf The narrow slot a saw blade cuts in a piece of lumber, usually about ⅛ inch thick.

Lag screw A large screw with a pointed tip and a hex head, generally used for bolting large timbers to posts.

Live load All the loads in and on a building that are not a permanent part of the structure—such as furniture, people, and wind.

Miter A joint in which two boards are joined at angles (usually 45 degrees) to form a corner.

Mortise-and-tenon Wood joint where a protrusion (tenon) fits into a recess (mortise), usually at a right angle.

Nailing flange An extension attached to a building component, usually predrilled for nails or screws—for example, around the sides of a window and on the edges of beam hanging hardware.

Nominal dimensions In lumber, the premilling measurement for which a piece of lumber is named (i.e., 2x4); in masonry, the measured dimensions of a masonry unit plus one mortar joint.

Nonload-bearing wall Partition or wall that does not carry a load from above.

O.C. An abbreviation for on center, typically referring to layout measurements taken from the center of one stud to the center of the next stud in line.

Oriented-strand board (OSB) Panel material made of wood strands purposely aligned for strength and bonded together with adhesive.

Outrigger A projecting framing member run out from a main structure to provide additional stability or nailing for another framing component.

Overhang Typically, the extension of a roof beyond the perimeter walls; also any projection, such as a deck platform that extends beyond it's supporting girder.

Particleboard Panel material made from wood flakes held together by resin.

Partition wall A nonload-bearing wall built to divide up interior space.

Penny (Abbreviation: d.) Unit of measure for nail length, such as a 10d nail, which is 3 inches long.

Pier A concrete base used to support columns, posts, girders, or joists.

Pigtail A short piece of wire used to make a short connection between electrical components.

Pilot hole A hole drilled before a screw is inserted to defeat splitting.

Pitch Loosely, the slope or angle of a roof; technically, the rise of a roof over its span.

Platform framing The framing method in

which walls are built one story at a time on top of decked platforms over the story below.

Plumb Vertically straight. A line 90 degrees to a level line.

Point load The downward force exerted by a single heavy object inside or on top of the structure, such as a fireplace, hot tub, or water heater.

Pole class Rating by the American Wood Preservers Association, which puts poles into one of ten classes depending on their load-bearing capacity (for loads delivered on a vertical pole) and for span (for loads on a horizontal pole or girt).

Pole framing Structures without standard masonry foundations that consist of construction poles set in the ground in select locations and regular intervals. Popular on barns, especially livestock barns designed to have large open central spaces.

Prehung door A door that's already set in a jamb, with hinges (and sometimes a lockset) preassembled, ready to be installed in a rough opening.

Pressure treated Wood that has preservatives forced into it under pressure.

Pump jack A working platform system that is raised and lowered along vertical 4x4s using a pumping action.

Purlin Roof timbers spanning between principal rafters, typically set on edge to derive maximum strength in the unsupported span.

Quality mark An ink stamp or end tag label that is applied to pressure-treated lumber (and some other lumber). The quality mark provides important information, including the type of preservative used and the water retention level.

Quarter-round molding Molding whose section is that of a quarter of a circle.

Rake trim Trim boards applied to the fascia along the gable ends of a roof projection.

Rafter Any of the parallel framing members that support a roof.

R-value The measure of a substance's resist-ance to heat flow. An R-value is a number assigned to insulation and printed on all insulation products. The higher the number, the greater the insulating value.

Rebar Short for reinforcement bar, or metal bars laid in a grid used to reinforce concrete.

Ridge The horizontal crest of a roof.

Ridgeboard The horizontal board that defines the roof frame's highest point, or ridge.

Ridge cut The cut at the uphill end of a rafter, along the ridge plumb line, that allows the rafter's end grain to sit flush against the ridgeboard.

Rim joists Joists that define the outside edges of a platform. Joists that run perpendicular to floor joists and are end-nailed to joist ends are also known as header joists.

Rise In a roof, the vertical distance between the supporting wall's cap plate and the point where a line, drawn through the outside edge of the cap plate and parallel to the roof's slope, intersects the centerline of the ridgeboard.

Riser In plumbing, a water-supply pipe that carries water vertically; in carpentry, the vertical part of a stair installed on edge, across the front of the step.

Run In a roof with a ridge, the horizotal distance between the edge of an outside wall's cap plate and the centerline of the ridgeboard.

Sapwood The living wood near the outside of a tree trunk that carries sap.

Scarf joint Where the end grain of two pieces of lumber meet in the same plane at a 45-degree angle, or in a jagged, overlapped cut, typically backed up by another board or hardware to secure the joint.

Setback A local building code that requires structures to be built a certain distance from the street, sidewalk, or property line.

Shakes Similar to cedar shingles, but rougher in texture because they are split rather than sawn.

Sheathing Panel material, typically plywood, applied to the outside of a structure. Siding is installed over it.

Shed roof A roof that slopes in one direction only.

Sill anchor Threaded metal anchors set in concrete to which sills are attached with washers and nuts.

Sill The horizontal two-by lumber attached directly to the masonry foundation. It supports the building's walls. Also, the piece of wood at the bottom of a window frame, typically angled to shed water.

Skirt boards In pole framing, pressure-treated 2x6s that run along the ground of the structure.

Slope The rise of a roof over its run, expressed as the number of inches of rise per unit of run (usually 12 inches). For example: 6-in-12 means a roof rises 6 inches for every 12 inches of run.

Snow load The downward stress on a sturcture's roof from accumaltions of snow.

Soffit The boards or plywood panels that run the length of a wall on the underside of the rafters, covering the space between the wall and the fascia.

Soil-cement mixture An equal-parts combination of soil and cement that is used to provide support for a pole or post being set into the ground.

Soleplate The horizontal two-by lumber that forms the base of framed walls, also called a shoe.

Span Distance between supports, such as the outside walls of a building or a structural wall and a beam.

Spikes 8-inch (or larger) ring nails usually grouped in fours, used to attach lumber to a pole.

Spread load The outward force on walls caused by the downward-and-outward force of rafters.

Spring brace A piece of wood that is wedged diagonally between two cleates—

one on the floor and one on the wall—used to fix a bow in a stud wall.

Stool A narrow shelf that butts against a windowsill.

Stringer On stairs, the diagonal boards that support the treads and risers.

Subfloor The flooring underneath a finished floor, usually plywood or OSB decking installed on floor joists or sleepers.

Through-bolt A bolt that extends completely through material, typically secured with a nut.

Timber framing A traditional building system that uses a skeletal framework of large wooden members, often joined together with strong intricate joints.

Toenailing Driving a nail at an angle into the face of a board so that it penetrates another board beneath or above it.

Top plate The horizontal two-by board nailed to the top of wall studs, almost always consisting of two boards that overlap at corners.

Total rise The ridge height of a roof measured from the top plate of the structure's wall.

Total run One half the building span, used in the calculation of roof angles.

Trap The water-filled curved pipe that prevents sewer gas from entering the house through the drainage network.

Trim Typically one-by lumber used as siding corner boards or as finish materials around windows and doors, under eaves, or with other architectural elements.

Trimmer Another term for a jack stud, or the short stud (nailed onto a full stud) that supports a header.

Truss A rigid assembly of timbers relying on triangulation to span distances impractical for a single member.

Valley flashing Material used to prevent leaks at the intersection of two pitched roofs that form an internal angle.

Water hammer A knocking in water pipes caused by a sudden change in pressure after a faucet or water valve shuts off.

Watt Unit of measurement of electrical power required or consumed by a fixture or appliance.

Web The inner members of a truss that carry loads from the chords, or perimeter members.

Wind load The stress on a structure due to gusting winds.

Z-brace door Door construction typically consisting of boards joined together and strengthened by a series of braces screwed to the backs of the boards in a Z-shaped pattern.

PHOTO CREDITS

Metric Conversions

Length

1 inch	25.4 mm
1 foot	0.3048 m
1 yard	0.9144 m
1 mile	1.61 km

Area

1 square inch	645 mm²
1 square foot	0.0929 m²
1 square yard	0.84 m²
1 acre	4046.86 m²
1 square mile	2.59 km²

Volume

1 cubic inch	16.39 cm³
1 cubic foot	0.03 m³
1 cubic yard	0.77 m³

Common Lumber Equivalents

Sizes: Metric cross sections are so close to their nearest U.S. sizes, as noted below, that for most purposes they may be considered equivalents.

Dimensional lumber		
	1 x 2	19 x 38 mm
	1 x 4	19 x 89 mm
	2 x 2	38 x 38 mm
	2 x 4	38 x 89 mm
	2 x 6	38 x 140 mm
	2 x 8	38 x 184 mm
	2 x 10	38 x 235 mm
	2 x 12	38 x 286 mm

Sheet sizes		
	4 x 8 ft.	1200 x 2400 mm
	4 x 10 ft.	1200 x 3000 mm

Sheet thicknesses		
	¼ in.	6 mm
	⅜ in.	9 mm
	½ in.	12 mm
	¾ in.	19 mm

Stud/joist spacing		
	16 in. o.c.	400 mm o.c.
	24 in. o.c.	600 mm o.c.

Capacity

1 fluid ounce	29.57 mL
1 pint	473.18 mL
1 quart	1.14 L
1 gallon	3.79 L

Temperature

(Celsius = Fahrenheit – 32 x ⅝)

°F	°C
0	–18
10	–12.22
20	–6.67
30	–1.11
32	0
40	4.44
50	10.00
60	15.56
70	21.11
80	26.67
90	32.22
100	37.78

Have a home improvement, decorating, or gardening project? Look for these and other fine Creative Homeowner books wherever books are sold.

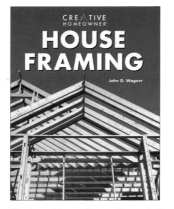

Designed to walk you through the framing basics. Over 400 illustrations. 208 pp.; 8¹/₂"×10⁷/₈"
BOOK #: 277655

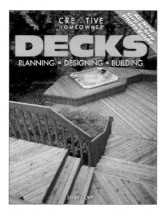

How to improve your home by adding a deck. Over 350 photos and illustrations. 192 pp.; 8¹/₂"×10⅞"
BOOK #: 277162

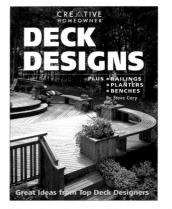

25 designs from 4 of the top deck designers. More than 300 photos and illustrations. 192 pp.; 8¹/₂"×10⁷/₈"
BOOK #: 277369

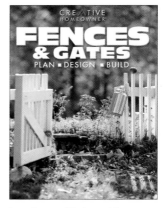

Install a prefabricated fence, or build your own. Over 350 color photos. 144 pp.; 8¹/₂"×10⁷/₈"
BOOK #: 277985

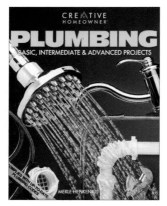

Take the guesswork out of plumbing repair. More than 750 photos and illustrations. 272 pp.; 8¹/₂"×10⁷/₈"
BOOK #: 278210

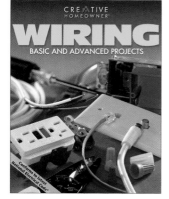

Best-selling house-wiring manual. Over 700 color photos and illustrations. 256 pp.; 8¹/₂"×10⁷/₈"
BOOK #: 277049

Complete DIY tile instruction. Over 350 color photos and illustrations. 160 pp.; 8¹/₂"×10⁷/₈"
BOOK #: 277524

How to work with concrete brick and stone. Over 850 illustrations. 272 pp.; 8¹/₂"×10⁷/₈"
BOOK #: 277110

How to create kitchen style like a pro. Over 260 color photographs. 208 pp.; 9"×10"
BOOK #: 279946

How to work with space, color, pattern, texture. Over 400 photos. 288 pp.; 9"×10"
BOOK #: 279672

Impressive guide to garden design and plant selection. More than 600 photos. 320 pp.; 9"×10"
BOOK #: 274615

Lavishly illustrated with portraits of over 100 flowering plants; more than 500 photos. 208 pp.; 9"×10"
BOOK #: 274032

For more information, and to order direct, call 800-631-7795; in New Jersey 201-934-7100.
Please visit our Web site at www.creativehomeowner.com